D0329142

MINICOMPUTERS
Low-Cost Computer Power for Management

MINICOMPUTERS
Low-Cost Computer Power
for Management

Revised Edition

Donald P. Kenney

A DIVISION OF AMERICAN MANAGEMENT ASSOCIATIONS

Library of Congress Cataloging in Publication Data

Kenney, Donald P
  Minicomputers.

  Bibliography: p.
  Includes index.
  1. Minicomputers. I. Title.
TK7888.3.K45 1978   001.6'4'04   78-14413
ISBN 0-8144-5484-4

© 1973, 1978 AMACOM
A division of American Management Associations, New York.

First Printing

PREFACE

In recent years, business management has become more aware of the potential benefits of data processing, but at the same time has become increasingly dissatisfied with the costs and lack of responsiveness of traditional processing methods. Large businesses have found it difficult to modify existing systems and impossible to install new ones in a reasonable time span. Small businesses have been squeezed between rising clerical costs and high entrance costs in the form of special skills and training required for data processing systems. However, the application of new electronic technology is making new approaches possible. The minicomputer, and the related products evolved from modern electronic technology, of which the minicomputer is the forerunner, provide the potential solutions to many business problems.

When technology coincides with demand there is inevitably an explosion of activity. New technology receives much attention and promises many advantages, not all of which can be fulfilled or accomplished within reasonable cost. Thus, those who contemplate the addition to, or the reorganization of, their data processing facilities are faced with a maze of decision-making factors that may confuse or discourage them. It is the purpose of this book to stimulate the imagination of those in business who have not yet recognized the promise of this new technology. It is also the intent to expose the risks, analyze the trade-offs, and suggest the methods by which the technical, organization, and operational problems can be solved in a way that gains the promised benefits.

Throughout this presentation certain key points will be repeatedly mentioned—for example, the low-cost electronic technology that made the minicomputer possible and attractive, and the hidden costs of its use that are the basis for its problems. These points recur in almost all minicomputer trade-off considerations.

v

The minicomputer apparently is not the greatest gift to mankind, as some claim, nor is it the most troublesome technology, as still others contend; it is possibly a little of both.

Advances in the electronic technology that produced the minicomputer also produced many other advances related to the entire data processing technology. These include the intelligent terminals, microprocessors, and error-correcting printers and peripherals. The technology that brings about exponentially increasing capabilities at exponentially decreasing cost is likely to continue for a considerable number of years, making developments of today the forerunner of technology of tomorrow. The extrapolated end points of today's technology trend suggest that infinite capacity at zero cost will occur in the early 1990s. This absurdity only dramatizes the dynamic changes facing us today.

But technology is only one part of the issue; another continuing theme that appears when evaluating the minicomputer and considering its application is that the low cost is deceptive. The price of the computer is small, but the operating cost to the indiscriminate user may be very high. The hardware may be inexpensive, but when the required software, training, and support are added, the initial cost justification may be invalid. There is more to solving a business problem than plugging it in a computer, but if the selected computer is the best one for the job and all other support factors are economically and thoroughly implemented, then the system could be extremely beneficial for the company.

Many things have happened to the minicomputer field in the past few years. The computers are more powerful, have a much broader range of capabilities, and cost considerably less than was thought possible just a few years ago. Although considerable use and growth were predicted, even the strongest supporter of the minicomputer philosophy underestimated the actual growth that has occurred in the past five years. The progress predicted by the most optimistic ten-year market forecasts was actually achieved in five years.

While software and language support was scanty in the past, it is becoming more plentiful today. Major manufacturers—such as IBM, Burroughs, Univac, and NCR—have joined the original minicomputer manufacturers and have contributed stability and prestige to the field. A whole new range of peripherals has sprung up. A few years ago the user had a limited choice of printers, but now there is a complete range of speeds that fill in the processing gap between the low-cost character printer and the expensive high-speed line printer.

Similarly, the cassette, cartridge, and floppy disks have extended the low end of file storage technology, while the largest data processing disk drives are extending the capacity at the high end. At the same time the size of the minicomputer has been expanding to the point where it cannot be differentiated from the mid-size computer, as well as decreasing to the microprocessor level.

There is an order-of-magnitude cost difference between the processing per dollar achieved by the minicomputer and traditional data processing methods of only a few years ago. An order-of-magnitude difference means that there is a discontinuity in the data processing spectrum—the principles that apply at one end of the spectrum do not necessarily apply at the other end. Therefore, the minicomputer is not just another low-cost computer, but is a whole new way of doing things. It requires a fresh approach toward solving the business problem, and allows processing to start much earlier in the data-capture function. It requires a new evaluation technique that rightfully considers the user and returns data processing to its true service functions. The writing of this book has been motivated by the need in business to coordinate this modern computer philosophy with established management principles and practices so that maximum benefit may be derived.

It is impossible to acknowledge everyone who helped make this book possible, or to recall all those who have contributed to the coalescing of ideas that formed the basis of this presentation. Contributions have been made by associates, friends, clients, vendors, engineers, and salesmen. To all these people I give my sincere thanks for the enlightening, stimulating, frustrating, informative, difficult, provocative (but always valuable) give-and-take sessions relating to these topics. In particular I would like to thank my associate Charles K. Pearson for his valuable suggestions regarding the organization and content of this book, and Susan E. Kenney for her tireless editing and clerical contributions.

Donald P. Kenney

CONTENTS

INTRODUCING
THE MINICOMPUTER

The minicomputer is more than a low-cost computer. Despite the fact that it can be programmed and that all kinds of data processing input and output equipment and peripherals can be attached to it, the minicomputer presents much more than simply a new method of data processing. It changes the philosophy of data processing by forcing economic consideration of the entire business process rather than concentrating solely on the computer. It also presents the possibility of fulfilling the promise of the computer—the promise that it will truly be an extension of a human being's power and intelligence, which has been in the air since the electronic computer was first used as a tool for business in 1951, but which has never been fulfilled.

The replacement of vacuum tube technology with solid-state electronic devices—first transistors and then integrated circuits— has brought the computer industry from the large expensive machines of the 1950s with relatively poor reliability, by modern standards, to high-speed reliable computers that do a thousand times more calculations in the same time for less cost. Advances in integrated-circuit design and manufacture concentrated more functions in a smaller space and brought about even lower prices, smaller size, and higher-speed computers, called *minicomputers*.

But electronic technology did not stop with the minicomputer. Further advances in increasing the density of the integrated-circuit chip with the added (and most important) ability to actually program these chips led the industry to devices called *microcomputers* and *microprocessors*. Truly, the processor in a single chip is with us today. It is no longer a high-technology device used in the laboratory, but a functional device with significant utility in industry and commerce.

The mini's low cost allows many new techniques to be economically justified for the first time. Rather than requiring many data processing jobs to be batched so that they can be run simultaneously in order to utilize computer power effectively, the low-cost minicomputer can be cost effective even when it is improving only the production of a single person. It can be a personal data processor to be used in a conversational fashion with the user, and as such can truly serve the needs of the user. It can be used in many situations without requiring an operator or technical staff, thus taking a big step toward universal use in small business organizations and in the home.

One step down from the minicomputer in capability is a device that is very much like the first minicomputer developed. This device, the microcomputer, is basically the result of the technological advances that produced extremely densely packaged electronic logic chips. The microcomputer contains on a single chip all the functions of a computer central processing unit. In addition, these chips can now be programmed to perform the same functions performed by large computers. The difference between a minicomputer and a microcomputer at the present time is one that is totally related to size. The minicomputer has larger data paths and capabilities than the microcomputer, and can process at a higher speed. However, both devices have the ability to use peripheral devices such as printers and data entry devices wired into them.

The microprocessor is a device with all the logical capabilities of the microcomputer, but without the ability to handle peripheral devices. It is a component of many types of equipment, such as the data input terminals now being employed at retail stores to record purchases and validate credits. In this form, the microcomputer is finding more and more use in industrial applications. It is being used in automobiles, and in our homes to monitor and control a number of everyday appliances such as washing machines and microwave ovens. Soon it will probably be used to facilitate shopping and banking from the home. The programmable logic capability of these devices makes them valuable for performing many functions, and their low cost assures that they will be adopted widely.

Reasons for Recent Emergence

Today's minicomputer has virtually exploded onto the market. The reasons for this sudden acceptance are many and encompass economic, technical, social, and psychological factors. Some of the more important are discussed below.

Low-Cost Electronic Circuitry

Certainly, the rapid advance in electronic technology that resulted in more than a thousandfold price decrease since 1968 has been the most important reason for increased use of minicomputers. The low cost of the processors has made possible the automation of many applications that previously were never considered economically justifiable.

Circuitry advances, especially the integrated circuit, have been a prime factor. Computer generations are classified by the types of components used in their manufacture. The first-generation computer used vacuum tubes, which limited processing performance in terms of speed and reliability. Heat generated by the vacuum tubes resulted in their having a relatively short operating life, placing an upper bound on the size of computers. The first completely electronic computer, ENIAC, was developed at the University of Pennsylvania in 1945. It had 18,000 vacuum tubes. Larger machines were clearly impractical, since it would have taken almost an entire day to find and replace the defective tubes.

Transistors replaced vacuum tubes in the second-generation computer. The transistors and other discrete components were individually wired and assembled into the functional logic circuits of the computer. Transistors are solid-state components, require little power, and are much more reliable than vacuum tubes. Their use saved the computer from a premature end, or at least allowed the computer to grow in size, reliability, and capability.

The development of cost-effective integrated circuits in the 1960s moved the computer into its third generation. The reductions in size, as well as increased power and capabilities that appeared with the third-generation computers, were made possible by the development of the integrated-circuit (IC) chip. The IC chip combines many functions in one component, resulting in a faster and more effective circuit at lower cost.

The design of computers and other electronic devices has again been transformed by large-scale integration (LSI), the process whereby tens of thousands of transistors and their interconnections are manufactured simultaneously and packaged in one chip. As a result, virtually all logic elements of a digital computer can be fitted onto a thin chip of silicon no more than a quarter-inch square. The redesign of circuits made possible by these advances throughout the 1960s, and their rapid integration in small-computer technology, provided the economic impetus for the industry's growth.

The cost of the minicomputer central processor has decreased considerably over the years. In 1966, for example, the processor cost approximately $30,000. Six years later, in 1972, its price was only 20 percent of that cost, about $6,500. In 1978 its cost has dropped below $1,000, while the performance, capability, and internal speed of the processor have increased.

Since the development of the integrated circuit, improvements in speed, costs, and reliability have been truly astounding. A single integrated circuit on a chip can encompass all elements of the most complex piece of electronic equipment that could have been built in 1950. Today's microcomputer, at a cost of about $300, has more computing capacity than the first large electronic computer, the ENIAC. It is 20 times faster, has a larger memory, is thousands of times more reliable, consumes a minute fraction of the power needed for the ENIAC, occupies one thirty-thousandth the volume, and costs one ten-thousandth as much. Availability of the IC chip is so widespread that it can be ordered by mail or bought at a local hobby shop.

More Sophisticated Users

Computers have become an integral part of all businesses and are now commonplace in our personal lives. We are familiar with computer-produced credit purchase statements, bank statements, and invoices, and also have learned something about the computer's power and its shortcomings.

People in business have been served by computers for many years. They know what the computer can do. While they are usually satisfied, the addition of more and more applications on the computer has resulted in an increasingly rigid, less responsive data processing function. Many users became impatient with the long application development time and were discouraged by the high costs. And at times after the development had been completed, the product did not function in the manner expected. Thus, when the minicomputer was introduced, the computer was ready for some new data processing method that returned the control of the application to him.

Economic Recession

Until 1969 it appeared that the entire date processing field expanded almost without regard to consequences. Hardware was constantly upgraded merely to take advantage of the most recently announced technology; and new, exotic systems were proposed and installed with inflated expectations of benefits. However, the industry matured suddenly.

The slowdown of business during the 1969–1971 period caused business to look carefully at all expenses. Data processing expenses were not excluded. As a result, new applications were carefully reevaluated and started only if the economic benefits were definitely obtainable. Reduction of operating expenses was also sought. Therefore, when new systems were needed, more modest approaches were chosen to assure easier development and control.

For all these reasons, existing computer users were more likely to choose minicomputers because they provided a low-cost, more rapid installation of a necessary system. Nonusers became extremely cost conscious and looked for ways to reduce expenses. One way was to identify areas where automation would effect savings. The minicomputer, because of its low price, was frequently considered for the automation of these applications. As a result, during the slow business period the minicomputers were the only rapidly growing segment of the previously dynamic computer industry.

Available Technology

Before the 1970 decade, the maturing computer industry had developed the skills to take advantage of the emerging new technology and had designed new equipment that provided means of realizing greater computer capabilities through improved peripherals. Although the objective was to augment the capabilities of large computers at an acceptable performance/price ratio, much of this technology was also applied to minicomputer peripherals. This resulted in the development of very competent but small and less costly peripheral equipment for minicomputers.

Convergence of Events

Technological advances and the business slowdown at the end of the 1960s stimulated the use of the minicomputers. It was stated in an *Auerbach Technology Report** as early as 1970 that the astonishing growth of minicomputers in the preceding years was a logical development of new computer technology and manufacturing economics. "The success of the minicomputer is due to developments in four general areas: hardware, software, cost, and people's attitudes." The characteristics that produced that point of view continue to the present day.

Segments of the Industry

The computer industry is made up of a number of different segments that must be understood in order for the potential user to determine a proper course of action.

Manufacturers. The manufacturers of computer mainframes market their products in a number of different ways. Some prefer to sell only equipment and others supply the entire system, including peripherals and software. In addition, some large manufacturers produce much of the peripheral equipment for their computers, whereas many others buy all associated equipment from independent suppliers of peripherals.

Original equipment manufacturers. Organizations that systematize the computer equipment package play a very important role in the minicomputer field. They provide the expertise to combine a computer and peripherals bought from the manufacturers with whatever is necessary to supply a complete working system for end users. This is especially important in an industry where many manufacturers prefer not to get involved in systems and in fact do not provide strong support, and where end users are frequently unsophisticated.

The services of original equipment manufacturers (OEM) vary. An OEM might develop its own programs, peripherals, or interfaces, or it might buy them. It might sell only a minicomputer that is a slightly modified version (some special features added, made more rugged, and so forth) of the computer purchased. An OEM invariably sells to end users and, because it has expert knowledge

---

Auerbach Computer Technology Report (September 1970), p. 1003. Auerbach Info, Inc., Philadelphia.

of the equipment, can supply good system performance at low cost.

Systems houses. Systems houses offer a capability based primarily on detailed knowledge of a specific application area. A typical systems house will develop all required software for an application, but will purchase all equipment from established computer manufacturers, usually from a single source if at all possible. These houses produce a complete working system—frequently called a *turnkey system* because they take complete responsibility for it. They provide training of the user's operators and often offer maintenance service in conjunction with the manufacturer.

Systems houses provide an important service to end users and at times to OEMs, but their existence is quite tenuous. They actually compete with many manufacturers, and there is no assurance that the manufacturers which presently choose not to produce systems will not change, thus threatening the survival of these systems companies.

Software suppliers. Software for minicomputers is produced by just about all segments of the industry. All minicomputer manufacturers supply the basic system software (executive systems, assemblers, editors, compilers, loaders, and so forth), and usually provide the more common types of software routines. In addition, more companies are developing or having developed application-oriented software support. A software house often supplies specialized software to the manufacturer to ease his development load, provides application-oriented programs to an OEM, and supplies special types of software such as cross assemblers or cross compilers to manufacturers or users. Their most common service and most important function, however, is to supply the software—application or system software—to the end user. This is usually done on a contract basis and thus differs from the systems house, which usually supplies a turnkey system.

End users. There are end users at all levels of sophistication, but the manner in which they buy minicomputers and associated equipment and services allows classifying them into two categories.

Sophisticated end users are knowledgeable and confident that they can assemble and program a system. The sophisticated end user can operate in a manner quite similar to an OEM. Depending on his own skills or those of the company's development staff, the knowledgeable user may choose to assemble all system components and develop required software. More likely, however, even the sophisticated end user will want the added support that comes with obtaining the computer, peripherals, and software from a single manufacturer.

Unsophisticated end users and those who want to minimize risk, either because of lack of skills or lack of desire, or both, want a complete system programmed and installed on a turnkey basis. This group will contract with an OEM, a systems house, or with the computer manufacturer to obtain a complete system.

Spectrum of Products

The minicomputer is one product in a large field of computing equipment where distinctions between various products are either hazy or nonexistent. It is difficult at times to indicate precisely into which of the following categories a particular product belongs:

Programmable calculator
Microprocessor
Microcomputer
Electronic accounting machine
Small-business computer
Intelligent terminal
Minicomputer
Computer

These types of machines form almost a continuous spectrum in the field of program-directed calculating and processing equipment. Literature of the field and even of manufacturers have not agreed on precise definitions; thus, there is a degree of confusion and, as a result, many inaccuracies in market statistics.

The nature of electronic technology causes the technical distinctions between different logic devices to become blurred or to completely disappear, leaving price as the primary difference between a minicomputer and other computers. This is hardly a criterion on which any choice between products should be based, and its value is additionally diminished in today's world of large price decreases. But, because of the absence of any other distinguishing characteristics, all definitions use price to differentiate between computer types.

Further uncertainty is introduced when the functions of a microprocessor or a microcomputer are compared with those of the minicomputer. While not universally accepted, the following definitions are intended to help distinguish between these similar types of logical processors.

A *microprocessor* is a semiconductor chip that is designed to perform logical functions. Fixed logic is inscribed in the device during its fabrication. It can be used as the central arithmetic and logic unit of a computer, together with associated circuitry, scaled down so it fits on a single silicon chip. About 20 companies in the United States are now manufacturing 30 different designs of microprocessor chips ranging in price from $10 to $300.

A *microcomputer* includes one or more microprocessors that perform logical and arithmetic functions under program control (firmware and/or software), with one or more LSI chips to provide timing, program memory, interfaces for input-output (I/O) signals, and other ancillary functions. Some read-only memory and/or random-access memory is also included. Today, most microcomputers are limited to 65K or less words of 4, 8, 12, or 16 bit size. They provide some I/O interface logic for a limited complement of devices. Typical prices for microcomputer chip sets without I/O devices or power supplies range roughly from $100 to $1,000 each, depending on functional capability and memory size characteristics. Examples include the widely accepted Intel 8080 chip, Texas Instruments' TMS-1000, and the Motorola 2901.

The minicomputer includes a processor and may, in addition, incorporate one or more microprocessors. It performs logical arithmetic and I/O functions under program control at speeds typically five to ten times faster than microprocessors. The memory address range is usually wider than that found in microprocessors, with sizes extending to over 260K bytes. The minicomputer price range varies considerably, depending on features included; from a low-end figure of about $10,000, the cost may rise to something considerably in excess of $100,000 for the processor with some storage and interfacing. In general, the mini price is under $50,000.

The boundaries between these devices, as for so many other devices struggling to maintian their integrity in today's fluid data processing environment, will certainly change in the next few years. In fact, it is likely that even our definition of a computer will change within the next decade.

In addition to the absence of distinctive features, it is even more difficult to distinguish a minicomputer from what is known as a small-business computer. To add to the complication, minicomputers are used in small-business systems, microprocessors are used in minicomputers, and microprocessors and minicomputers are also part of intelligent terminals, programmable calculators, and many other related devices.

Electronic accounting machines. The latest group of accounting machines to appear on the market have a central processing unit and can be programmed like any computer. They are always programmed by the manufacturer in some relatively permanent fashion, in a language that is unique to the particular machine.

The electronic accounting machines, also known as programmable billing machines, accounting computers, or (quite commonly) office computers, combine the capabilities of a typewriter, calculator, and billing machine, but operate under program control.

The accounting machine is ledger-output oriented. The operator types in information on special alphanumeric keyboards; then, under program control, the machine produces invoices, checks, ledgers, and other necessary business forms.

Application programs are loaded into the machine usually by changing an entire program board. Data such as customer and product information is usually maintained on magnetic ledger cards. Most manufacturers maintain program libraries of the most common business applications, which are available to the user at nominal or no cost.

Small-business computers. The next higher level of machines in the processing spectrum—the small-business computer—is a stored-program computer. Except that it is configured to handle specific commercial data processing applications, it is similar in function and capability to the small standard data processing computer.

This category also encompasses a wide variety of products. The smaller machines provide only specific functions, but the larger ones are highly sophisticated and provide most of the same capabilities as large-scale computer systems. Generally, these machines have very powerful processors. In fact, many of them use a standard minicomputer as the central processor. The difference in capability between the small-business computer and a minicomputer is the lack of flexibility of the business computer, due to its being configured in a very particular way. It is usual for manufacturers to design these systems for only a specific class of business applications. In doing this, some of the capability needed for applications other than the strictly commercial ones is lost. Also, the operating system, the master program that controls the operation of the computer, is frequently modified to handle the heavy imput/output load, thus sacrificing some other capabilities. The operating systems in some of the systems are even completely implemented in hardware rather than in software (programming). These restrictions produce beneficial results when used in the applications for which they were designed, but they do decrease performance if used for different or more complex applications.

To be called a small-business computer, the system must be able to perform sorting and have on-line access to large data files. In addition, it should have the ability to establish a rudimentary information retrieval system. Therefore, the major distinction between the small-business computer and the electronic accounting machine is the data storage and retrieval capability. The accounting machine commonly uses magnetic ledger cards, whereas the small-business computer uses random-access disk files or magnetic tape.

To be considered a small-business computer, the system should supply the user with the means to program his application. This requires the availability of a high-level language compiler such as COBOL or RPG (report program generator). In addition to user-developed programs, the supplier usually provides off-the-shelf programs for the basic commercial applications such as payroll, accounts receivable, and inventory.

These systems usually have standard data processing input/output equipment such as card readers and line printers, and also some special type of auxiliary equipment such as a keyboard cathode-ray tube (CRT), job station, or special point-of-sale terminals. The system shown in Figure 1–1 features a high-powered minicomputer as the processor, configured with keyboard input, disk file, and printer.

The market for automation of small businesses. Until 1970, which brought the minicomputer into many business applications, computer use was concentrated in large organizations. Less than 1 percent of the businesses in the United States having less than 50 people had an on-site data processing facility, although this group comprised 96 percent of all businesses. There are almost two million business establishments in the United States, but only 50,000 companies have had computers installed. It is evident that the computer could not be afforded or was not accepted in the small-business area. But the small-business computer and the minicom-

Figure 1–1. Minicomputer system configured for business applications. I-8130 interactive direct processing system from NCR Corporation combines interactive processing with low cost, a library of industry-oriented applications, and full compatibility with larger members of the NCR 8000 series of computer systems. The system shown here features 48K memory, multiple processors, integrated flexible disk drives, visual display terminal, keyboard, and visual record printer, which can accommodate continuous computer forms and journal rolls as well as cut forms such as ledger cards. Photo courtesy of NCR Corporation, Dayton, Ohio.

puter may open up this untouched market. With almost 99.3 percent of businesses having fewer than 250 people and 89 percent having fewer than 20 people, many, many companies will be looking for data processing assistance. The following distribution clearly shows in which areas the market potential is concentrated.

No. of Employees	Percent of Businesses
1–3	54
4–7	19
8–19	16
20–49	7
50–99	2
100–249	1.3
250–499	0.4
500 up	0.3

The small-business computers are designed primarily to serve the business data processing needs of small companies. The principal sales targets are the more than 500,000 U.S. business and government organizations with between 10 and 500 employees. Smaller companies will usually find it difficult to justify the price tags on these machines, while larger organizations will usually prefer more powerful computers. The smaller computers are also being productively used in some of the nation's largest corporations in a variety of specialized applications such as these.

- Local processing of some or all data generated in branch offices, divisions, and/or small subsidiaries.
- Individual, "dedicated" applications and specific functions of a larger, centrally processed application that involves extensive keyboard input and printed output, such as the preparation of accounts payable checks, insurance claim checks, and stock transfer certificates.
- "Intelligent terminal" applications, in which the small computers perform limited local data processing functions and communications control functions in company-wide data communications networks.

Minicomputers. The minicomputer covers the widest range in this continuous spectrum of programmable calculation and processing equipment. The minicomputer has all the basic capabilities of the standard computers. All types of standard data processing input, output, and storage devices can be attached to the minicomputer and integrated into the system. Because of its great capabilities and high processing speed, low-speed equipment such as a ledger card reader is not normally used with the minicomputer.

All minicomputers can be programmed, and all suppliers provide either assembler or compiler programs. Usually, several versions of these are available, allowing the user or supplier to develop almost any kind of application program desired. These same words might also apply to the microcomputer, except for application versatility. It, too, has all the basic capabilities of standard computers and can support input/output devices as well as programming languages, but it has a smaller memory capacity and at present does not interface with as wide a range of peripherals. Also, its programming language capabilities are at present very limited. However, these features are constantly being enhanced, and therefore it is almost certain that before long there will be minimal (if any) distinction between minicomputers and microcomputers.

Because of its great capabilities—its flexibility permits it to be used in a multitude of applications, including all the business applications for which the accounting and small-business computers have been designed—the minicomputer is the prime concern of this text. The minicomputer encompasses all functions that are provided by the business and accounting computers and provides many more capabilities in addition. It is a general-purpose device; it can be used where any business computer, accounting computer, intelligent terminal, or calculator is used, but the reverse is not possible.

The minicomputer can take a number of physical forms, from a stripped-down controller version consisting of only the central processor and a small amount of memory, similar to existing microcomputers, to a complete data processing system. When used in a large system, a minicomputer may contain 500K characters (or bytes) of memory, massive disk files, line printers, magnetic tapes, and data-input terminals. Stripped-down minicomputers, microprocessors, or microcomputers are very frequently built into other devices such as optical readers, computer output microfilm equipment, and intelligent terminals. In these applications the computers are an integral part of a larger system and are not visible to the user.

Figures 1–2, 1–3, and 1–4 illustrate the variety of minicomputer sizes and the different ways in which the minicomputer is configured.

Acceptance of the Minicomputer

The reasons for the acceptance of the minicomputer to date and its expected continued success are many and are very complex. As in any other issue, the reasons can be sorted out according to

Figure 1–2. Wang Laboratories' 2200 PCS computer is light enough to be carried almost anywhere and powerful enough to provide an alternative to time-sharing services. The new low-end model in the 2200 series of small computers from Wang is sold into distributed processing as well as personal computing applications. Photo courtesy of Wang Laboratories, Inc., Lowell, Mass.

whether they favor the mini or oppose the alternatives. The positive reasons for minicomputer use outweigh, in the estimation of many users, its disadvantages. In addition, a number of negative arguments against the data processing alternatives have caused users to modify their preferences in data processing methods and choose the minicomputer in increasingly large numbers.

Figure 1–3. The Digital PDP 8/E, a small, low-cost, high-speed minicomputer from Digital Equipment Corporation, is the latest model of a line of computers introduced in 1965. Photo courtesy of Digital Equipment Corporation, Maynard, Mass.

Computer Solutions of the 1960s

With the growing use of computers, expenditures for data processing increased from less than $2 billion in 1960 to $8.3 billion in 1965 to $25.5 billion in 1970 to $55 billion in 1977. These growing expenses caused data processing managers to attempt to maximize the efficiency of the computer operation, but their attempts to

Figure 1–4. Digital's PDP-11/70 features large-scale computer operations in a medium-scale system. The system has internal memory expansion capabilities of up to 2 million bytes and features a new and advanced operating system. It is upward-software-compatible with other members of the PDP-11 computer family, but can run existing programs at two to three times the speed of the previous top of the PDP-11 line. Photo courtesy of Digital Equipment Corporation, Maynard, Mass.

increase efficiencies had a number of results that (from the vantage point of hindsight) were not always favorable.

Increased data preparation costs. In an effort to maximize computer processing, more work had to be done before the computer received the data. Since this task usually falls outside the data processing department, users' expenses were increased.

Slower service. Data is batched and processed by the computer only periodically (weekly or monthly), resulting in poor service to the user. Using this method of operation, re-runs for additional information become impossible.

The data processing mystique. The highly sophisticated systems required to obtain maximum computer through-put added a new level of complexity to computer operation. Skilled computer technicians who can understand the highly specialized computer systems do not have the time to get involved in users' problems, thus widening the service gap and promoting lack of understanding.

The "super" syndrome. Being associated with the biggest and newest piece of computer hardware brings great satisfaction (and usually increased salaries) to many computer specialists. Unfortunately, it is usually these same people who are asked to evaluate the possibility of upgrading to a new computer. This causes an ever-increasing spiral: bigger machines and bigger systems to fill them.

Long development times. Electronic data processing (EDP) budgets indicate that approximately 70 percent of the data processing resources were spent either on continuing operations or on conversion, and only 30 percent on new development. With all these resources required just to maintain operations (70 percent of the current EDP expenditures is over $30 billion), the development of new applications suffers, resulting in the frustration of potential users.

Lack of flexibility. The highly complex systems developed for the large computers are also dependent upon them. Changes or additions to the systems require compatibility of all details. This causes the loss of any opportunity to capitalize on or adjust to sudden changes in the business environment and results in a rigid, unresponsive system.

Other characteristics. Numerous other characteristics can be traced to the concept of bigness, all of which have had a negative impact on the success of data processing services. Problems increase exponentially with size. A 2,000-statement program takes about four times the resources required for a 1,000-statement program. As system size increases, problems can be expected to increase and reliability to decrease, thus negating theoretical efficiencies of scale.

People's attitudes also cause a problem. There is a tendency on the part of data processing people to equate bigness with goodness. There is also a proclivity to overpower the problem rather than to solve it by the best method possible.

Resulting Problems

In an attempt to raise effectiveness, data processing management has carefully measured the computer performance and instituted procedures to improve its operation. These measures and procedures are directed by the economy-of-scale concept and have established that the processing performance—through-put per unit cost—increases as the volume increases. While these procedures have made computer internal processing more efficient, the effect on the entire data processing operation has been less than spectacular, a logical outcome because the objectives of service and efficiency are contradictory. With the accent on formalized procedures, increased structuralization, and lack of options to improve efficiency, service has to suffer. The problems that resulted from this approach for reducing costs were a lack of responsiveness and service to the user and the reliance on through-put as the measure of efficiency.

Through-put measures and the economy-of-scale philosophy are myopic management approaches. These concepts concentrate on the processor to the exclusion of all other parts of the system. Although there is no doubt that attempting to maximize performance of the processor is important, it is clearly suboptimizing. If, in order to accomplish optimal processor functions, the efficiency of other parts of the system chain decreases, the result will be to decrease rather than to improve overall system performance.

In the early days of data processing this approach was surely correct. In the early 1960s the cost of the computer hardware was much more than the personnel costs associated with computer operation. By 1970 a crossover point had been reached, after which the costs of computer personnel and services were greater than the computer hardware costs.

Measures that use computer through-put as the sole criterion for judging system performance are, at best, incomplete. If the means used to improve the through-put of the processor have a negative effect on personnel expenses, which is by far the major cost area, then these performance measures may well be incorrect. When a minicomputer is used in its typical fashion, dedicated to a specific application, its processor may be almost idle and still the system can be very effective and also very efficient. Therefore, minicomputer use should not be judged by the presently existing standards. The use of the minicomputer calls for a return to basics in evaluating performance. Evaluation of systems should consider the full life-cycle costs and benefits, and these include not only the data processing department's expenses but also the user's costs and benefits.

The User's Environment

Control of data processing. From the user's point of view, many trends that have been evident since the 1960s make it appear that he is losing control over his operation. With the ever-increasing data processing costs, many users have welcomed the use of computing equipment that allows them to retain full control of the system and of their operation.

Relaxation of rigid operation standards. With the smaller, dedicated minicomputer systems, it is no longer essential to conform to every operation standard. The relative economics decide whether it is preferable to handle all matters in a standard fashion or to satisfy each user's requirement.

Earlier capture of data. The automation of data capture applications provides users with many benefits, including lower costs, accuracy of data, timeliness of data, and accurate assignment of responsibility for the data collection operation. The first employee who handles the data should be the one that enters it into the system, since no one knows that particular operation better.

Anticipating the future. The acceptance of the minicomputer concept is likely to continue because of the need for automation aids for future business requirements. There are many clerical operations in present-day businesses that management will have increasing difficulty in filling. Even today, businesses have problems when the reliable old clerk who knows all company procedures finally retires. It is literally true that such well-informed personnel are no longer available. The solution is to use the logic of the computer to aid and guide a not so knowledgeable and not so motivated clerk through the same clerical operation. This type of automation requires a low-cost processor such as a minicomputer.

Business requirements for information are also expected to change. As business develops more sophisticated planning and control systems, more pertinent and more accurate data will be necessary. Distributed computing power can analyze and sift the data at the lower organization levels and pass only the appropriate data to the higher organization and data processing levels. The quantities of data that have to be scanned to obtain the necessary information might be too great to be accomplished in any other fashion.

Problems

Minicomputers are low-cost systems and therefore their use can be justified by relatively small savings. When small, absolute quantities are involved, the margin for error is small. The use of the minicomputer has many hidden traps for the user. Failing to recognize and resolve the problems, and to do this rapidly, could very easily dissipate all potential benefits.

The low-cost problem. The low cost of the minicomputer is deceiving because the figures normally quoted apply only to the central processor, and the spiral of ever-increasing system development and software costs can soon overwhelm the user. Systems and software that account for about 50 percent of the large-computer expenses may exceed 90 percent of the quoted cost of a minicomputer. Peripherals essential to a business system may very easily cost four or five times the computer price. This cost "iceberg" is more dramatic simply because potential users may be misled by the basic quotation and are not aware that minicomputers have most of the same requirements as the larger systems. Programming, systems analysis, testing, conversion, and many similar functions are required, regardless of the size of the system.

Other potential problems may also arise. These include reliability, service, software support, backup considerations, support of dispersed computer sites, control of corporate accounting and data processing procedures, and security considerations. The data processing philosophy of the company—that is, the level of experience in data processing and method of doing business—is a particularly important consideration.

Minicomputers are being used in many applications, and many surveys of the industry dwell on numerous other applications possible in the future. However, too often in discussions of applications the emphasis is on what can be done, without due consideration of the economics of such action. The minicomputer is a new tool and must be treated as such. It is not everyone's solution, but its very existence indicates that, at least for some businesses, it satisfies a search for a less costly and more effective way to solve business data processing and information problems.

THE MINICOMPUTER
MANUFACTURERS

History of the Minicomputer

The rationale for the use of the minicomputer is its low cost, which allows the computer to be utilized economically even when it performs only one application. By dedicating it to one application, highly complex operational problems are reduced. This application—the dedication of the minicomputer to a single operation—is a motivating force that promises wide and increasing utilization. Moreover, such dedication of minicomputers to a specific function is an indication of how it should be used. This type of use has been successfully applied in the process control and aerospace industries.

Process control usage. Minicomputers were first used in the process industries. Until they became available, electromechanical hard-wired equipment was used in the measurement and control of the processes. Because the control functions of different processes differed somewhat and because minor changes were frequent, hard-wired controllers had to go through repeated reconstruction. By designing a small computer with a programmable memory, the controller hardware need be developed only once, and its use is determined by a program that is rewritten for each application. Although programming is not inexpensive, it is much cheaper than designing a new controller every time a change is made.

The philosophy that started the minicomputer field is still valid today. The minicomputer is frequently used in changeable data-entry applications and in integrating diverse systems. Other characteristics of the process control computer have also been adapted to the minicomputer. These process control systems now operate on-line rather than in a batch fashion, as do the majority of large data processors.

The small minicomputer memory has resulted in the development of effective methods for rolling in programming segments from auxiliary storage, to be held in the machine memory only when that program segment is actually in use. These efficient techniques have not only been adapted successfully to present-day minicomputer applications, but have also contributed importantly to development and acknowledgment of its versatility.

Aerospace industry contributions. In the early 1960s the aerospace industry required specialized airborne computers. From these designs, many of the features of the minicomputer evolved. The size, weight, and power constraints of the aerospace industry forced designers to compensate for the enforced hardware limitations. As a result, paging techniques and multiple precision arithmetic subroutines developed for the Apollo guidance computer and similar computers in the mid-1960s became important contributions to the minicomputer field.

The early companies. Digital Equipment Corporation of Maynard, Mass., began delivering minicomputers in 1963, and to this date it is the leading supplier. Digital Equipment was followed into the field by Computer Control Company, which, in 1966, became the Computer Control Division of Honeywell. Until the end of 1965, these two companies had the field to themselves, with Digital Equipment having the much larger portion.

The early years. Minicomputer users of these early years were a very expert group. Since most of these early systems were delivered to technical users in the control industries, much of the support familiar to today's computer users was not available and, to a large extent, was not necessary. Part of the reason for the low price was that the manufacturer did not have to supply training, detailed documentation, or even much software. It was even not uncommon for the user to perform his own repairs. These early users were truly pioneers.

However, it was evident that the minicomputer field could not fulfill its potential growth unless support, maintenance, and particularly software were made available. Developments in these areas contributed to the explosion of the field almost as much as the reduction in price.

The second group of companies. Starting in 1966, many new companies entered the field. Some of these companies, such as Varian and Hewlett-Packard, were established in technical or instrumentation areas, but others such as Interdata, General Automation, and Data General were formed specifically to produce minicomputers. Interdata started operations in 1966, as did Varian Data Machines. Hewlett-Packard, General Automation, Computer Automation, and Micro Systems are some of the more important minicomputer companies that started in 1967; Data General and Lockheed entered the field in 1968.

Proliferation of companies. It took very little capital to get started in the minicomputer field. Using the newly developed components, design of a high-powered computer was rather easy and could be done in a relatively short time. The difficulty, however, lay in customers' demands for support and particularly for software, which required more of an investment than could be supplied by new companies that were underfunded. Users' uncertainty of the survivability of these manufacturers was also a deterrent, for naturally they wanted to do business only with those companies whose stability assured continuing maintenance and supply of spare parts for the computers.

As a result, the proliferation of new companies in 1968 and 1969 was followed by a rapid decline in 1970. In 1969 new companies were emerging at the rate of about one per week. At one time during 1969 there were over a hundred companies that advertised they could supply minicomputers. Harder economic times, fewer sales, and the decreasing supply of capital caused many of these suppliers to halt operations during 1969–1970. IBM's System/3, which competed at the high end of the minicomputer capability scale, was introduced in 1969. It was not generally considered to be a minicomputer, however, because it was larger and more expensive than other available minicomputers and also lacked support of on-line terminals.

The 1970s. After this initial explosion and subsequent decline, there were approximately 52 manufacturers remaining in the field at the end of 1970. In 1970 IBM also introduced the System/7, a sensor-based minicomputer more suitable for industrial application than for business purposes. A year later the number of minicomputer manufacturers was on the rise again, and the increase continues today. With the use of microelectronics, the inclusion of processing logic in terminals and other devices, and the blurring of distinctions between computers of all sizes, it is just about impossible to identify all of the present-day original minicomputer manufacturers. However, in 1977 it was estimated that 90 U.S. and 30 foreign manufacturers supplied approximately 450 minicomputer models (see Figure 2–1).

Most people in the field agree that many of the smaller companies will be acquired by larger companies or will merge in order to continue competing, a judgment supported by realignments made in 1972. In the future there will undoubtedly be less than 50 companies in the field, including those associated with larger companies. It is expected that each of these manufacturers will have two to five models of minicomputers available at any time.

The 1970s were dominated by the original manufacturers such as Digital Equipment, Data General, and General Automation. The large computer manufacturers such as IBM, Burroughs, NCR, and Univac joined Honeywell in making their presence known. The entry of systems houses that build complete business-oriented systems around purchased minicomputers and peripherals became very common in the 1970s.

Figure 2–1. Minicomputer suppliers.

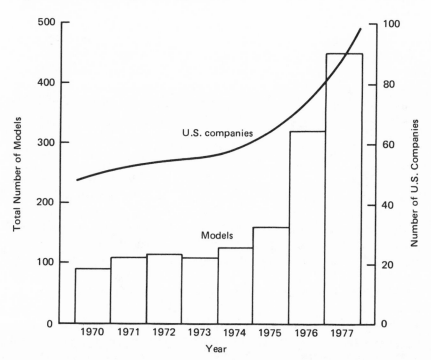

The mid-1970s. IBM truly entered the minicomputer field with the System/32 and Series/1 minicomputers introduced in 1975 and 1976, respectively. These were highly successful and were followed by the System/34 and the 5100 and 5110 portable minicomputers. IBM also added terminal input capabilities to the System/3, decreased its price, and made it more adaptable to small business use.

In the mid-1970s the major companies, building on their strong base of hardware, fleshed out their minicomputer lines by providing:

- Expanded systems: increase in memory sizes from a maximum of 64K (K = 1,000 characters) of internal storage to 256K, and more, characters. Internal cycle speeds, previously on the order of one-millionth of a second, were increased, often by a factor of 4.
- Increased peripheral interfacing: increases in the number and range of sizes of printers, tapes, disks, and other equipment were provided.
- Software support: numerous application packages and language processors were developed and made available, generally on a rental basis.

Microprocessors and microcomputers. The semiconductor logic integrated circuit used by the minicomputer contained the seed of the microcomputer. The circuit chips had logic elements in them, but were a combination of transistors designed to perform specific and limited tasks. Accordingly, central processing units of large computers were made up of hundreds or even thousands of the circuit chips.

Logic chips were also employed for control or arithmetic functions in specialized applications. In what became known as "hard-wired logic systems," chips and other individual components were soldered into a rigid pattern on a printed circuit board.

In 1969 Intel Corporation envisioned a different way of employing the new electronic capability. A customer wanted calculator chips of a specific design, but Intel saw a way to improve on the original design by making a bold technological leap. The company found it was possible to store a program that could run a microscopic computing circuit in the intricate inside of the memory chip. Instead of fabricating the problem into the integrated circuit chip, an entire central processing unit (CPU)—the computer's brain— was inscribed on a single thin chip of silicon no greater than a quarter-inch square.

The CPU on the chip became known as the "microprocessor." Attached to the microprocessor were two other memory chips: one to move data in and out of the CPU and the other to provide the program to drive the CPU. This now made available a rudimentary general-purpose microcomputer that could not only run the complex calculator but could also do many other functions depending on its program.

The microcomputer was slower than the minicomputer, but it could be mass-produced as a component on the same high-volume production line where Intel made memory chips—a surprising development that suddenly put semiconductor companies into the computer business. After some slight improvements, Intel's invention contained 2,250 microminiaturized transistors on a chip slightly less than one-sixth of an inch long and one-eighth of an inch wide, and each of those microscopic transistors could outperform the vacuum tubes used in the ENIAC computer developed in 1947.

The microprocessor chip, labeled the "4004," could possibly be as famous as the ENIAC. Despite its small size, the 4004 just about matched ENIAC's computational power. It also matched the capability of early 1960 computers that sold for $30,000 and up, and in which the central processing unit took up the space of several desks. The 4004 was upgraded in capacity to the 8008 in 1972 and then to the 8080 at the end of 1973. The 8080 was 20 times faster than the 4004 and was the prototype for the computer on a chip.

With the arrival of the microprocessor on a chip, the end of the costly search for ways to reduce the complicated technology to more general applications was achieved. Microprocessors and microcomputers are presently supplied by the big semiconductor companies: Texas Instruments, Motorola, Fairchild, General Instruments, Pro-log, and others. The microcomputers presently supplied are in many ways very similar to the initial minicomputers that were introduced in the 1960s. They usually have at least 16K characters of internal memory, allow interfacing with standard terminals, disks, and controllers, and can even be programmed in some limited higher-level languages.

Companies and Offerings

Although some well-known large computer manufacturers are in the minicomputer business, most of the manufacturers have minicomputers as their main or only product and are relatively unknown for other reasons. Largest in the field is Digital Equip-

ment Corporation (DEC) with more than 70,000 minicomputers
installed worldwide. The first minicomputer was DEC's Model
PDP-5, which was introduced in 1963, a hand-wired machine that
cost $27,000. The PDP-8, introduced in 1965, was the first mass-
produced minicomputer. It cost about $17,000 and opened up the
field. The PDP-8 was the first of a family of similar machines that
are still being produced and sold. Twelve years after its introduction, the PDP-8 was still accounting for 8 percent of DEC's shipments. DEC has since developed several new improved lines. The
one of primary interest is the PDP-11 line of 16-bit minicomputers,
which have been installed in 45,000 businesses since their introduction in 1970. The PDP-11 is the mainstay of the company's
small-computer line and is one of the most widely used computers.
In 1977, about 30 percent of the existing minicomputer installations
were DEC machines, as indicated in Table 2–1. Despite the fact
that DEC installs more computers than any of its competitors (with
the possible exception of IBM), its share of the market has decreased to about 25 or 30 percent from its 50 percent portion in 1970
because of the enlarging market.

Table 2–1. Minicomputer installations.

	1977		Cumulative Through 1977	
Manufacturer	Installations*	Percent Instal- lations	Total Instal- lations*	Percent Instal- lations
Digital Equipment	27,000	26.4	103,000	31.7
IBM†	23,000	22.5	40,000	12.3
Data General	11,000	10.7	37,000	11.4
Hewlett-Packard	6,000	5.9	24,000	7.4
Computer Automation	4,500	4.4	20,000	6.2
General Automation	4,500	4.4	19,000	5.8
Texas Instruments	4,000	4.0	13,000	4.0
Microdata	2,500	2.5	11,000	3.4
Interdata (Perkin-Elmer)	2,000	2.0	9,500	2.9
Honeywell	2,000	2.0	9,500	2.9
Varian (Sperry Univac)	2,000	2.0	9,000	2.8
All others	12,500	12.2	30,000	9.2
Total	102,000	100.0	325,000	100.0

*Estimated.
†Includes Series/1, System/7, 5100, System/32.
SOURCE: *Electronic News*, "Spotlight on Small Computers," August 22, 1977;
manufacturers and other industry sources.

Rounding out the top tier of minicomputer builders are Honeywell, Hewlett-Packard, IBM, and Data General. Each of these companies has already delivered more than 10,000 minicomputers, and Data General managed the unprecedented feat of delivering its two-thousandth computer after only three years of existence as a company.

In the second echelon of minicomputer makers are innovative young companies such as Computer Automation, General Automation, Interdata (now a division of Perkin-Elmer), and Microdata. It is very difficult to track the performance of the large computer companies in the minicomputer field, but it is known that Burroughs, NCR, Honeywell, and recently Univac have a significant and growing market size. In addition, minicomputers are also being built by divisions of large, well-established companies such as General Telephone and Electronics, Lockheed, Varian (now part of Sperry Univac), and Texas Instruments. And then there are dozens of comparatively small, unproven companies whose survival will depend upon their ability to back up their imaginative hardware ideas with effective marketing, production, software, and customer support.

The IBM Offerings

IBM, the dominant supplier of large-scale computers, was a late entry into the minicomputer and small business computer field. However, with the introduction of the System/32 and the more recent Series/1 and System/34, its presence is now strongly felt. IBM's entry is significant to the minicomputer industry in several ways. It adds the company that has the finest reputation for customer service and support to an industry with a reputation of frequently delivering hardware rather than systems or solutions.

The presence of IBM puts the stamp of acceptance on the many novel practices—the personal computer, programmerless systems, and distributed processing—introduced with the minicomputer. IBM's presence will increase the dollar volume of the market significantly, not only because of the sales made by IBM but also because of a stimulation effect produced by its strong marketing efforts to bring these techniques to many businesses previously unaware of them, thus widening the field for all suppliers. It is quite likely that IBM will dominate this field in the future just as it has done in the large-computer-system field.

System/3. The first IBM offering that had some characteristics resembling a minicomputer was delivered in 1969. The System/3 computer, although smaller in size than the standard large-size computer, was oriented toward data processing. It was primarily a card input, batch data processor without the capability for multi-terminal on-line input. As such it was not considered a minicomputer and was not included in industry figures on minicomputer sales.

Model 10 was the first of the System/3 offerings. It stressed direct-access disk files but, like most larger computers, was still oriented toward batch processing. The 96-column punched card was introduced with the System/3 and was the primary data input medium.

System/3 grew at both the low and the high end, and now consists of six distinct versions. In October 1970, Model 6 was introduced. This machine was oriented toward data processing and most suitable for commercial applications. It employed keyboard data entry for use in interactive problem solving and for limited data entry. For a long period of time, only these two models of the System/3 line were in production. They are no longer made, but refurbished models can be obtained. Together, Model 6 and Model 10 account for over 25,000 computers sold until the present time.

In July 1973, the very powerful Model 15 was introduced at system prices ranging from about $40,000 to over $300,000. Approximately 6,000 Model 15 computers were delivered through 1977.

Model 8, a disk-based system featuring cardless batch processing, was introduced in September 1974. About 6,000 of this model were delivered over the short life of this computer, which is no longer in production.

Model 12, an updated version of Model 10 using a new faster type of integrated circuit, was brought on the market in July 1975. It had greater processing speed than previous models and was frequently used in telecommunication applications.

In January 1976, the smallest model of the System/3 line, Model 4, appeared. This work-station oriented system for the first time fully qualified System/3 as representative of the philosophy and standard use of the minicomputer.

Overall, through 1977, over 50,000 of the System/3 computers were sold, making it one of the most popular computers in history.

System/7. In 1970 IBM introduced the System/7 minicomputer. This was a true minicomputer, but again was not oriented to business applications. It is primarily a sensor-input computer that has great utility in process control and in technically oriented environmental control applications. It also has been frequently used in communication applications, interfacing a voice response or data entry application with a large computer. It can be on line to IBM 1130, 1800, 360, and 370 computers. There are three models of this System 7; a typical minimum system costs about $12,000.

Series/1. A computer that is probably the replacement for the highly successful System/7, the Series/1, was introduced by IBM in late 1976. In addition to its sensor base capabilities and communication orientation, it also has utility in the commercial environment when provided with the proper software. It can function in a distributed processing environment with an IBM host computer or as a stand-alone system. It can be assembled into an extensive array of configurations; however, IBM did not initially supply much software support for it. As a result, until recently it was not considered to be a machine for the unsophisticated user. Until it is further enhanced with system and application software and other support packages, it will be a favorite of the OEM and turnkey system supplier. IBM is constantly adding to the software repertoire, making the Series/1 increasingly enticing to the end user.

The IBM Series/1 is offered in several models and in several different processor versions. The system prices range from slightly more than $4,000 for a stripped Model 3 with 16 bytes of memory to over $100,000 for the large Model 5 with the 256K Model E processor. A typical basic business-oriented system consisting of a 64K byte CPU, disk drive, a diskette (floppy disk) unit, and a character printer would cost close to $40,000. Such a system is shown in Figure 2–2. In addition to Fortran IV, PL/I, and Assembler language, the Series/1 supports standard COBOL that is compatible with the 370 OS/VS COBOL, providing an upward migration path to IBM's largest computers.

System/32. The IBM System/32, unveiled in January 1975, is one of IBM's smallest computers. It is a work-station computer system, designed for unsophisticated end users, and satisfies all characteristics of the minicomputer. All components of the System/32—the printer, the disk, and the central processing unit—are housed in a single desk-size cabinet, as shown in Figure 2–3. Applications can be programmed in RPG II, but IBM has strongly endorsed the application package approach, causing IBM to bill this as a "programmerless" computer.

Application programs designed to satisfy specific industry requirements are available for various industries and can be tailored to meet individual company needs. The system supports on-line CRT display terminals as well as communications for sending and receiving data to another System/32, a System/3, System/7, or Sys-

Figure 2–2. IBM Series/1. CPU, large disk, diskette unit, and communication and other units are contained in the rack enclosure. A matrix printer and display station with user-supplied keyboard appear at right.

Figure 2–3. IBM System/32. Shown with operator console, serial printer, and operator display screen. Programmable CPU, large-capacity disk storage, and diskette are housed in cabinet.

tem 360 or 370 computers. The 32 has bidirectional serial print capability as well as line printers. It can use either punched card or magnetic card input and output. It supports large disk storage as well as diskettes.

A typical purchase price of System/32 begins at about $30,000, or rents at about $680 monthly. Although very successful (approximately 20,000 were delivered by the end of 1977), the System/32 has one major drawback: it can serve only one user at a time.

System/34. The IBM System/34, introduced in April 1977 for first delivery in January 1978, represented the next step upward in IBM's participation in the small-business computer market. Figure 2–4 shows a typical System/34 configuration. As compared with the System/32, the 34 offers more processing power, larger memory capacity, larger disk storage, and multiple input terminals. Although the 34 is basically un upgrade of the highly successful System/32, its most significant difference is its ability to add to the basic system as many as 7 local but independent work stations and 64 work stations linked through communication lines. Thus, with the System/34 IBM has endorsed the concept of multiuser, mul-

Figure 2–4. IBM System/34. Shown with CRT keyboard terminal work station with serial printer. Line printer, programmable CPU, large disk storage, and other work stations having terminals and diskettes are shown in the background.

titerminal, small-business computer systems of the type that has been offered with considerable success by independent vendors such as Basic-4, Burroughs, Microdata, Four-Phase, and GRI.

As opposed to the batch-oriented System/32, the System/34 is interactive, or transaction-oriented, and hence is a completely multiprogrammable, multiterminal on-line system. While it is theoretically possible to have all 72 work stations running different programs simultaneously, users would typically have six or less going at one time.

A basic System/34 processor with 32K bytes of memory, a fixed disk drive, and a diskette has a purchase price of approximately $25,000. The system also includes a printer and display unit. The 72 work stations consisting of printers or display units may be attached to a single processor. Some 16 versions of the System/34 are being offered with variations in memory, disk, and diskette storage size.

With the System/34 computer, IBM again has endorsed the application program-package approach. Separately priced programs for billing, inventory control, accounts receivable, sales analysis, and many other uses are available at a price from $35 to $50 per month. Other industry-oriented packages are also available. The machine can also be programmed in RPG II and in Assembler language. The RPG II language is compatible with other machines, which allows upward mobility of these programs to the System 3 or smaller 370 computers.

With its competitive price, the multiterminal, work-station oriented, on-line, multiprogramming small-business computer System/34 is priced and configured to land right in the middle of the current first-time-user market.

The 5100. In September 1975, IBM made the initial delivery of the 5100 portable minicomputer. This small, 50-pound, desk-top computer, which takes little more space than a typical typewriter, was a new departure for IBM. The computer is programmable and is primarily designed to handle scientific problem-solving applications. In addition to supporting APL and BASIC programming languages for user-developed programs, it also has available a large library of mathematical and scientific program packages. A cartridge tape unit, used for storing data and programs, is an integral part of the 5100 system. The 5100 also has optional telecommunication capabilities for transmitting and receiving programs and data to and from large IBM computers. A bidirectional 80-character-per-second matrix printer and CRT display terminals may be used with

Figure 2–5. IBM 5100. In a single desk-top unit the 5100 contains up to 64K characters of storage, a cartridge for large-capacity storage, functional keyboard, and display screen. Other features are optional.

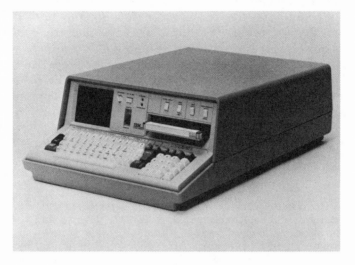

the computer. An estimated 3,000 systems have been installed through the end of 1977. A typical system, such as that shown in Figure 2–5, costs approximately $9,000. An interactive version, the IBM 5110, introduced in 1978, added random-access storage and communication capability making it suitable for distributed processing.

Small-Business Computers

The small-business computer market consists of four main segments. The first group consists of the large computer manufacturers such as Burroughs, NCR, Sperry Univac, and IBM. These companies offer small-business computers as only one part of a very large range of computer offerings. However, companies like NCR and Burroughs, after specializing in the office equipment and machines market for many years, continue their concentration on office automation with small-business computer offerings. Sales of these new machines now comprise a good segment of their income.

A second group consists of the major minicomputer manufacturers such as Digital Equipment Corporation, Data General, General Automation, GRI, Computer Automation, and Hewlett-Packard.

These companies have, in the past, supplied minicomputers that ended up in business-oriented applications, although this was not their primary market. With the exploding new market for small-business computers, they are now packaging the minicomputer with peripherals, usually of their own manufacture, with some application software, and are marketing them as complete systems. Usually included with the systems are language processors such as BASIC, RPG-II, or some form of COBOL that allows the user to program his own business applications. Small-business computer configurations of Data General (a) and GRI (b) are shown in Figure 2–6.

The third group of suppliers of small-business systems consists

Figure 2–6a. Data General's CS/40 small-business system. Equipment shown includes a 64K-character CPU, with diskette drive and 10-million-character disk, a Dasher™ video display, and a printer in a work station environment. Approximate price $33,400. Reproduced by permission of Data General Corporation, Westboro, Mass. Dasher is a trademark of Data General Corporation.

Figure 2–6b. Small-business computer by GRI. 64K byte GRI SYSTEM 99 by GRI Computer Corporation shown supporting 4–10.6 million character disk drives, 9-track magnetic tape, 3 printers, and 3 terminals. Typical prices for a system with 32K byte CPU, 10.6 Mbyte disk drive, 1 printer, and 1 terminal start at $33,333. Photo courtesy of GRI Computer Corp., Newton, Mass.

of systems houses and turnkey vendors. These include companies such as Basic/Four, Four-Phase, Mini-Computer Systems, and Ultimacc. This group is similar to the second group except that they do not manufacture the minicomputers. They bring together computers and peripherals from many different vendors, supply the application software, and sell the complete package as an application system. A typical system of this type is shown in Figure 2–7. The prime appeal of this approach is that the vendor writes all software, removing that task and responsibility from the user. This approach is particularly attractive to first-time users.

The fourth group consists of the integrated circuit chip manufacturers. The semiconductor manufacturers who specialize in making the integrated-circuit and microprocessor chips that go into minicomputers have now branched out to supply full application-

Figure 2–7. Small-business system from Minicomputer Systems, Inc. The system shown includes a 65K character CPU, disk drive with fixed and removable disks, serial matrix printers, and CRT keyboard terminals. Complete system costs less than $50,000. Photo courtesy of Minicomputer Systems, Inc., Hartsdale, N.Y.

oriented systems. However, because of the limited support for programming and application development available by the microprocessor companies, the sales are more commonly made to the systems and turnkey houses, where a complete system is fashioned from the bare-bones equipment originally supplied.

Table 2–2 indicates the estimated small-business computer shipments for 1977. Since minicomputer manufacturers supply equipment to small-business computer companies and also at times ship entire business systems, the figures shown in this table duplicate some of the numbers shown in Table 2–1 as minicomputer installations.

A very large number of small-business computer systems are now on the market. Whether they are sold as complete turnkey systems or as equipment configurations to be programmed by the users, their capabilities and capacities are quite similar. The costs usually fall in a range from approximately $25,000 to $40,000 for a complete system. Typical of these systems are the Burroughs B-80, Data General's microcomputer-based CS series, the NCR 499, the Digital Equipment Corporation Data System 324, the Univac BC-7, and the Microdata Reality 2.

The small-business systems have a wide range of capabilities. They can support communication terminals for on-site data entry and data processing, as well as for communicating with larger com-

Table 2–2. Small-business computer installations.

Manufacturer	1977 Installations*	1977 Percent Instal-lations	Cumulative Through 1977 Total Instal-lations*	Cumulative Through 1977 Percent Instal-lations
IBM	8,600	27.5	20,600	22.4
Wang	4,700	15.0	9,900	10.8
Burroughs	2,000	6.4	3,000	3.3
Digital Equipment	1,700	5.4	5,700	6.2
Basic Four	1,400	4.5	5,400	5.9
NCR	1,200	3.8	4,200	4.6
Data Point	1,100	3.5	3,100	3.4
Univac	1,000	3.2	1,500	1.6
Honeywell	1,000	3.2	1,800	2.0
Data General	900	2.9	1,400	1.5
Lockheed	850	2.7	2,050	2.2
Microdata	850	2.7	2,250	2.4
All others	6,000	19.2	31,000	33.7
Total	31,300	100.0	91,900	100.0

*Estimated.
SOURCE: *Electronic News*, November 14, 1977; and other industry sources.

puters in a distributed system network. They typically support multiple CRT and data entry work stations, large disk-storage systems, diskette storage, magnetic tape storage systems, line printers, and slower-speed character printers. The computer systems usually come with a comprehensive set of industry-specific application programs. Among these are programs for manufacturing, accounting, accounts payable, accounts receivable, and payroll. The software is unbundled, and costs from $35 to $100 per application. Language processors, invariably including RPG-II, are available for those desiring to develop their own application.

These small-business computer systems are easy to use and do not require a technical support staff to assure continuous operations. They are designed and configured for the first-time computer user, and provide a reasonably easy, trouble-free method of automating the basic business functions of a small business.

Super minicomputers. Running counter to the trend toward ever smaller and cheaper minicomputers is a current expansion toward a class of super minicomputers whose power and flexibility rival those of far more costly medium-scale computers. These systems feature large main-storage capacity, fast semiconductor memory, advanced memory management facilities, multiprogramming operating systems, and other big computer software facilities at central processing unit prices ranging from about $15,000 upward. Among the high-performance minicomputers that adhere to the

Figure 2–8a. Data General ECLIPSE S/130. This large business configuration includes a 192K-character CPU, 96-million-character disk, magnetic tape, communications subsystems, line printer, and serial printer. Price is approximately $100,000. Reproduced by permission of Data General Corporation, Westboro, Mass. ECLIPSE is a registered trademark of Data General Corporation.

traditional 16-bit word length are the DEC PDP 11-70, the Data General Nova Eclipse Series, and the Varian V-76. Meanwhile, the increased computational power and flexibility made possible by the use of a 32-bit word length are being emphasized in such systems as the DEC VAX 11/780, the Interdata 8-32 Mega-Mini, the SEL 32-50 and 32-55, and the Wang WCS 60 and 80. Two of these superminis are shown in Figure 2–8 (a) and (b).

Many of the offerings of the semiconductor companies fall into the super minicomputer category. In fact, some of these computers are so powerful that their designation as minis is strained. The computers of National Semiconductor Corp. run unmodified IBM System 370 operating system software making them completely compatible with the largest data processing computer. National's medium-scale Model 400 is comparable in performance to the IBM 370/145, and its complete software and I/O compatibility makes it suitable not only as a stand-alone computer but also as a remote-

Figure 2–8b. Interdata 8-32 Mega-Mini. Shown are dual Mega-Mini® processors with tape drives, disks, line printers, several keyboard display stations, and a serial printer. Photo courtesy of Interdata, Inc., Oceanport, N.J.

computing facility in IBM 370 based distributed processing networks. National CSS, Inc., Magnusen Computer Systems, and others, jointly with semiconductor manufacturers, have developed IBM 370 compatible super minis. These and other similar companies illustrate the entry of the semiconductor industry directly into the manufacture of end-user super minicomputer systems.

Microcomputers. Having solidified their position as cheaper alternatives to the large general-purpose computers for many applications, the minicomputers are in turn being threatened by a newer and still cheaper class of computers called *microcomputers.* The microcomputer field is in a development stage very similar to that of the minicomputers in 1970. The processors are highly capable, but the software support and application knowledge are not presently available from the microcomputer manufacturers. As a result, microprocessors and microcomputers are primarily used by original equipment manufacturers, who assemble them into complete, functional, business-oriented systems. It appears that at least for the next few years, microcomputers will not have the full range of peripherals such as those used by minicomputers. In addition, the processing speeds will be somewhat lower. Therefore, instead of displacing large numbers of minicomputers, the microcomputers can be expected to open up vast new application areas for which even the cheapest minicomputers have been economically unjustifiable.

Packaged systems. Many original minicomputer manufacturers either build complete packaged systems or supply their minicomputers to other original equipment manufacturers to be incorporated into their packaged products. Many of the recently announced small-business computer systems are, in fact, configurations that consist of previously available minicomputer processors, with standard peripheral equipment and integrated with software designed for specific types of applications. Digital Equipment Corporation (DEC) offers its business-oriented users its Data System 300 and 500 series, which are based on the popular DEC PDP-8 and PDP-11 minicomputers, respectively. In addition to the DEC business systems, there are many others, including the offerings from General Automation (DM 100), Burroughs (B-80), Univac (BC-7—see Figure 2–9), Data General (Eclipse), and GRI (System 99).

Foreign suppliers. European equipment is making a much greater impact on the small-business computer market than on any other segment of the U.S. computer market. Honeywell, International Computers, Olivetti, Philips, and Nixdorf are marketing

Figure 2–9. Sperry Univac BC/7. The BC/7 system shown includes a 65K character CPU, ¼ million character diskette storage, CRT display with printer in a workstation configuration, line printer, and optional communications interface. The system is designed to be operated by personnel untrained in computers. Reproduced by permission of Sperry Univac, Blue Bell, PA.

equipment that they manufacture in France, Great Britain, Italy, The Netherlands, and Germany, respectively.

The Japanese, who are active in the large-computer mainframe area, are also starting to produce microcomputer systems, minicomputer systems, and small-business systems. They are expected to be a major force in the market very shortly.

The Minicomputer Market

It is very difficult to obtain a reliable estimate of the minicomputer market. Indeed, even the statistics of present and past sales are difficult to acquire. This difficulty is not surprising because existing estimates of the market are made unreliable by a mass of uncertainties, which include the following:

- Lack of agreement on precisely what a minicomputer is.
- A rapidly changing technology.

- The future availability of presently unknown alternatives.
- The extent of minicomputer hardware price deterioration.
- The extent to which minicomputer hardware techniques will replace programming techniques.
- The extent to which programming techniques will advance, thus reducing software costs.
- The extent to which minicomputers will be accepted for large business applications where software support is essential.
- The likely duplication in counting computers, since manufacturers sell the computer to other suppliers who include it in equipment such as small-business computers.

Although it is difficult to estimate the size of the market, it is commonly agreed that minicomputers constitute the fastest growing segment of one of the fastest growing industries. The 1977 worldwide minicomputer shipments are estimated to be approximately $2.8 billion, having increased at an annual rate of 40 percent for each of the two preceding years. The 1976 leaders (excluding IBM, for which separate minicomputer figures are not available) were Data General with a 60 percent increase in revenues over 1975, DEC with a 42 percent growth, and Hewlett-Packard with 27 percent.

Table 2–3 indicates the estimated revenues for selected minicomputer manufacturers for 1980.

Table 2–3. Revenues of selected minicomputer manufacturers (estimated for 1980).

Manufacturers	Revenues ($ millions)
Digital Equipment	1,200*
Hewlett-Packard	600
Data General	500
Interdata (Perkin-Elmer)	180
Texas Instruments	150
General Automation	120
Mod Comp	70
Computer Automation	65
Honeywell	60
Varian (Sperry Univac)	60
Microdata	50
Systems Engineering Labs	50

*Excludes large computer systems.
SOURCE: *Electronic News*, September 12, 1977; manufacturers and other industry sources.

MINICOMPUTER HARDWARE

A definition of the term "minicomputer" would be a good starting point. However, it is very difficult to define a minicomputer so that it is uniquely distinguished from other computers, since all computers are functionally the same. The most common definition of a minicomputer uses price as the criterion that differentiates it from other types of computers. In general, a cost of the central processing unit (that is, cost of the basic computer without peripherals) of less than $25,000 usually distinguishes the minicomputer from the traditional computer.

There are other ways to define the minicomputer, and these definitions are probably just as valid or invalid as the definition based on price. It is often defined in terms of its use or, more precisely, in terms of the philosophy of its use. Traditionally, it has been used where it is dedicated to a single application. That is, it has been used to handle one application, such as order entry or information retrieval, rather than a mixed job stream of completely different applications. Its use in this manner not only brings about a new way of using computers, it also makes the user evaluate computer performance only in terms of system economics. Thus, a definition based on philosophy of use is a valid one, possibly the best one, but it does not encompass all uses of the minicomputer.

A strictly technical definition of a minicomputer, which is valuable because it is precise and will always be valid regardless of the price range or how the computer is used, is based on *word size*. The word size is the basic unit of internal design and operation within the computer. Many of the economies of the minicomputer derive from the smaller word size and corresponding smaller data paths. If this criterion is used, a minicomputer may be defined as a computer having a word size of 18 bits or less. This definition fails, however, when applied to many older, second-generation computers, which have smaller word size but whose cost was an order of magnitude more than the present-day minicomputer. In addition, a number of new computers using a 32-bit internal structure have appeared in the industry. Although they are sometimes referred to as "midicomputers" or "mega-minis," the industry usually considers these machines minicomputers. The advantage of the definition is that it is precise and will hold regardless of future price changes.

The most commonly used definition, however, the one used in most literature and throughout industry, is based on price. As early as 1970 *Auerbach Minicomputer Reports** defined a minicomputer as a computer that costs less than $25,000, has at least a 4K memory, uses stored program control, can be programmed, and is not restricted to specialized applications. The key points illustrated by this and many other similar definitions still apply and will be adhered to in this book.

1. It is a general-purpose computer and not restricted to specific applications.
2. It operates through programming.
3. It has a versatile input and output capability.
4. The central processor costs less than $25,000.

Reasons for Existence

The minicomputer has come upon the scene largely because of the dramatic changes in electronic technology that started during the 1960s and continued through the 1970s. During this period, the components used in computers and other electronic equipment shifted from vacuum tubes to transistors, then to integrated circuits (ICs), then to medium-scale and large-scale integration (MSI and LSI), and most recently to extremely densely packed LSI chips called microprocessors.

Although we are not overly concerned with how a computer is made, these developments are important because they are the motivating force behind the development of the whole minicompu-

*Auerbach Minicomputer Reports, Vol. 10, 1970. Auerbach Info, Inc., Philadelphia.

ter industry. Not only are these new components able to perform thousands more functions than those done by the single discrete component of the early 1950s, but they also perform each function better and hundreds of times faster. In addition, the use of these components reduces the production cost of computers to a very large extent. Use of integrated circuits permits large reductions in the cost per circuit. The integrated circuit also accomplishes hundreds of times as much as the transistor. Functions that require many discrete components—such as transistors, resistors, capacitors, and diodes—are combined in a single integrated-circuit chip.

This circuit miniaturization has a number of important benefits. It allows the performance of the equipment to be improved. That is, it reduces physical distances, thus allowing greater speeds of internal computing to be achieved. It reduces size and weight. Even more important than these advantages is the fact that use of this technology allows a manyfold reduction in assembly and production costs, since each wiring operation now accomplishes hundreds of times as much as those needed when individual transistors were used. Product reliability is very dependent upon the number of physical and electronic connections. The concentrated multifunction components lead to greatly reduced production costs and allow for the automation of many of the assembly functions. The effectiveness of the production process and the reliability of the product are therefore greatly increased. Along with low assembly costs there are also lower testing and quality-control costs. The philosophy of design is also somewhat influenced by the ease of production.

Minicomputers, like many other space-age electronic devices, use the plug-in assembly technology. This type of design, which has always been desirable and effective, now becomes economically feasible. Modular construction may not in itself make the minicomputer different from other computers, but in this case major segments such as memory, arithmetic logic, and even the power supply are separable.

Through the selection of the proper modular features, minicomputers can be, and usually are, directed to a broad but specific application area. For example, by adding a module for decimal arithmetic, the standard minicomputer can be made very efficient for business applications; double-precision hardware features and hardware multiply-and-divide modules make it ideal for scientific applications. Similarly, the computers can be tailored by the proper selection of standard hardware modules for use as a communications controller, a power machine tool controller, and many other specific functions. As a result, the machine adapted to do a particular job can be very efficient in that application, and because the machine is usually dedicated to a single application, the user obtains maximum value for his money. The user does not have to buy a general-purpose computer model that was designed to satisfy everyone's needs at once. He can buy just enough computer power to do his specific job.

The design philosophy carries over to simpler data paths. Many of these computers operate internally off a single bus line, and all operating parts of the computer are plugged into that circuit bus. This simplifies the design and construction, and provides for easy replacement of components that fail. The simpler data paths and logical construction bring about a new level of understanding of computers.

The nature of the companies in the field has also had a large effect on the development of minicomputers in the past year and a half. These companies are generally small or are a small division of a large company, and because of their size and small investment in historical or traditional techniques, they can respond very rapidly to the new technology.

The acceptance of minicomputers by business and industry is strongly tied to the economics of the marketplace. Regardless of the technical capabilities of the computer, its use is evidently cost-justified. Moreover, the benefits must surely be significant to gain such great acceptance in so short a time. While many computer costs continue to fall, labor costs continue to rise. Each increment of these changes introduces a situation where automation becomes more attractive, and increases the number of applications where automation can be justified. (See Figure 3–1 for a comparison of minicomputer costs and labor costs.)

Many of the characteristics mentioned here as common items in the minicomputer have been available in some large computers. However, these features are a much more integral part of small computers because the dynamic nature of the small companies permits design philosophy to be changed very rapidly.

The effect of all the foregoing factors is cumulative. The philosophy of use affects the design, which affects the production, improves the cost/benefit characteristics, and in turn changes and modifies the original concept of what is feasible. And all these changes can take place in a relatively short period of time because of the nature of the developing companies and because of the simpler design concepts involved.

Figure 3–1. Monthly costs—average minicomputer system versus clerical labor.

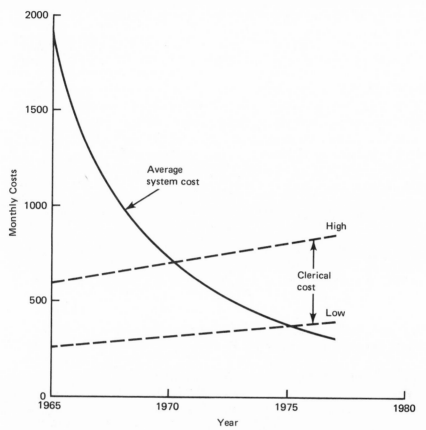

Range of Capabilities

What can minicomputers do? Are they as capable as the large computers? It has been stated that if you overcome the connotation of the term "mini," keep an open mind, and evaluate the minicomputer objectively, you will find this class of equipment compares favorably with a machine as large as the IBM 370/135. If you ignore the "mini" prefix, you will find that these machines could just as well be named "compact computers."

Table 3–1, which lists some technical processor statistics such as memory size, cycle speed, transfer rates, and minimum add time, shows that the characteristics of the typical high-performance minicomputer compare very favorably with those of commonly

Table 3–1. Central processor characteristics of selected computers.

Computer	Year of Model Delivery	Memory Capacity (thousands of characters)	Cycle Speed (micro-sec.)	I/O Transfer Rate (millions characters per sec.)	Min. Add Time* (micro-sec.)	Purchase Price ($000)
Digital Equipment PDP 11/45	1972	16–124	0.3	3.8	0.3	38
Data General ECLIPSE C/300	1975	32–128	0.2	1.25	0.2	30.7
General Automation GA-16/330	1975	4–65	0.45	2.50	0.78	4.0
Honeywell 6/36	1976	8–128	0.65	1.5	1.90	5.6
IBM Series/1	1977	16–128	0.80	1.6	1.32	5
Interdata 8/16	1976	16–64	0.75	2.66	0.75	6.25
Microdata 3200	1973	4–128	0.35	5.0	0.4	9.63
Texas Instruments 990-10	1975	8–1024	0.75	6.0	3.6	2.2
Varian V-76	1976	16–1024	0.66	6.0	1.32	8.6
IBM 370/125	1973	98–262	0.48	2.4	9.8	385
IBM 370/138	1976	524–2100	0.71	1.3	2.14	350
IBM 370/145	1971	164–2097	0.54	5.3	2.14	800
Honeywell 66/80	1976	262–1048	0.75	4.05	0.63	2,600
Univac 1100/80	1977	524–4200	0.48	2.0	0.20	2,600

*Minimum execution time for binary add of two-digit number.

Source: Cost and performance derived from manufacturer-supplied data and various industry publications.

used large computers. These comparisons involve nine common minicomputers and five standard computers.

Comparisons of computers' performance can be very inaccurate and misleading. General-purpose computer processing performance can be measured in terms of add time, multiplications executed per second, transfer rate, and even cycle time, but these parameters may not be meaningful when comparing computers' use. Such comparisons do not take into consideration the size (in number of digits) of the arithmetic problem, I/O efficiency, or software capability, not to mention user environments; therefore, none of these characteristics should be the yardstick to use in the evaluation of total systems.

In particular, the add-time comparison can be very misleading because of the minicomputers' small word size. For 16-bit minicomputers the add time provided would be merely for adding 2-digit numbers, while the computers having larger words could

Table 3–2. Calculations per dollar.

Computer	Additions per Microsec.	Purchase Price, $	Calculations per Dollar
Digital Equipment PDP 11/45	3.33	$ 38,000	86
Data General ECLIPSE C/300	5.0M	30,700	160
General Automation GA 16/330	1.28	4,000	230
Honeywell 6/36	.526	5,600	94
IBM Series/1, Model 3	.758	5,000	150
Interdata 8/16	1.33	6,250	213
Microdata 3200	2.50	9,630	260
Texas Instruments 990-10	.278	2,200	130
Varian V-76	.758	8,600	88
IBM 370/125	.102	385,000	0.26
IBM 370/138	.467	350,000	1.3
IBM 370/145	.467	800,000	0.58
Honeywell 66/80	1.58	2.6M	0.61
Univac 1100/80	5.0	2.6M	1.9

SOURCE: Derived from manufacturer-supplied data and various industry publications.

add numbers of many more digits without requiring any additional time. However, one interesting exercise relates the internal processor characteristics to price. In Table 3–2 the minimum add time is the number of bits transferred per microsecond divided by the price of the minimum usable configuration. This result can be taken as an extremely rough guide to the per-unit cost of processor power. The figures indicate at least an order of magnitude in favor of the minicomputers. Figure 3–2, which includes the characteristics of several other computers in addition to those shown in Table 3–2, illustrates this point very graphically. Of course there are other factors that modify or, for some uses, reverse the favorable comparison. The large computer can do many things at the same time. The scheduling and loading functions and the general-purpose operating system allow an operator to load many types of programs, which are then run without further thought to the allocation of the computer resources and facilities.

The smaller word size of the computer means that fewer instructions or less powerful instructions can be used and less main mem-

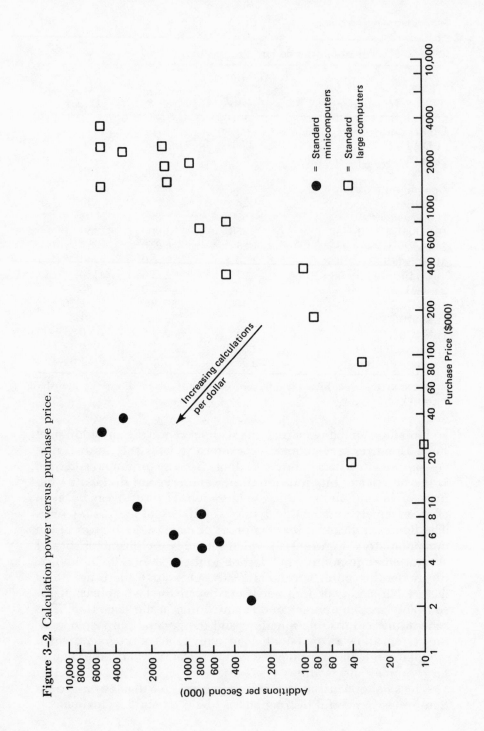

Figure 3–2. Calculation power versus purchase price.

ory can be directly addressed. This results in more instructions and computer cycles for accomplishing the same job, modifying the speed advantage the mini might have had. In addition, some functions such as high accuracy and floating-point arithmetic that are needed in scientific calculations cannot be done in a practical manner on the small machine. Large linear programs for scientific allocation or modeling applications require large amounts of internal storage and therefore cannot be readily done on the minicomputer. Large compilers such as those needed for standard COBOL require large amounts of memory to be efficient and cannot be handled in the small computer. Moreover, most (but not all) minicomputers use binary arithmetic in their internal calculations. When this is the case, additional computing is required to change the decimal numbers of the real world to, and from, the binary notation used internally.

Although the primary and most advanced uses of the minicomputer have it operating in a dedicated application, its economies, low cost, and high capability have justified its use in the standard data processing environment as well. However, even when it is used as the main processor in a data processing environment, the user buys and pays only for the amount of system (internal memory, data channels, internal hardware features) that he really needs.

Disk-operating systems are supplied without charge by most of the major manufacturers. These software systems handle the batch processing of many jobs in a manner similar to large computers. Foreground-background monitors are also available, but it is much more common to have the minicomputer used in a multiterminal time-sharing environment. For those applications where the user interacts directly with the computer—a real-time operation as opposed to a batch-processing operation—there are many very competent real-time or time-sharing operating systems. Almost without exception, each minicomputer manufacturer can supply a real-time or time-sharing operating system. Such an operating system not only has a multiuser time-sharing monitor, but also supports many different input/output terminals. It invariably supports both BASIC, a programming language developed for people who needed to use the computer but had no desire or need to learn the formal, professional programming languages, and RPG II, a simple business-oriented language. All application programming can be done in these user-oriented languages, which use common English and simple mathematics statements.

The characteristic of being designed for a specific job is very

much evident when a microprocessor or a stripped-down mini
is used in some kind of controller or in a data-input terminal such as
the so-called intelligent terminal. For example, an intelligent terminal could be designed to operate in a very specific data-capture
application. Inside that terminal would be a microprocessor, which
is essentially a computer without its input/output devices and
channels but containing the central processing unit, a small programmable memory, and usually a buffer memory to hold the processed data for ultimate delivery to a communication line or
another computer. Besides the advantage of low price, the resulting
terminal would have extremely high hardware and software
reliability.

Internally, the minicomputer would likely contain some microprogrammed modules that perform specific functions on that
input data. Microprogramming is a hardware technique built into
the machine, and which with one input instruction will trigger the
execution of a series of operations. The program can be set for a
specific application. It can be designed to aid the person entering
the data by checking the validity of the information as it is entered
and then either correcting it or informing the user of any inconsis-
tency. It could also be used to tailor the minicomputer to a specific
application area such as for use as a communication processor. All
this can be done by a set program designed for that particular
application and included in the intelligent terminal as a hardware
or computer function rather than a programming or software function. This produces a highly reliable, error-proof, and efficient device designed specifically for that application. This area of use of a
minimum-sized, microprogrammed computer in the data input or
intelligent-terminal application, while common today, is expected to be one of the largest and most important types of applications in the very near future.

Another important illustration of how the minicomputer is designed for the job relates to the use of read-only memory. Instead of
modifying the instruction set or allowing one instruction to perform
very many operations, as is done in microprogramming, a somewhat
related technique is used to put the exact equivalent of a software
program into a wired-core memory of the computer. This allows the
programming of the system to be done by traditional means, but at
its completion the program is wired into the main memory of the
machine. This type of memory is called *read-only memory* (ROM)
because it can be always read and used, but no one can alter it or
write on it, thus preventing its logic contents from being changed.

Use of the read-only technique to put the operating instructions (the program) into unalterable memory prevents the accidental changing of that program. An unauthorized intrusion into the program of any computer is not too common, but it can happen and may be caused by natural or human interference. Accidental change of a program can be caused by static electricity, high-frequency transients on a power line, programming errors, or tampering with the program. On the other hand, changing a program that is contained in read-only memory can be done only by removing the entire board, and this is precisely what is done when a change in the program is desired. A new board is wired to reflect the new program and is slipped into the place vacated by the obsolete board.

Although physically changing boards is an easy operation, taking less than an hour, modifying boards for a standard-sized program costs several thousands of dollars. Thus, the read-only-memory technique is not used if the program is expected to be modified. It is used where the nature of the computer operation is so critical that any means must be taken to insure continuing operation. This technique aids the operation of computers in many poor environment locations such as a factory in which heavy electrical equipment is being turned on and off frequently, or in locations that experience unusual temperature or humidity conditions.

Microprogramming and some uses of read-only memory result in a special type of computer, one that is designed to operate very efficiently in a specific application. It also means that it will not be software-compatible with any other computer. Therefore, the use of these specialized techniques should be chosen carefully. Microprogramming and specialized read-only-memory techniques are primarily used when the computer is to be used over and over again in the same types of applications.

Computer System Components

Peripheral Equipment

A general-purpose minicomputer is useless without peripherals. When used for business purposes, the computer system requires peripheral equipment for input, output, and storage, the cost of which will frequently exceed the price of the computer.

Some minicomputer companies also manufacture peripherals. Few of the minicomputer manufacturers produce all their peripherals, but all major companies supply a full range of peripherals and support and provide maintenance. A very large range of peripherals is available for minicomputer systems. In addition to the standard data processing peripherals that have been interfaced to all major minicomputers, a new range of peripherals with slightly degraded performance at a much lower price is also presently available. Also there are some peripherals that are used only with minicomputers and are priced accordingly. In this category are cassette tape drives, which are too slow and inconvenient for the large data processors, but are very useful and effective in many small systems. Diskettes, or floppy disks, a low-cost random-access storage medium, are also used for minicomputer systems, but rarely for large computer systems. The features and characteristics of some typical peripherals important to minicomputers are discussed below.

Main memory storage. The main storage of every computer is called memory and is contained internally. It has frequently been called "core," but this name is no longer appropriate because the magnetic toroid core memory has been replaced by semiconductors in most computers.

A memory extension that increases the main storage beyond the normal capacity of the machine is usually considered as a computer peripheral. Although available for a few minicomputers, memory add-ons are used only by the most sophisticated users. They are, however, quite commonly used in large computer systems.

Auxiliary storage. The computer's main storage is expensive. Large main memories affect the price of the computer directly and also indirectly through increases necessary in the internal electronic logic and circuitry. Therefore, large masses of information are stored in auxiliary devices such as tapes or disks and brought into main memory only when actually being worked upon. Auxiliary storage may be categorized in many ways, but it is felt that the best one relates to the method of data access, either random or sequential.

A random-access (also called *direct-access)* device is one in which an individual set of data can be located and retrieved without searching through the entire file. Either by an addressing scheme or logic arrangement, the reading mechanism is directed to the location of the desired data and retrieves only that data. Because of its random-access nature, it is not essential to maintain data in any prescribed order in this type of file.

Sequential-access devices make a continuous search of the file, record by record, to locate the desired information. As a result, the time to locate and retrieve specific data is long, on the order of minutes, making sequential devices inappropriate for use in on-line systems.

Random-access storage. Almost all random-access auxiliary storage in use today utilizes "rotating" memory. Information is stored on many tracks on a magnetic surface of a drum or disk, which continuously rotates. As the data is rotated, read-write heads located over the tracks read or record the data. Two devices are used: moving-head and head-per-track.

The moving-head disk uses flat platter-like surfaces as the recording medium. In the most common configuration, the read-write heads move radially across the surface of the disk until the correct track is located; then the data is retrieved in the next revolution of the disk. Figure 3–3 illustrates this construction. The larger disks rotate rapidly, typically at 1,800 to 3,600 revolutions per

Figure 3–3. Moving-head disk.

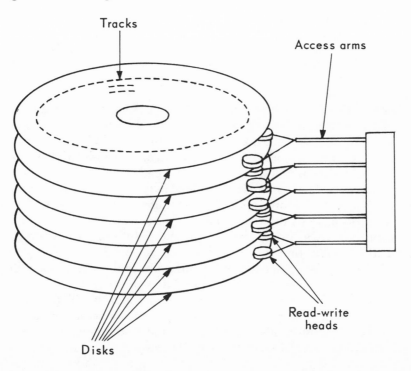

minute or approximately one revolution every 15 to 30 milliseconds. The time required to retrieve data from a moving-head
disk consists of the time to position the arm over the appropriate
track *(seek time)* and the time required for the disk to rotate to the
proper position *(latency)*. The total access time is dependent upon
the particular disk drive, but 30 to 60 milliseconds is typical for a
good-quality, large-capacity disk.

Disk drives with removable storage units, called *disk packs* or
cartridges, are available and are very useful and very popular. The
disks can be removed from the mechanical drives and reading
heads. This means that very large data bases can be used, provided
all data is not required to be on line at all times. Several different
application data files may be maintained on separate disks, thus
expanding the system capacity and usefulness tremendously.

The head-per-track device does not require the read-write head
to move and thus provides certain advantages over the moving-
head disk:

- Faster access: The time required to position the head over the
  proper track is eliminated.
- The device is more reliable, since a major moving part is
  eliminated.
- The storage and reading mechanism can be entirely sealed,
  making it impervious to many adverse environmental
  conditions.

As the name indicates, a head-per-track device has a fixed head
positioned over each track, requiring only the electronic start sig-
nal. The recording medium is either the surface of a drum or a disk.
The drum predates both the moving-head and fixed-head disks, but
has largely been replaced by the fixed-head disk because of lower
fabrication costs. These devices normally have smaller storage
capacity and cost more per unit of storage than the moving-head
variety. Because of their high speed, they are frequently used as
swapping disks to bring program modules into main memory for
execution in real-time systems.

Diskettes (floppy disks). In the early part of the 1970s, a smaller
version of the single-platter removable disk drive came into use for
data and program storage. It was quickly labeled the "floppy disk"
because its recording medium was a disk of mylar plastic, unlike
the rigid aluminum disk and drums that had been used in all
previously successful mass-storage devices.

The floppy disk was actually introduced in 1970 by IBM, buried in the 370 system as a microprogram loader for the big 3330 disks. Similar microcode storage applications of the floppy disk followed in the 370 system. Thus buried, the new storage medium attracted little notice until 1971 when IBM began test marketing in Europe a data entry terminal using the floppy disk.

In the second quarter of 1972, three independent manufacturers announced floppy disk drives using the standard IBM medium. Almost instantly in the fall of 1972, IBM announced the 3740 data entry station with a new diskette or floppy disk cartridge. Three distinct segments of the market appeared. The IBM-manufactured disk retained a continuing large portion. In addition, there were a large number of independent manufacturers who followed the IBM design and developed fully compatible diskette drives. Finally there were the pioneers, the technical innovators, who offered noncompatible equipment, generally opting for improved features such as moving heads, faster media rotation, a combination of one fixed and one removable disk, and others.

The diskette has continued in use by IBM as a microprogram storage device. However, its use in the mid-1970s as a data entry storage medium was by far the largest volume application for this device. The diskettes have also made heavy inroads into the intelligent-terminal market and into key data entry systems supplied by independent manufacturers. They are routinely offered as optional peripherals with most minicomputers, although the larger hard disks are more commonly purchased. They are also offered as part of word-processing systems, which have long been the enclave of magnetic cards and cartridge tape. As minicomputers penetrate more new areas such as process control, engineering, and building automation, the diskettes will follow in the same ratio. Table 3–3 indicates the applications in which diskettes are used and their percentage absorption of the market.

The diskette has taken its place, together with cassettes and cartridge tapes, as one of the big three of small-scale removable storage devices. Table 3–4 provides some typical disk costs and performance information.

Random-access devices are the most useful storage equipment. Because of their frequent use in on-line systems, the great variety of disks available, and their tumbling prices, disks are used in most minicomputer systems as the major storage medium.

Sequential storage. Magnetic tape has historically been the most commonly used storage medium in data processing. A tape

Table 3–3. Estimated 1980 diskette (floppy disk) drive shipments by market. (Total estimate = 470,000 units.*)

Market	Percent of Total Shipments
Small-business systems	20.1
Data entry	17.4
Minicomputers/microcomputers	16.1
Communication terminals	15.7
Word processing	9.6
Point-of-sale terminals	8.2
Programmable calculators	3.7
Program store	3.5
All others	5.7

*This total comprises three approximately equal segments: IBM manufacture, IBM compatible, and noncompatible independent.

Table 3–4. Typical disk storage units.*

Disk Type	Price ($000)	Average Access Time (millisec)	Transfer Rate (K characters/ sec)	Capacity (millions of characters)	Storage Cost (cents/ character)
Fixed head	9.8	8.4	116	0.524	1.87
Diskette	3.9	355	30	1.26	0.310
Movable head	12.5	35	312	10.0	0.125
Fixed head	9.5	8.5	1,070	0.512	1.85
Movable head	15	63	405	30.7	0.049
Diskette	4.1	483	56	0.512	0.801
Fixed head	30	30	300	2.048	1.46
Movable head	140	30	806	200	0.070
Diskette	40	35	885	140	0.029
Fixed head	33.5	17	500	4.3	0.779
Fixed head	13	17	105	0.256	5.08
Diskette	6	35	184	2.34	0.260
Fixed head	7.9	10	910	1.0	3.25
Diskette	1.25	162	250	0.512	0.240
Diskette	0.855	91	250	0.512	0.167

*Costs and performance data on disk units available from minicomputer manufacturers.

unit consists of seven or nine tracks of data recorded on a strip of plastic tape coated with a magnetic medium. Data is recorded in densities of 200 to 1,600 bits per inch (bpi) in blocks of various lengths. The tape moves past fixed read-write heads where data is transferred to, or read from, the tape.

Magnetic tapes still present one of the most economical means of auxiliary storage, but because they are sequential devices, they have limited value as data file storage for a class of systems that normally operates on line. Standard magnetic tapes (200 to 1,600 bpi, 7 and 9 channels) for the computer industry are available and are supported by most of the larger minicomputer manufacturers. It appears that the only nonstandard data processing type of magnetic tape available is Digital Equipment's DEC tape.

Tapes are easy to handle and store a large quantity of data at relatively low cost. Their disadvantage is that they have to be read sequentially. For an inexpensive, slow tape drive, as might be used in a small minicomputer system, reading a full-sized tape could take ten minutes or more.

Many of the nonstandard tapes, such as DEC tapes, compensate by being shorter and by having addressable blocks for quick location, reverse read, and (in the case of cassettes) a faster search speed than a read-write speed. This often brings average access time to a fraction of a minute.

Cassette and cartridge tapes. Magnetic tapes that have become popular because of the need for low-cost storage to go with low-cost computers and terminals are the cassette and cartridge tapes. The cassette and the cartridge each have the same physical form as their equivalents used in home entertainment machines, but have been modified for greater reliability. Cassettes are more popular by a wide margin and are used in many different types of data processing and related applications. The estimated 1980 dollar market for cassettes, by application, is shown in Table 3–5.

Cartridges and cassettes are very commonly used in data collection applications and also have great value when used to store programs. There is complete ease of loading and storing of the programs in either form, and the sequential reading, a detriment in many other applications, is necessary in loading programs.

Together with the diskette or floppy disk, the cartridge and cassette form the main small-scale removable storage for microcomputers and minicomputers. All three are used in data collection, data processing, terminals, and in all sizes of computers. All three media can be conveniently transported and can even be safely

Table 3–5. Estimated 1980 cassette drive market by application. (Total market = $120 million.)

Application	Percent of Total Market
General-purpose minicomputers	28
Communication terminals	22.5
Small-business computers	19.5
Programmable calculators	12
Word processors	10
Industrial	5
Miscellaneous	3

mailed to a data processing location. Table 3–6 provides a cost comparison of the three devices.

Although Table 3–6 indicates the unit cost of storage, in general, makes cassettes not as competitive as cartridges and diskettes, cost-per-bit figures cannot take into consideration such factors as how much data is needed for an application. Using the cartridge for an application that stores only as much data as can be stored on a cassette, for example, raises the cartridge cost per bit by several times.

The first step in deciding what type of unit to use is to determine the amount of data that must be stored. If it is below two million characters, a diskette or a cassette should be considered. If the volume is higher, a cartridge could be used, if using multiple units is not feasible. Whenever access speed is important, cartridges and

Table 3–6. Cost comparisons of cassette, cartridge, and diskette.*

Characteristic	Cassette	Cartridge	Diskette
Price of drive (min.)	$450	$700	$700
Price of media	$ 8	$ 20	$ 8
Average capacity (characters)	675K	3M	512K
Average access time	18.8 sec.	20 sec.	250 millisec.
Average transfer rate (char/sec)	1K	6K	30K
Storage cost:			
Drive (cents/char.)	.067	.023	.137
Media (cents/char.)	.0013	.00067	.0016

*Cost and performance data available from manufacturers.

cassettes are not applicable, leaving the diskette as the only viable device in this category. Table 3–7 gives some typical cost and performance information on the various types of tape units available from minicomputer manufacturers.

In the spectrum of minicomputer storage devices, main computer memory is the most expensive. In auxiliary memory, although the per-unit storage costs of the very large moving-head disks are very close to tape costs, in general the tape storage is cheaper. However, the less expensive medium (tape) has the slower access

Table 3–7. Typical tape storage units.*

Type	Tape Speed (inch/ sec)	Capacity (millions of characters)	Average Access Time (min)	Write Speed (K characters/sec)	Price	Storage Costs (cents/ character)
Cartridge	30	2.5	.3	6	$ 1,450	.058
Cassette	6	1.0	.3	1.3	450	.045
Cassette	7.5	.90	.8	.75	2,825	.31
Cassette	24	.62	.25	2.60	3,650	.59
Cassette	30	.25	.2	1.20	1,250	.50
DEC tape†	100	2.08	.25	10	12,600	.61
Standard‡	25	2.5	10	7	7,000	.28
Standard‡	25	38	10	40	8,900	.023
Standard‡	45	19	5.5	36	8,900	.047
Standard‡	12.5	38	20	20	7,200	.019
Standard‡	37.5	19	7	30	11,000	.058
Standard‡	45	13	5.5	72	20,000	.15
Standard‡	75	13	2.6	60	9,000	.076

*Cost and performance data on magnetic tape units available from minicomputer manufacturers.

†Nonstandard data processing type.

‡Industry standard 7- and 9-track computer tape.

time. This characteristic—the device with the faster access speed is more expensive—holds for all types of storage. This effect is illustrated for tapes and various types of disks in Figure 3–4.

Current usage recognizes the advantages and disadvantages of disks and tapes. A common arrangement that utilizes several forms of auxiliary storage to best advantage in the same system is the combination of a high-speed fixed-head disk for program storage, a movable-head disk for file storage, and a magnetic tape for backup.

Figure 3–4. Access time versus storage costs for common auxiliary storage.

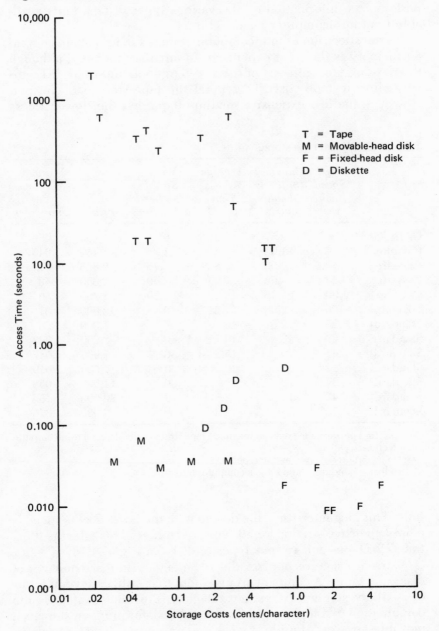

Data-Input Devices

There are available an almost infinitely large range of data-input devices, from the automatic sensing type (such as automatic product weighing) to the keyboard. These are useful over a wide range of data processing and automatic applications.

Data recording devices. Most of the standard noninteractive data recording devices have been used for many years in data processing applications, are quite familiar, and all have value in the proper application. The following are those available for minicomputer systems:

Keypunch.

Paper tape punch.

Keyboard to magnetic tape, disk (diskette), cassette, or cartridge.

Magnetic-ink character recognition (MICR).

Optical character recognition (OCR).

Touchtone telephone.

Special readers: credit cards; work stations; optical or magnetic codes.

Conversational terminals. Because of the preference and value of using the minicomputer in on-line operations, conversational keyboard terminals are of major interest. The two important terminals are the printers and the cathode-ray tube (CRT) displays.

Printing terminals, also known as keyboard printers, usually employ serial character printing mechanisms and impact techniques. They provide output directly onto hard copy at 10 to 100 characters per second. Teletype Corporation, a subsidiary of AT&T, manufactures the most commonly used terminal in this field. The Teletype and printing terminals based on the IBM Selectric typewriter mechanism encompass the largest portion of the conversational terminal market. These devices have the following characteristics:

- Low prices are available. Some Teletypes are available for $500.
- No memory or control logic. The computer to which the terminal is connected does most of the work.
- Hard copy is a natural by-product of the terminal.
- They have long-time use, resulting in established techniques and software.

- The devices, some of which are identical to typewriters, are very familiar, thereby overcoming user resistance.
- Communication capabilities are available and well established. The machines have low speed and therefore provide low-cost communication facilities.
- Portable devices are available.
- They have slow printout of computer-produced information.

Alphanumeric terminals, better known as CRTs, produce a visual display of up to about 1,000 characters on a TV-like screen. (The cathode-ray tube, or CRT, is in fact a television tube.) The terminal includes a typewriter-style keyboard and some special keys for control, such as editing commands, transmission control, and end-of-message indications. There are also special keys for control of the cursor, which is a movable symbol indicating a particular character position on the screen.

The CRTs can be connected to the computer in clusters through one controller or can be tied in individually. They have storage buffers, and logic capabilities are also available. They have no hard-copy capability, and attempts to solve this problem have not been completely satisfactory because of low speed or high cost, or both.

The logic capabilities of CRTs are constantly being enhanced (again because of the low cost and the powerful features available through the use of microprocessors and logic chips) to a point where the intelligent CRT has much of the power, though not the versatility, of a small minicomputer. CRT terminals of the Dataspeed line have versatile logic capabilities and are also compatible with Teletype Corporation's other terminals.

Other important characteristics of the CRTs which make them attractive are:

- Instantaneous information display. A full screen, approximately 1,000 characters, can be displayed essentially instantaneously. The speed is limited only by the communication-line capability.
- Compatibility. Many CRTs have been designed to be completely compatible with Teletypes, allowing easy interchange in application.
- Split-screen capability. Computer-gathered information can be displayed side by side with manually entered data for easy sight verification.

- Conversational processing is encouraged. The high speed facilitates question-and-answer conversational processing.
- Noiseless. Its quiet operation makes it more suitable in office environments.
- No paper is required.
- High reliability. This all-electronic equipment is more reliable than its electromechanical counterpart.
- CRTs have well-developed communication capabilities and software.
- Logic capabilities. The performance of editing and control logic at each terminal removes a processing load from the computer.
- Relatively low cost. CRT terminals vary in price from about $1,000 to $8,000, depending on the built-in capability. For most applications, a suitable alphanumeric CRT terminal can be found for under $2,500.

Printing Equipment

Most applications end with a printed document—a report, an invoice, a listing, or some other form. Visual displays are occasionally sufficient for output purposes, but most applications, particularly in business, require a large amount of printing.

Printing may be performed by impact or by nonimpact methods. It is rare when a multiple copy of an output document is not required; therefore, systems almost always find an impact printer necessary. Output impact-printing units are usually classified according to whether they print a character at a time or print an entire line. The line printer is the typical data processing printer and is faster and more expensive then the character printers.

Character printers. Most character printers in use are of a serial type in which the print mechanism moves across the line. The Teletype and printers such as the IBM 2741 terminal and others that use a Selectric mechanism are quite common. These are the same terminals used in conversational applications. In fact, a great many small systems use nothing more than one of these devices to take care of all input and output requirements. Output speeds are usually 10 to 60 characters per second. Cost is generally in the area of $1,000 to $4,000.

Until recently, if the user's requirements exceeded the capabilities of these keyboard printers, he had to go to a much more expensive line printer. The requirements of small-scale business

Table 3–8. Line printers: characteristics and price.*

Speed (lines/min)	Character Set	Print Positions	Price ($000)
60	64	132	4.6
200	96	132	11.5
230	96	132	10.5
300	64	132	11.5
300	96	132	7.9
356	64	80	9.8
600	64	136	18.0
1,200	64	132	35.0

*Cost and performance data on line printers available from minicomputer manufacturers.

processing have necessitated development of new techniques to fill this gap. Several of the recent printers introduced can space at comparatively high speeds or print in the reverse direction on alternate lines. These and other techniques increase the effective speed of the serial printers. Many additional impact and nonimpact techniques such as dot-matrix, thermal, and inkjet spray have been developed to accommodate the wide range of printing needs.

Line printers. The standard printers for data processing applications have existed for many years, and low-priced units have become available to fill the needs of the minicomputer systems. The price of printers depends on the width of the print line, the number of characters in the print set, and particularly the speed. A typical large data processing system line printer prints at speeds of about 1,200 lines per minute, has a set of 64 characters, and prints over 132 positions. Printers supplied by minicomputer manufacturers have speeds typically in the 300-line-per-minute range. Some typical prices and characteristics of these line printers are shown in Table 3–8.

Cost of Minicomputers

The dramatic reduction of costs is the true motivating force for the minicomputer industry. Businessmen are taking a look at minicomputers and are finding that these computers can help them. Because of the low price tag, the small computers are supplying EDP power to small firms that previously had none or used time-sharing and service bureau operations. For a relatively modest price, say, $30,000, or less than $1,000 per month, the small businessman finds he can do something constructive, valuable, and economic. Frequently, the cost of a minicomputer system is less than a single clerk's salary. As a result, the displacement of just one person provides the manager with a highly effective, accurate business aid without additional cost.

However, it should not be assumed that minicomputer systems always mean "mini" costs. The most commonly quoted figure, the one used in the definition of minicomputers, is $20,000 or $25,000, but this applies only to the basic computer price. When operating in a functional system, peripherals (or additional equipment) are frequently required. Additional memory, which costs up to $1,000 for each 8,000 characters, is usually needed. Also, file or data base storage is very likely to be needed. This could typically cost $20,000 for each unit. And this does not even start to consider the software.

A typical system might have several terminals for input of data, magnetic tapes, or (more commonly) disk devices for the storage of data, and would have some kind of output printer or output display device, probably both. In addition, the user might want a card reader and punch card or paper tape equipment for loading and maintaining the programs because it is usually very inconvenient and time-consuming to enter programs via a keyboard terminal. As a result, the basic $25,000 purchase price could blossom into possibly $100,000 for an entire system. A factory automation or a communication minicomputer system, with its multiple disks, printers, and communication interfaces, could cost in excess of $200,000. Figure 3–5 illustrates this point with a system that could be used for on-line data entry with simultaneous background batch processing.

In a large data processing system the cost of the peripherals commonly equals the cost of the computer, but in a minicomputer system the costs of the peripherals commonly far outstrip the cost of the computer. The great reductions that have occurred in computer costs have not affected the peripheral costs as much, since all are largely electromechanical devices rather than totally electronic, as is the computer. The peripherals used on the minicomputer may be, and usually are, the same size and often the same devices that are used on the large computers. A system that has large data storage requirements is still going to be costly even though it uses a minicomputer as the central processing unit (CPU). However, be-

Figure 3-5. Stand-alone business system 1.

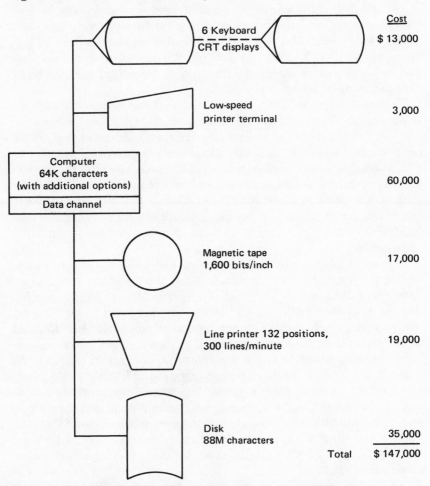

	Cost
6 Keyboard CRT displays	$ 13,000
Low-speed printer terminal	3,000
Computer 64K characters (with additional options) Data channel	60,000
Magnetic tape 1,600 bits/inch	17,000
Line printer 132 positions, 300 lines/minute	19,000
Disk 88M characters	35,000
Total	$ 147,000

$3,000/month, 5-year lease, $950/month maintenance

cause of the minicomputer, there are low-price systems that can do a very effective job for the businessman.

Figure 3-6 illustrates a simple stand-alone business system based on a minicomputer. This system has one terminal, a CRT keyboard display unit for data input and visual display output. It has a disk file that can store up to half a million characters of data. It also has a printer terminal, which is used as the console to instruct the computer, as an additional input device, and as a printer for

Figure 3–6. Stand-alone business system 2.

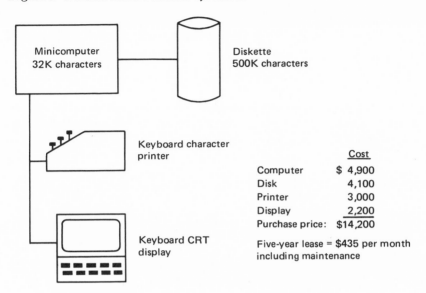

Minicomputer
32K characters

Diskette
500K characters

Keyboard character
printer

Keyboard CRT
display

	Cost
Computer	$ 4,900
Disk	4,100
Printer	3,000
Display	2,200
Purchase price:	$14,200

Five-year lease = $435 per month
including maintenance

output information. A minicomputer with 32,000 characters of internal storage is the center of the system. The monthly charge for this system would be about $435, including maintenance, on a five-year lease.

The simple system in Figure 3–6 is basically an information retrieval system. It could be very valuable in personnel, sales reporting, management information, and inventory control applications. For example, it could be programmed to store, update, select, retrieve, and display personnel records. Or it could be used to select and instantly display or print a list of all employees who had a particular type of experience, or of all salesmen who exceeded a certain value of sales, provided this type of data was maintained in the file. It is possible that a simple, low-cost system of this type could pay for itself in reduced personnel expenses in less than a year.

The systems described here are realistic minicomputer systems although their costs differ by a factor of 10, which is fairly typical for these types of systems. It is very pertinent to note that an effective computer system, a cost-effective one that will help reduce operating costs, can be purchased for as little as $30,000. In either case the buyer pays only for as much computer system as he needs to do the job.

BUSINESS ORGANIZATIONS
AND THE MINICOMPUTER

A business organization exists for the purpose of accomplishing predetermined objectives. To accomplish these objectives, management must provide guidance and direction, must motivate and stimulate new ideas, and must monitor and control operations.

Management of any organization requires information and data. Superimposed on every business organizational structure is a data processing organization. The method and effectiveness of the interaction between these two organizations has major effects on the results achieved by the company. The company structure may be independent of the data processing structure as long as the organization information needs are adequately satisfied. The data supplied must be accurate and timely, and the cost to retrieve and process the data must be reasonable. Because of the cost involved, careful planning and control is essential to assure that managers get the information they need when they need it. Because storing and retrieving data is expensive, this process must fulfill management's needs, but it must be selective.

Timely data is also important, but there is rarely a need for instant information at any level. The cost and complexity of data systems rise exponentially as the time from source to use is reduced. The term "management information" has been used to entice companies into expensive and usually unnecessary data systems. The need for instant information is rare, since the information provided and the decision rendered are usually not sensitive to small variations in time.

Modern technology is making available new, economic means of communication and data transfer. These means—the hardware part of the system—are the economic part, and can draw users into a system without full consideration of all the expenses and pitfalls involved. Management must exert strong control to insure that costly resources are not wasted and that new developments proceed with some long-range objective in mind.

Sometimes conflicting organization objectives cannot be satisfied through existing structures. A common management dilemma is the preservation of autonomy in remote divisions where expertise in specific user needs is located while still achieving the economies of scale that central management can produce. An important question is how to develop managers or make managers responsible for profit centers when systems and data services needed for their business area are designed and controlled by central staffs. Solutions for these problems are now being provided by advanced facilities in the form of local, economic, flexible data processing systems and cheap, reliable communication means. These systems allow a company to implement a system of management and control that is largely independent of the data system or geographic considerations.

Whether the organization is strongly hierarchical with rigid chains of command and firmly embedded procedures, or cellular with short lines of command and more autonomy in the various cells, information needs appropriate to the environment can be satisfied through the proper choice of data system support. Even in the past, control of the systems based on new technology has been difficult and not always effective. But today, with very low-cost equipment available, the possibility of a more autonomous organization, and the possibility of small, remote locations using the equipment, firm organizational control is essential.

Company Characteristics and Data Processing Innovation

The expected benefits and consequences of any deviation from traditional methods of doing business or conducting internal company processing must be fully evaluated. Although the final outcome cannot be predicted with certainty, management should be at least aware of all possible results.

The use of the minicomputer deviates from tradition and must be considered as a precedent-establishing technique. Minicomputer use for business applications is new. Companies with established data processing systems must develop new policies and techniques for evaluating and using them. For companies without established data processing organizations, the consideration of computer systems brings them to an important and crucial crossroad. A decision at this point to adopt the data processing installation approach rather than the user-computer approach is just about irreversible. The problems are very different for large and small companies, but the minicomputer touches in some way the processing problems of all companies. The minicomputer is now in use for business applications in billion-dollar companies and in companies whose annual gross income is under $8 million. But the small and large companies have different problems and different alternatives.

In terms of systems and computer applications, the billion-dollar company is not just the small company with larger volume, for a difference in an order of magnitude produces an entirely new entity. The difference in costs of any process is not commensurate with the difference in size. This is particularly true of computer applications. Consider a payroll application. The systems analysis and programming work for a system that will run a payroll for 50,000 people is, at most, only slightly greater than that required for a system that will process a payroll for 1,000 employees. The equipment and operating expense differences are greater, but are not even close to being proportional to size.

The small company generally has fewer applications that can benefit from an automated approach because of the relatively smaller economic benefits to be derived from new systems. However, in some large companies, there is no alternative to a data processing system. In large commercial organizations, banks, and insurance companies, the processing has become so great that to do without the computer would be impossible. The increase in growth and services in these companies, due to the use of automated systems, stimulates more automation and this increases the dependency on computers.

The small company has several alternatives to installing a computer. Once a computer application is justified, the company has a feasible option of letting someone else do the job for it. A service bureau could provide the data processing competence, or an external time-sharing service could handle all its processing. If a large company were to do this, the cost would be prohibitive. Most companies of any considerable size have had a data processing organization for some years. This organization includes a large professional staff that has been trained on the large computer, and therefore its point of view and experience is oriented in this direction. When an application is proposed, the method of solution naturally tends to incorporate the techniques with which the staff is familiar. A small company that has not established such precedents or does not have a computer philosophy so firmly rooted can be much freer in its choice of alternatives.

The mere fact that a company does have a computer inhibits the development of new, innovative computer systems and the acquisition of additional data processing methods. No computer is ever utilized 100 percent of the time. Time is always available to care for emergencies or to provide a reasonable schedule. Moreover, whenever an upgrade is necessary, it is upgraded in quantum jumps. When additional processing is required, the increased capacity generates more spare capacity. This makes it very easy to add another job to the system, even though the job is not justified by the full equivalent cost, but by the incremental cost of the additional resources required for the particular job. Of course a day of reckoning finally comes when an upgrading is essential. However, this is easily justified by showing how close to absolute capacity the computer is being utilized. Such high utilization surely indicates user satisfaction (to the DP manager at least) and there is no problem in obtaining approval for upgrading.

Control of data processing systems and expenditures is a major area of concern for every company, regardless of size. It is much more difficult and also much more important in the large company that has many locations. The kind of control and how it is exercised has a great impact on the nature of new systems. A large company frequently has a centralized control over data processing where the solution is decided by the central staff. The smaller company is usually just the opposite insofar as staff is concerned. Rather than a large professional staff, the small company or the remote divisions of a large company have a small staff whose strong point is their familiarity with the application and the business of the company. As a result, their point of view is somewhat different and is oriented more toward the user. Therefore, although there are many similarities between all business organizations—their applications are the same—the way the company reacts to system problems can be very different.

However, many systems used in a remote environment in the large company are identical with typical systems of the small company. An information storage and retrieval system has value in many departments of a large company, such as in the personnel department or a sales office keeping track of salesmen performance. A small company has need for systems performing similar functions. Or a computer system of a similar concept could be used to handle basic company functions such as accounts payable, which would operate in an interactive, self-checking, on-line manner. Although the framework for the data processing function is quite different, many of the applications of small and large companies are the same.

Evaluating the Minicomputer System

The computer industry is relatively new. The first electronic computer was invented during the life span of most people alive today, and the first computer business application was dedicated in the Bureau of Census of June 14, 1951, less than 30 years ago. But the industry has applied certain yardsticks, certain judgments for determining the performance of a computer, which have a historical base. When we look at the computers developed by the new technology of the 1970s and the resulting new philosophy of use, we find that these traditional yardsticks are no longer always valid. The criterion for judging performance of computers is evident from the use of monitoring techniques whereby activity of the computer components (CPU, channels, and so forth) can be measured to determine their utilization. This measurement approach, directed at the computer itself, assumes that the computer is the universe. Monitoring methods aid in improving the efficiency of each important area of the process, but they are clearly suboptimizing when the complete system is considered.

A valid evaluation technique must take into consideration all links in the system chain. The use and philosophy of the dedicated minicomputer is validated by viewing the entire system and judging its performance on its capability of solving basic business problems. Full utilization of the central processor is not so important as the degree to which the user's needs are satisfied and the minimum cost of doing this.

In judging the performance of the computer, we must look beyond the immediate area the computer is serving. We must look at the overall effect on the company services and costs. Benefits are provided to the user and must be counted. The system, in addition, has associated costs. It has direct costs such as the computer cost. It also has some indirect costs that are very difficult to identify. Every facet of the operation should be appraised. We must look at the cost of alternatives, the cost of training, and the cost of maintaining the skills of an accomplished staff. The difficulties in keeping files and programs for remote computers in step, and the complicated logistics of transferring information among many locations, must also be considered. The difficulties and cost of corporate control and security in the multiple small-computer environment must not be overlooked. We must consider the possible degradation of the large computer, which is possible if more and more jobs are drawn away from it. On the other hand, we must consider the full costs of the large computer—including costs for maintaining it and its large operating system—so that in judging alternate approaches we are cognizant of all cost factors that could affect the data processing decision.

Centralization versus Decentralization Controversy

As long as there have been organization studies, there have been controversies over which organization type is more effective—centralized or decentralized. It seems that, at any point in time, many companies are centralizing while an equal number are decentralizing. To add to the confusion, styles and company management change, and companies that moved in one direction ten years ago could be moving the opposite way now.

Arguments for the centralized approach are centered around the control exercised by the top management of the company. There are also strong arguments for a decentralized approach, one of which is that the ability of managers is developed by giving them some degree of autonomy at the lower organization levels. This contributes to the profit-center concept. The capable regional manager in the multidivisional company can be given profit responsibility for his area, thus providing performance incentive and a means for performance evaluation.

There is also controversy regarding the centralization or decentralization of the data processing function in the large company. However, evidence indicates a tendency toward a centralized authority. Proponents for centralized data processing also claim control as an important reason, but their major argument centers around economies of scale. Those who argue for decentralization usually cite the service to the user as the justification for any additional costs decentralization might incur.

When a company analyzes the situation in preparation for a possible change to or from a centralized data processing organization, the analysis is typically performed by the professional corporate data processing staff. Thus, some loss of objectivity may occur because a few computer professionals have been known to be blinded and dazzled by the exotic features of a new piece of hardware that only a large central operation can afford. In addition, due to insensitivity to the users' many problems, which can result from dealing with corporate computer problems, users' needs usually take second place to the desire and prestige attached to working with large computers.

The economies of scale cited by the proponents for centralization are reflected in the internal accounting reports. These economies are obtained from the reduction in purchase or lease costs effected by the replacement of two computers with one slightly larger one and by consolidating systems and programming staffs. These costs are identifiable on expense reports and budget projections, and are therefore obvious targets for those who have responsibility for keeping costs low. On the other hand, as proponents for decentralization point out, not all company costs show up on the accounting forms. Service to the user means providing the local manager with information for running his profit center at the time he needs it. It is difficult to exercise proper control over escalating costs if the manager has to wait months for his operating expense reports. In addition, late inventory or credit account payment reports could lead to customer dissatisfaction, a loss factor that does not show up in a short-term expense report. Service to the user and rapid response to local data processing needs—major arguments in the decentralized approach—are benefits that are practically impossible to quantify. As a result, these objectives are not promoted as much as the ones that appear on the financial reports.

Many companies, despite having a centralized data processing organization, have adopted the decentralized profit-center approach in company management. However, implementation and selection of computer projects in the data processing center have a great bearing on local profits. This strongly supports the argument for decentralized data processing, but it also causes problems in the centralized organization. Possibly, in the future, when computer operations are more stabilized and become better understood, middle managers at the local level will insist that local data processing talent be available and responsible to them.

Organizational Control

An important reason for establishing a centralized data processing organization is that control is maintained over all parts of the computer-related operations. This control is effectively exercised in the following areas:

Establishing policy and long-range goals.
Establishing priorities.
Project selection.
Selection of hardware.
Selection of programming languages.
Uniformity of coding systems.
Common applications and programming (no duplication of programming efforts).
Common reporting methods and data.

There are an infinite number of possible data processing organizations and policies—a continuous spectrum—that can reflect the degree of centralization desired. In reality, we rarely see the two extremes of either the totally and absolutely centralized or decentralized organizations. Normally, organizations are mostly centralized with only a few decentralized functions or are decentralized with central coordination.

Mostly centralized. A central group will have authority and responsibility for planning, project selection, selection of hardware, and programming. If the company functions are sufficiently homogeneous, the central group will also have responsibility for operating the computing facilities. The local group will be responsible for modifications due to local procedures and maintenance programming.

Decentralized with central coordination. Individual users have their own systems, programming, and operations staff, and operate their own computers. Central coordination is provided in terms of programming and data standards. Authority is exercised over types and manufacturers of equipment. Audit of operations and coordination of development activity to avoid duplication of effort are provided by the central group.

Use of the Minicomputer

Minicomputers in the multilocation organization must be controlled by the central organization. As illustrated by the analysis of data processing responsibility, this control is no greater than is normally performed in the existing organization, although exercising and enforcing thāt control will be more difficult. In principle, the organization to maximize the benefits and control the use of minicomputers is already in existence in almost all large companies.

The minicomputer application in business is designed to satisfy the users' needs. If the corporate group does not respond to these needs of the remote organizations, the local groups will resort to clandestine methods. If a user is determined to solve a problem and sees the means for solution but does not get acceptable legal assistance, he will seek and find illegal means. This is very easy to accomplish with minicomputer systems. The systems are relatively inexpensive, there are many systems houses that will take in the entire development and installation job if desired, and it is relatively easy to hide the development and even the installation from the corporate group until the operations and benefits have been proved. (For a number of years many minicomputer manufacturers called their machines "digital processors" or "programmed controllers" so that local users could circumvent the top-management approval required for all computer acquisitions.)

Control is essential with minicomputer systems. Systems analysis and programming, while accounting for 50 percent of a large computer system expense, may cost two or even ten times the expense of minicomputer hardware. A centrally controlled group can take advantage of the economies of software development by re-using software modules, particularly the operating system or real-time monitor. Central control is also essential to limit the types of hardware within the company. Since the programming is not generally transferable between computers, limiting the number of different types of computers in use is necessary to eliminate duplication of effort and to reduce costs for learning and maintaining programming skills. Other savings could result from combining purchases by all company units in a corporate contract, to attain greater influence and support from the manufacturers and to receive the significant quantity discounts that are available on the minicomputer hardware.

The central staff acts almost as a systems house in that it gets the computer equipment from the manufacturer(s), assembles the system, and does all basic system programming for it. Additional application programming can be done by the central staff with the assistance of people who are familiar with the user application. This application part of the system may be programmed in a user-oriented language such as RPG-II, BASIC, or other English-like programming languages, making it very easy for the users' staffs to develop the application portion of the entire package under central staff direction and assistance.

Central control or coordination of minicomputer developments is essential to obtain the major portion of the benefits that are available. It is important to note that present-day corporations are organized and operated within the economic framework required to maximize the benefits of minicomputers. An unresponsive organization cannot keep the applications from developing, but it may lose the benefits to be achieved now and prevent easy expansion or integration in the future.

Issues in Data Processing

Before a small company installs its first computer, before it takes the jump into data processing, alternate systems and their consequences should be investigated. The large computer in the data processing installation and the minicomputer are not, in general, alternatives for the same type of processing. However, they do overlap functionally. Before the businessman contracts for his first computer application, he should be aware that he can avoid being drawn into the high-overhead data processing environment for quite a period of time. The economics and advantages of the data processing environment and the user-oriented computer system should be compared. A minicomputer installation allows many applications to be handled without hiring and training a professional data processing staff. On the other hand, some applications require a large computer, and when this is the situation, it is natural to add more jobs on that same computer.

The typical objectives of the computer operation department are (1) effective and efficient use of the computer and associated resources, and (2) rapid and effective service in solving a wide range of user problems at low cost. Unfortunately, these two objectives are in direct conflict. The efficiencies brought about by large computers have generally not resulted in both greater responsiveness to users' needs and lower costs. Frequently just the opposite has occurred.

Computers have been steadily growing in size and capability, and their processing power has increased at a much faster rate than their cost. Advances in electronic technology have reduced the unit cost for all processing—for large computers as well as for microcomputers and minis. But, while the economies of scale of processing power apply, much of the advantage is dissipated by general-purpose software and by interfaces required to make the large computer suitable for handling processing of all types.

Special hardware and software are needed for telecommunication applications, for data-base applications, and for time-sharing applications, and lots of special software is needed to perform all these functions at the same time. Minicomputers cannot do all these things at one time, so simpler software, which occupies a much smaller portion of the computer, is used for its dedicated functions. Even in a multiprogramming environment, the minicomputer must operate in a much simpler fashion because of its reduced facilities and data-path limitations. While hardware economies increase with size, there are exponential diseconomies associated with increasing the size and the amount of software.

To be able to handle the ever-increasing variety of data processing jobs, and to process them simultaneously, the computer requires a massive amount of special programs, called *system software*. System software includes all the programs that interface between the application programs and the computer hardware as well as the operating system that makes everything else work.

The operating system is designed to provide highly efficient use of very powerful computers. It acts as a traffic cop—directing the transfer of data from input to output. It allows the computer to work with many different I/O devices and special system software.

An operating system resides in the computer at all times. Even a small standard computer operating system requires more than 100,000 characters of memory. Larger operating systems can require a million or more characters of the computer's internal memory—corresponding to a cost of about $200,000 at IBM Model 370 prices. This large block of money is spent, not to directly serve the user, but just to provide the residing place of the operating system. The space requirement not only is expensive but also reduces the system capability, since fewer simultaneous users can be handled by the remaining portion of internal memory.

When the requirements for other software support packages are added to that required for the operating system, it can be seen that a truly large computer is necessary to provide sufficient space for running the user's applications. Table 4–1 lists the space requirement needed for the system software resident in the internal memory of a large, but not atypical, dual-processor IBM 370/165 computer system. (Other parts of the computer system software reside in

Table 4–1. Use of internal memory in dual IBM Model 370/165.

Software Component	Characters Required × 1,000		
	System 1	*System 2*	*Total*
Operating system	708	694	
Input scheduling and output spooling	750	—	
Data base management system	530	—	
Communication line control	—	270	
Communication application control	—	128	
Total system software	1,988	1,092	3,080
Available for user applications	1,084	1,980	3,064
Total system internal memory	3,072	3,072	6,144

SOURCE: Carl H. Reynolds, "Issues in Centralization," *Datamation*, March 1977.

off-line disk storage and are brought into main memory only as needed.) It can be seen that 50 percent of six million characters of internal memory is used solely for the resident system software.

In addition to the space requirement, there is significant processing overhead incurred by each of the system software components. Internal control of data transfer operations uses a great proportion of the available CPU cycles. Just the operating system can take, and has taken, as much as 50 percent of the available machine cycles for internal routine servicing functions.

Use of the operating system has made it necessary for all users to master a new, difficult job-control language (JCL). This contributes nothing directly to serving the user, but in fact adds another level of complexity and a training and operational problem. Also, generating an operating system that takes several man-days is no task to be written off lightly. With the numerous versions of improved and corrected operating systems that are issued, a sizable effort is spent in generations over the year.

Reasons for adding more jobs to the large processor are justified by the logic of economy of scale, which implies that the per-unit processing cost decreases for each additional job run on that computer. Economies of scale in computer processing originate in the economies of scale attained in manufacturing the computers. As the electronic component technology advances, the economies of scale in manufacturing naturally decrease. Also, with the more powerful computers that are physically smaller and require less power, the economies of scale with regard to site and environment (raised floors, air conditioning) also decrease. Most of the arguments for economy of scale, however, center on the efficiency of the processor, but efficient computers do not necessarily produce effective operations. Today, many highly efficient computers bring great satisfaction to their caretakers but do so at considerable cost to the organization.

To be meaningful, data processing costs must consider more than just internal computer performance. Full life-cycle system costs—which include systems analysis, systems development, programming, operating, equipment maintenance, downtime, program maintenance, program and systems modification, staff expenses, and physical site overhead—should ideally be considered for all new systems. There is evidence to indicate the existence of diseconomies of scale among staff, programming, and systems analysis. Since data processing hardware costs are now less than the money spent on staff, the efficient use of computers should not be maintained at the expense of the more costly functions—that is, increased staff or training.

Efficiently operated programs may be developed at the expense of internal memory, but unless the entire program code is frequently accessed, it becomes inefficient to have the program reside entirely in memory. The larger and newer data processors use virtual paging and overlay techniques to limit the size of the program that resides in internal memory. Most minicomputer systems, being limited in total memory available, have always used these techniques when large programs had to be implemented. In addition, small programs, or program modules, can be written and debugged at a lower per-statement cost than a large program, illustrating the diseconomies of scale with regard to program size. Other issues in data processing are mostly qualitative and affect decisions between minicomputers and large-scale data processing.

Personal Computer Philosophy

The business office of the future has frequently been projected as a place where fewer people, with the assistance of a computer, will be able to make more decisions, more important decisions, in a shorter period than can now be done. The computer would be shared by many workers, but because of its great speed relative to the speed of the workers, each employee would feel that the computer was his alone. There is little doubt that this will definitely be the way in which much of daily business processing will be performed. The low cost and availability of logic built into reliable systems will make it not only operationally but also economically preferable to many other alternatives. This trend toward future simplification has started now, but at present the economies of the approach are not always decisive and incur some risks for the uninitiated.

It is ironic that the new, unsophisticated user of data processing is the one who really needs to have a computer completely at his service, while at the same time he is the one who presently takes the greatest risk in adopting this approach. However, despite the inherent risks of support and reliability, this personal computer system is being used by many small users who find that the economic and operational advantages outweigh the disadvantages.

The personal computer approach has less attraction for the large established companies that have mature data processing organizations. By means of the low incremental cost of adding a new small application to their existing computer, they are able to adopt a low-cost alternative. Any operational advantages often relate to nonquantifiable benefits, such as servicing customers faster, and unless they reduce direct costs, benefits are often not significant enough to overcome the confidence earned by the large computer systems. It becomes difficult, then, for the large company to modify its approach. There have been, of course, a number of personal computer systems in large companies where operational, security, or economic advantages were evident.

The main advantage of personal computer systems is the ease of operation. No data processing skills are required, although this is a mixed blessing because there are no systems that are incapable of having a hardware or software failure. When a system fails, professional assistance is required to diagnose the fault, correct it, analyze and correct the processed data, and make the system operative again. A company without a professional data processing staff must rely on outside services for this support. While there are many competent and responsive systems and maintenance organizations, the control, knowledge, and dedication that an in-house staff could supply are missing.

The small company will have no problem in the future when this approach is more established and the companies that develop these systems have the stability and tenure to generate complete confidence—but the problem exists today. Still, many small companies find that being relieved of the requirement for a trained data processing staff is more important than any other consideration. They solve their problem by having sufficient backup, by dealing with a well-established systems house, or by dealing solely with a major, established hardware company that can provide complete and dependable support.

Data Processing Decisions

The potential use of minicomputers presents a number of problems to organizations, but probably no opportunity is without its problems. The minicomputer is new, and the technology it epitomizes is new and growing. This technology will affect organizations of all sizes, but all will ultimately adjust to its use. The opportunities and benefits that are available are many, but proper care and control must be exercised to realize them. The large company, in general, already has the organization to exercise the degree of control necessary for obtaining optimal benefits from recent technological advances.

Care must be exercised to assure that the small computer is appraised in a proper fashion. Its cost seems low, but other important aspects must be considered—such as training in new programming techniques, vulnerability, and its effect on the present data processing operation and organization. However, data processing is again being seen in its original and proper role, as a service to the user. This means that the full system rather than the computer processor alone must become the unit of evaluation. When this is done, the minicomputer will offer an economically feasible solution even when compared to a system whose only data processing cost is the incremental expense of the large computer.

This user-oriented approach is usually more attractive operationally. It puts the user directly in the processing cycle. The clerk who enters data into the system is the one who knows the operation. This method assures increased accuracy and responsibility. It also puts the computer into the situation as a true extension of human intelligence.

While this personal computer approach presents some hazards for the uninitiated in the area of support, even for the vulnerable small companies its benefits are frequently sufficient to make it desirable. With the constantly decreasing cost of computation, its acceptance and use are inevitable. The economies attained are too desirable to overlook. Because of these expectations, many companies are training their organizations to handle this development now so that future benefits will be achieved without unnecessary costs and loss of control.

MINICOMPUTER SYSTEMS AND THEIR USES

The data processing community has grown at a very rapid rate since the introduction of the third-generation computers in 1963. During this time, data processing has evolved from the simple adaption of card-oriented tabulating rooms to very sophisticated multiprogrammed computer systems, requiring installations manned by several hundred people. As a consequence of the rapid growth and change of emphasis in computer operations, and due to the increasing electronic data processing (EDP) sophistication these systems brought about, many end users feel that they are not receiving benefits commensurate with their costs.

Many companies find that their EDP systems lack compatibility, do not provide the response desired by the client, are too rigidly designed, or are too difficult and costly to change. Increasingly, efforts are made to integrate these information systems into what has become known as "Total systems." Usually, however, these efforts fail for the following reasons:

- Systems efforts and design at various field locations cannot be stopped while waiting three or four years for a system standardization effort to integrate the network.
- The cost of converting an existing system may be overwhelming.
- By the time the network is finished, it is already obsolete.
- Various field managers have different requirements for the system.

When properly used, the minicomputer can be an important part of the means of providing cost-effective data processing that is responsive to the needs of the user. The user of the mini makes it possible to dedicate a computer to a single function, serving the user in the manner most suitable to him.

With low-cost equipment, independent minicomputer systems designed to satisfy the specific needs of numerous businesses are now in use. And because they are programmable, they can interface with many different technologies. Low equipment costs and flexibility are primary reasons for their widespread use. Therefore, conceptually, it is possible for the minicomputer to provide the following benefits or improvements:

- Compatibility with all types of system organization.
- Compatibility with all types of equipment and computers.
- Ability to adapt to improved technology as this technology becomes economically feasible.
- Ability to serve the needs of decentralized field users while meeting the requirements of the centralized system.
- Ability to use more cost-effective equipment.
- Ability to retrieve selected summary information on command.
- Ability to operate under any set of system requirements— remote batch, on-line, or stand-alone configurations.
- Ability to improve the efficiency of the large computer by performing those jobs that waste power external to the data processing center.

These improvements, discussed in this chapter, will be related to applications of the minicomputer in a number of business environments, including the dedicated system, the data processing center, and the modification of existing systems, illustrating in each case how it can be used to provide cost-effective service to an organization.

Minicomputer Capabilities

The commonly accepted definition of a minicomputer relies on price to distinguish it from other types of computers. The definition gives an indication of the problem encountered in deciding when to use a minicomputer and when not to use it. If there is nothing

more than price (or size, or weight, or other criterion) to distinguish
it from other computers, then specific limitations of use are difficult
to identify.

As a generality, it can be said that the minicomputer does the
same jobs that the large computer can do, but it cannot do so many
jobs simultaneously. It cannot do many jobs so fast. And there are a
few specialized large computer jobs that it cannot do at all.

Assuming the validity of these qualifications, it is difficult or
almost impossible to define limitations of the minicomputer as the
ability to do all jobs up to a certain point but nothing beyond that
point. Its capability depends on the precise requirements of the
specific job. The nature of the computer processing required, the
urgency of the job, the reliability required, the security required,
the type of staff available, the company philosophy, and long-range
plans, all enter in the decision regarding the use of a minicomputer.

Most important to the decision is precise determination of the
requirements of the function in which the computer will be involved. There are very few applications for which the minicomputer is unequivocally unsuited. The technical features that could act
as a constraint are the internal storage, the processing capacity, and
the input/output capacity, but it is only in a few special circumstances that these constraints can be translated into application
limitations.

While the typical minicomputer has a range from 8K to 256K
characters of internal memory, many have larger capacity. The PDP
11/70, for example, can be expanded to 2 million characters. Widely
used medium-size computers such as the IBM 370-135 and -145
have 500K and 1,000K character memory capacity, respectively.
Therefore, although the minicomputer cannot handle some special
applications and programs, the memory size is not a limitation
when compared with that of many larger computers.

Input and output channel speeds of the most common minicomputers are normally higher than the medium-speed computers.
Some minicomputers do not have the ability to connect as many
high-speed peripherals as do the larger computers, but others do
have the same capacity. In any event, this feature is rarely a limitation; in fact, the higher-speed data transfer of the mini's input and
output is often an advantage.

The processing capacity depends on many factors, which vary
from machine to machine. These factors include the processor
speed, the instruction set, word size, and internal hardware features
of the machine. In general, the most popular minicomputers have

processor speeds just about equal to that of small and medium computers. They do have smaller-size words, which means that they are limited in either their addressing capability or the power of the instruction set. Therefore, jobs that require a lot of internal processing with very little input and output might take more time to run on the minicomputer. For many other jobs the additional processing time is not noticeable because of the heavy, time-consuming input/output processing. Or, even if the processing does take significantly longer than it would on a larger computer, the additional time for processing might be meaningless in the specific application.

Despite the fact that the minicomputer might take more time than the larger computer to do a specific calculation or to validate some amount of input data, it still might be the most efficient and effective way to do the job. If input data to be validated is being keyed into an on-line system by a worker, the speed of computer processing would not be important. Any computer would process so fast, relative to speed of human response, that it would be waiting constantly on the manual imput process. Thus, there would be no reason to use the most powerful computer. In fact, unless the computer were underutilized, and would always stay that way, it would be most inefficient to tie it up for such a job.

Dedicated Systems

Some systems are used equally in both the large and the small company. In the small company the use of these systems may be the basic way of processing data. In the large company the system would probably be used to handle some peripheral type of function. The dedicated system might be used in the small company for sequentially handling two or three of its applications, or several computers might be used, each dedicated to one of the tasks. One or more of the computers could be used for the on-line retrieval of information or possibly for an on-line production-reporting system. In any case, these systems are self-contained and there is no tie-in to any other system in the company. The same situation applies in the larger company.

A number of dedicated systems do not produce information for other systems. These may be located at company headquarters or at one or many field locations. The characteristics of these systems are quite similar, although the applications may not be. It makes little difference in the functioning of the system if the information contained is a skills inventory file of personnel in a large company or a file of open purchase orders. The systems, identical in design, might be located at a field sales office to keep track of salesmen performance and provide a rapid comparison of their current performance to their previous record.

There are also some common, large data processing applications that are really much better done on a free-standing minicomputer. For example, consider an application that is centered at a field location of a large manufacturing company. The information from this subsystem is needed only by the local manager. Except for one line of summary cost information that is included in the monthly expense reports, this application has no ties to any other data processing application.

Consider this real-life situation, which is not an isolated case, and decide if a dedicated system appears to be more attractive: The manager has profit responsibility for his installation, which consists of a warehouse, manufacturing plant, and shipping facility. The application in question deals with his shipping costs, both company and hired transportation. The present procedure, shown in Figure 5–1, is as follows:

The daily trip tickets are brought to the office each night. A clerk copies information onto tally sheets for company-owned trucks and hired transportation. This data is accumulated for a month, at which time the tally sheets are mailed to the company's closest data processing center. The data is then keypunched, verified, corrected, batched, and delivered to the computer room, where the data is copied on tape and the program is run (but only after the higher-priority jobs are completed), following the normal iterations for correcting errors. When the results are printed and checked out of the computer room, they are mailed back to the regional manager. (He presently receives the full reports because when he used to receive only exception reports, it would take two additional weeks to get details of the specific areas he needed.) The reports are paged through by his assistant, who picks out the pertinent cost figures and ratios of in-house to hired transportation costs. By this time the oldest data is more than 45 days old. As a result, the manager keeps his own handwritten record of transportation expenses so that he can react quickly to sudden increased costs and make correction meaningful.

There is a great amount of waste in the procedure, but from the data processing point of view it appears to be a good application. The computer center has all the facilities and time to handle this

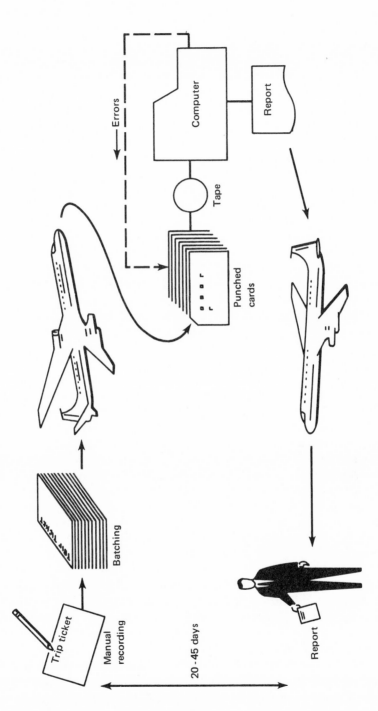

Figure 5–1. A 20- to 45-day batch-processing cycle.

job. It does not take much processing time, and since the computer is not running three shifts, the incremental data processing cost is very slight. But is the total cost small from the company's point of view? To the data processing cost must be added the costs of translating, keypunching, verifying, validating, correcting errors, shipping the information, and analyzing results. When this is done, it is realized that all this expense—and it is not small—is wasted because the manager must also keep his own records in order to respond alertly to current problems.

The use of a minicomputer as a dedicated system could be a fine operational solution in such a case. Much of the paper handling, data collection, and translation could be eliminated so that the information would be available to the manager whenever he wanted it. A system that could perform this function would cost less than $100,000, including software. The cost might be justified by just one application, and this application might be practicable in several plants or company locations with identical processing requirements. If the software development cost is prorated over three or four similar systems, the lower per-unit cost could result in a one- or two-year payout, meanwhile providing much more timely and accurate information for the manager.

The retrieval application is one that commonly employs the dedicated computer approach in both large and small companies in somewhat similar fashion. It is important to note that it is a common type of application. While it is acknowledged that software development costs can be distributed equally over a number of identical systems, it is also true that most of the development costs of nonidentical systems may be captured in succeeding installations, since the difficult retrieval portion can be left intact while only the less complicated user-application modules are modified.

These types of applications—the free-standing information storage and retrieval system and the data processing application which is not a mainline operation—are ideal for a dedicated minicomputer. These systems can benefit large and small companies equally.

Minicomputers in the Data Processing Center

Except for the fact that so many sophisticated people have asked, "Will the minicomputer ever replace the large computer?" the question would be considered naive. The minicomputer and the large computer each do a particular type of job best. They are complementary rather than competitive. The large, expensive computer processes great masses of data and is efficient only when kept busy. The small computer improves the efficiency of the large computer by relieving it of tasks that it does not do efficiently but which, until now, it had to do because of the lack of alternatives. The large computer is built to process large quantities of data. Many applications, particularly the many real-time applications that can now be justified, are not always suited to the capabilities of the large computers.

Initially, when communications functions were added to the computer, one or two lines of communication were interfaced. The computer usually handled these rather well and had them operating without too much difficulty and without noticeable degradation of performance. However, the very success of these applications caused more and more communication lines to be brought into the computer. As a result, the computer spent so much of its time handling communication lines that it literally had little time available to do any of the processing. But the minicomputer has alleviated this overload. It handles communication applications very well, serves many lines in a fast and efficient manner, assembles to characters, checks for errors, loads a buffer with the completed character or block of characters, and then, either through an intercept or by polling, sends the assembled, validated data into the computer. Thus, the large computer is relieved of these tasks and is free to do the things it does best in the data processing area. A minicomputer, costing one-tenth of the large computer, can relieve the large computer of a sizable portion of its processing load. The following section discusses computer systems specifically designed for communication processing.

Much of the costs in data processing, frequently a full 50 percent, are incurred in the data transcription function. By using the minicomputer for this function, a large portion of the system costs can be reduced. Data is usually prepared for the large computer by keypunching. It is then batched and totaled and entered into the computer, where it goes through certain error checking and data validation routines. Then error reports are produced and the input is returned to the sender for correction, perhaps a couple of days after it was originally submitted. Other applications achieve improved turnaround time by having the large computer function as an on-line system, in which smaller batches or individual transactions are submitted, checked by the computer, and returned to the sender much sooner. Both methods have drawbacks—the lack of timeliness of the former, and the tie-up of the computer in the latter. A minicomputer system combines the best features of each method. Because of its relatively low cost, it matters little if it is committed to only this work. Moreover, because the large computer can replace these demanding jobs with more productive work, the minicomputer increases the effectiveness of the larger system.

On the other end of the large computing system are high-speed printers, graphic devices, or some type of storage or output device. The minicomputer with tape input and line printer output can act as an off-line printer (programmable, if necessary) and relieve the large computer of this job. In fact, some editing and formatting functions can be added to extend the use of the minicomputer in this function. In other situations, it can be tied directly into the large system. This can be done in several ways. The least sophisticated way is through the use of compatible peripherals. An industry-compatible magnetic tape can be produced as the minicomputer output for input to the large computer.

Other techniques are available if the situation demands it. There is the communications option by which the small computer is tied to a communication line that transfers data to the large computer through its communications interface. Even more desirable in some cases is a direct transfer of data. Interfaces built for the minicomputer and connected to the high-speed channel cause it to appear as a standard tape controller to the large computer. This allows the minicomputer system to be integrated into the large computer without requiring any change in the software or operating system of the large computer. The large computer handles the data from the minicomputer just as it would handle data coming from one of its tapes. This provides a high-speed, heavy data-volume interface that does not require any changes to the large computer system, not even software modification.

Communication Processors

The minicomputer can be used in communication applications in several ways. It can be used as a remote concentrator, taking the data that flows from a large number of slow-speed lines and combining the output onto a smaller number of high-speed lines to reduce telephone line charges. It can also be used as a message switch computer for routing messages among interfacing communication lines, or as a powerful front-end processor (FEP). (See Figure 5–2.)

An FEP is a special kind of data communications computer, usually a minicomputer, that interfaces between one or more large centralized host computers and other devices such as terminals, concentrators, and peripherals. A diagram of a typical data communication network controlled by a front-end processor is shown in Figure 5–2 (c). The FEP relieves the large host computer of routine communication-handling chores like terminal polling, message assembly and disassembly, and error detection and correction, thus enhancing the centralized computer performance. FEPs can also be used in networks that have multiple hosts.

The FEP has several basic ingredients: a central processor, communications interface, and one or more host computer interfaces. Also, FEP computers come with an operator's console and always a mass-storage device such as a tape cassette, diskette, or hard disks.

The central processor is invariably a fast mini that has a substantial amount of main memory—up to 512K bytes. It is commonly configured to do multiprogramming. Most processors are interrupt-driven devices, with input/output operations given the highest interrupt priority to prevent data loss and keep response to a maximum.

The host interface is a high-speed direct line to the central computer. Many types of central computer serve as hosts, but most FEPs interface with large IBM 370-type computers, commonly replacing IBM's own 370X series of FEPs. At least one mass-storage unit is needed in an FEP; almost all have at least a tape cassette or a diskette (floppy disk). Many vendors offer large-capacity disk storage that serves to store the FEP's operational software, to store messages for forwarding to devices in the network, and to save critical parameters for restart or (if the host computer goes down) to record data for later recovery. Microprocessors are frequently used in the FEP to handle specific tasks, for example, the line interface function and high-demand activities relating to character-oriented operations such as packing and unpacking data, deleting characters, and checking for errors.

Users can turn to minicomputer-based FEPs to achieve significant benefits. For example, the large computer that is connected to a dozen or more communication lines that have no FEPs spends as much as half its operating time handling I/O routines. If such a CPU exhibits 60 percent utilization, then 30 percent may be ab-

Figure 5–2. Using minicomputers as communication processors.

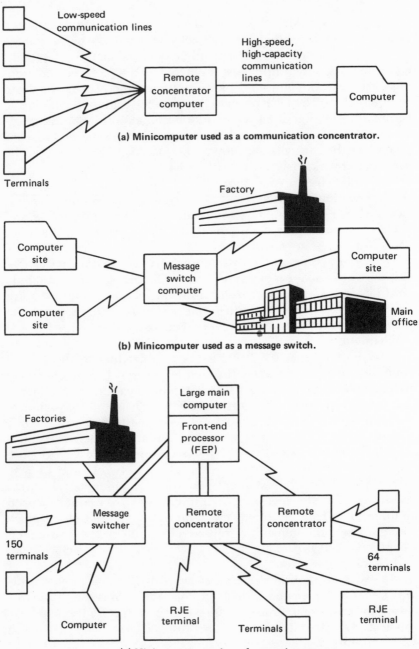

(a) Minicomputer used as a communication concentrator.

(b) Minicomputer used as a message switch.

(c) Minicomputer used as a front-end processor.

sorbed in internal application work and the other 30 percent in I/O. With a carefully selected FEP, mainframe computer utilization drops to 30 percent in this example, thus freeing it for more application-oriented activity.

There are other significant capabilities of the FEP. It can maintain essential message traffic and reroute high-priority messages should the host computer go down. It also provides capability to alter a network or add new terminals that are not usually supported by the host computer without having to change the host software.

Weighed against these advantages are some drawbacks that the user must assess. They include some probability of loss of data should an unforeseen burst of high-volume traffic occur; the difficulty of programming the FEP; the danger of using complex, perhaps untried software; and the traditional difficulties that may result when something goes wrong in a system composed of equipment supplied by several independent vendors.

Centralized and Decentralized Data Systems

A distinction can sometimes be made between the organizational philosophy and the data processing philosophy of the company. While it is possible to have a centralized organization with decentralized data processing, it is very rare. It is even rarer to have a decentralized organization with centralized data processing. Usually, the data processing organization follows the corporate organization philosophy. In fact, many management authorities claim that an important advantage achieved by the use of the minicomputer is that it allows the profit-center manager to have control of his own data processing, regardless of his position in the organization or physical location.

A centralized data processing organization always exercises corporate control of the information processing and usually, in addition, has centralized computers. A decentralized organization has fewer controls and reduced standards and is primarily motivated by the philosophy of service to the user. As a result, it usually has many data processing facilities, each primarily under control of local profit-oriented managers.

The distributed system is logically closer to the decentralized approach, since it uses dispersed data processing locations and allows local control over some processing. However, the distributed approach usually provides interaction with all other compu-

Figure 5–3. Data processing and information organizations.

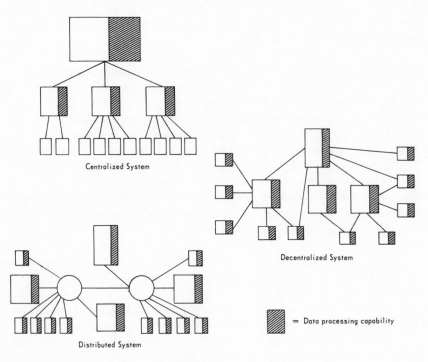

ter locations when needed, while the decentralized philosophy employs separate but broadly autonomous data processing centers. Illustrations of the centralized, decentralized, and distributed data systems are shown in Figure 5–3. The low-cost minicomputer is a viable distributed processing tool, and the distributed concept accentuates the value of the minicomputer, tying the two inexorably together. Because of its importance to minicomputers, distributed processing is addressed in detail in Chapter 6.

Modification of Existing Systems

Integrating the Minicomputer into the Large Company System

A major concern of anyone who has the responsibility and authority for maintaining the data systems within a company is the problem of intermixing various types of equipment. With the many new cost-effective terminals, computers, peripherals, and controllers now available, the systems designer who refuses to mix the equipment of different suppliers will miss out on many economic and operation benefits.

Since the minicomputer is a low-cost programmable device, it is ideally suited for integration into many different types of systems. The minicomputer can be programmed and modified to handle a variety of data coding—even at different speeds. In a communication system, for example, as long as the computer is programmed to recognize a particular code, it can convert that code to any other type. The program modules that perform the conversion function take the form of a table lookup and are resident in the computer. The table is entered, using the incoming character code as the index, and the translated value is extracted. The conversion table can be used for any translation. A system can be built with the capability to translate any code to any other code, including even those codes that may not be needed initially. As new applications or new equipment are added to the system, all that is required for integration is the unique means for identifying the specific code used in the input information. Once that input is identified as proper code, then that data can be processed by the programming modules, with little additional cost and no additional problems.

Because the minicomputer is a programmable device, it is possible to integrate it into many different systems, with confidence that future types of equipment can be handled in the same system. Most companies have some systems in existence, and for a variety of reasons these systems periodically require change. A change in concept or the integration of two major functional systems could require several years to complete. In addition to the expenses for developing and installing the revised system, the company would lose the potential benefits of the improvement.

Small-Business Computers

As the business grows, its information needs grow right along with it, in terms not only of quantity, but also of accuracy and timeliness. And the cost to organize, interpret, and further process the data grows at an increasing rate. The small-business computer allows managers and owners of small businesses to achieve many of the benefits that previously could be obtained only by companies that had the resources to use the large computers.

Many of the small-business computers are for first-time users; in fact, a supplier without the software and education support suitable for first-time users would not make a success in the small-business field. The computers generally perform basic business operations such as general accounting applications. Packaged software for applications such as accounts receivable, payroll, accounts payable, inventory control, general ledger, and others is usually provided with the small-business computers. They are generally easy to use, and while no computer system can be independent of technical assistance, the small-business computers are approaching that goal. First-time users can frequently install a packaged application in a very short period of time without the costly and time-consuming system analysis and programming that usually accompany such an installation.

The business computer puts updated information at the fingertips of people who need it. The system usually consists of display stations, desk-top printers for use whenever permanent records are required, a high-speed printer to turn out multiple-page reports, disk storage, and a powerful processing unit. Generally, the system is equipped with multiprocessing capability so that several people, all performing different jobs in different places, can use the computer simultaneously.

In an order entry application, for example, a clerk at a display station can check inventory for availability of the item, verify the customer's credit rating, and enter the order—all within seconds. At the same time, a printer in the warehouse can be automatically printing a packing slip. In addition, as the order is entered, the information in the computer files is automatically updated. This means that when the purchasing clerk needs to reorder, he will know the exact level of every inventory item. Accounts receivable and other company systems can also be updated. If desired, year-to-date sales figures can be supplied, with the very latest sale included in the figure.

The small-business computer is frequently used as a complete system for the small business. It is also often employed in large businesses for stand-alone applications, and it can be used as the central processor in an in-house time-sharing application. It can communicate with employees at remote sites—such as branch offices, plants, or warehouses—for data entry or retrieval, or it can function as part of a distributed network of remote computers. The computing needs of the user determine the configuration that is most appropriate.

The small-business computer, in general, enables users (frequently first-time users) to automate an application in a short period of time at a fairly reasonable cost. This automation should provide the business with more accurate, more timely information, and more comprehensive information—all at reduced costs.

The Microprocessor in Data Processing

The microprocessor is an electronic logic device that is the functional equivalent of the small stored-program computer. It is capable of being used both as a replacement for logic and as a processing element in a computing system. It has application in the data processing environment and in the larger nontechnical community as well.

Data capture. The microprocessor is commonly built into a terminal to provide validation logic in the data entry process. It would be programmed either in a hardware or software fashion to provide the logic necessary to test and validate that the data being entered into the system is accurate and complete. The so-called intelligent terminals have always had logic devices that provided their intelligence. With the use of microprocessors, more comprehensive logic tailored to the user's specific needs can be incorporated into terminals at low cost. The microprocessor can be also built into data acquisition devices used in complex laboratory and industrial applications.

Commercial data processing. Although it has not been generally accepted as such at this time, a prime use for a microprocessor is as a substitute for software. It has been envisioned that future computer programs will be assembled by selecting microprocessor-coded equivalents of programming routines. However, even if this extended use of microprocessing is not realized, it is very likely that in a few years, repetitive programming routines now performed in software will be built into special-purpose commercial data processing machines. As the cost for software development increases and microprocessor costs continue to decrease, this technique will see increasing use.

Manufacturing applications. The industrial uses of microprocessors are potentially infinite, since almost every aspect of modern manufacturing techniques is amenable to logical control by computer devices. These include the reading of badges to identify a particular worker, machine control data acquisition functions that measure the performance of a processing operation, automatic quality control, scheduling of manufacturing operations, and the data transmission that would tie into the corporate computers.

Consumer applications. Microprocessors are presently used in many consumer applications. At present they are used in microwave ovens and washing machines, in TV sets and TV games, and, most extensively perhaps, in the electronic ignition and monitoring of automobile engines.

Peripheral controllers. Microprocessors are replacing the hardwired logic now employed in disk, tape, and printer controllers, adding flexibility and new functions at lower costs. When used in this way the microprocessor provides error detection and correction logic in the controller, significantly increasing its utility and value.

The decreasing cost combined with increased flexibility due to their programmability will no doubt stimulate the use of microprocessors in all areas in the near future. Their use will be so extensive and will impact so greatly on our present data processing philosophy that the definition of what we now know as a computer will surely change in the near future.

Approach to System Modification

The preferred approach to system modification is to devise a method capable of realizing the following objectives:

- Modify the system rapidly and at low cost to capture the benefits of the proposed change immediately.
- Maintain the existing system without degradation while the changes are being made.
- Minimize the changes to the existing system.

The most beneficial method requires a device that can translate the data output of the new addition to the system into a form that will allow transparent integration into the existing system. Ideally, this device is capable of modification so that minor variations due to differences in user methods can be accommodated. In addition, the device should be capable of testing and validating the input data and locking out all but the desired data. And, hopefully, this device is low in cost. These are specifications for a device that has logic and can be modified readily to accommodate a number of variations. In other words, a low-cost programmable processor, a minicomputer, or microcomputer can do the job.

Consider the application illustrated in Figure 5–4(a). The input

Figure 5–4. Data processing system.

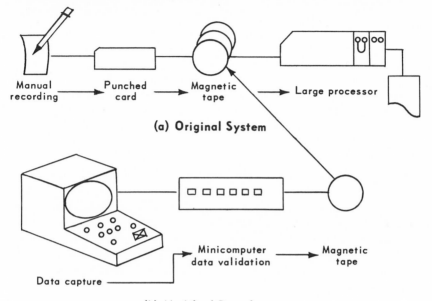

(a) Original System

(b) Modified Data Input

documents have been collected from a number of sources and sent to the company data center. The data is punched into cards, verified, and converted once a week to tape and processed. If errors are detected in the processing, an additional week is needed for correction. In Figure 5–4(b), the front part of this system—the data-input source—has been replaced by a small minicomputer configuration. The clerk, who previously completed the form, now enters the data directly into the minicomputer by means of a CRT input terminal. The computer program would guide the operator through the input procedure, validate and edit the input data if desired, format the output, and write the output on the industry-compatible magnetic tape in the format that is expected by the large computer. Thus, this tape can be used in the original system without any system or programming modifications.

The use of a minicomputer in this application facilitates integration. It allows piecemeal or partial system changes rather than requiring an entirely new development. It allows benefits to be achieved in a shorter time period, and it produces a flexible system. If, in the future, for some reason a decision is made to modify the company procedures completely in a way that requires major system changes, the minicomputer can be reprogrammed to accommodate them. Although this reprogramming does cost something, it surely costs much less and disrupts the system much less than other procedures that require replacement of computers and equipment.

Multiple Processor System

Another use of the small computer in the large data processing environment employs several processors in an integrated system. These multiprocessor systems, in which several computers are tied into one mass-storage system, give indications of great potential for effective operation and are most promising for the future. The processors in these multiprocessor systems are still almost exclusively devoted to a single function. This follows the standard minicomputer philosophy by using all its resources in a dedicated application. No operating system is needed (as would be essential if the functions performed by the multiple processors were combined into one large computer), the processing power is not diluted by the high overhead of a complex operating system, and each processor is employed solely to handle the user's problem.

Figure 5–5 describes a multiprocessor system of minicomputers. This system uses three processors in a task-oriented manner. Each processor has a set of tasks to do, and also has the peripherals to help do the work. In the topmost level of the figure is the communications processor, which handles all incoming and outgoing data. It also performs transmission-error checking and the editing (first CPU). The second CPU is the computation machine with arithmetic and floating-point hardware features. The third CPU is the input/output processor, which handles the mass-storage allocation and control. Each processor has its own local memory (private to itself), but also has access to the common data and programs in the mass-storage main memory. With this arrangement, the capacity and specific features of each CPU can be tailored to its task. Such systems are most efficient, however, if all CPUs are of the same family so that they can share common programs stored once in main memory.

Connections of minicomputers offer a great deal of potential for great improvements in cost performance of computing systems. They have the added advantage of sharing system components. The system is configured even more closely to the job to be done because it need call upon specific system resources only as required.

Figure 5–5. The multi-mini system.

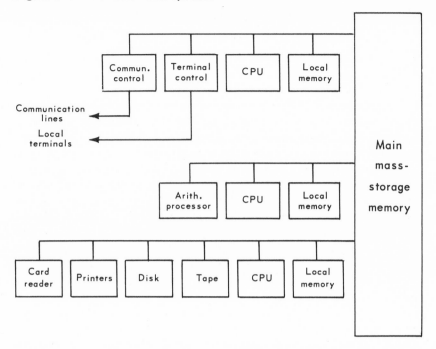

Advantages and Disadvantages of Minicomputer Systems

We have been looking at just what these systems can do. As a result, the attributes of the minicomputer system have been stressed. There are, of course, negative aspects as well.

The advantages of using minicomputers are summarized as follows:

Low cost.
Simplicity in design and operation.
Easily integrated into operating functions and systems.
Systems are operated by the user. No formal EDP staff is required.
The system can be custom-designed to the application. No overbuy is necessary.
Interactive system design may be accomplished as easily as a batch-processing system with wider use.
Attractive security conditions can be provided for critical data

by having these dedicated systems residing in the user department.

Small size; no special air conditioning or raised floor required.

Software languages supplied by vendors are compatible within a vendor's line.

Support for user-oriented language available.

No costly, high-overhead system software and operating system required.

Negative aspects of the minicomputer are not necessarily constant, nor are they equally pertinent to all situations.

Vulnerability. It does not require a large investment to produce minicomputers and similar types of hardware. As a result, some small companies in the field are not solidly funded. In general, the companies are smaller and newer than their larger computer competitors.

Technical limitations. The primary technical limitations of these computers are the 16-bit word and the maximum memory size. However, the small word size does not affect many applications; and with random-access, high-speed disks, and virtual memory systems, the memory limitations are not likely to handicap most business systems. However, there are still real restrictions. In particular, these computers cannot be used to handle large models, large linear programs, or large compilers.

Service, hardware maintenance, and support limitations. Since the market to date has been a seller's market, many manufacturers have been more interested in developing their hardware than in firming up their service or support capabilities. Therefore, manufacturer's support may be spotty and may vary by location. Investigation of the supplier's capability in each specific location is desirable before a commitment is made.

Use limitation. A dedicated system means dedicated peripherals. Physically separated systems each require their own storage and input/output equipment. Therefore, no sharing of peripherals is possible, as it would be in a data processing center.

Economics. "Economics" was listed as being on the positive side; however, some negative aspects of minicomputer costs should be mentioned. Since the large peripherals used with a mini are just as expensive as for the larger computer, the economic advantage of a minicomputer system decreases as the size of the system increases.

Also, although most minicomputers are claimed to be user-oriented, programmerless systems, there is usually some time when expansion or modifications must be considered. Technical personnel are needed at such times, and are also needed to diagnose problems and malfunctions. Building the technical staff to handle such problems could rapidly dissipate much of the expected savings.

Moreover, at times it is desirable to buy more than the minimum configuration so that program development will be easier. If the basic system does not require a printer or card reader, it would probably make sense to buy this additional equipment to make program assembly and compiling less time-consuming. Redundant equipment needed for backup purposes would likely be a significant portion of the total systems cost. And, if several stand-alone minicomputer systems are in use, this redundant equipment would be needed at each site, greatly inflating the costs.

System reliability. Custom-designed dedicated systems are vulnerable to system failure when a single peripheral element fails. In a multipurpose large-computer operation, peripheral device redundancy exists.

Software not transferable. Many of the existing programs have been written in Assembler language that is different for each machine vendor, and therefore not compatible. Higher-level languages are available (such as BASIC, RPG, ALGOL, FORTRAN, and COBOL), and therefore this problem may diffuse somewhat, but it will never completely disappear.

Software maintenance. Program maintenance could be a problem when numerous, remote, dedicated systems are used. These systems still require maintenance and updating. A problem arises because the technical staff is usually not at these locations but at the data processing center. When a requirement common to all systems is changed to accommodate, say, a new corporate report or a new tax rate, the programs at each location must be changed. This is accomplished at a multiple of the costs needed to change a single equivalent large-computer program. Also, because of the less sophisticated programming and debugging tools available, developing and maintaining minicomputer programs is more costly than for equivalent large computer functions.

User inertia. In order to accomplish acceptance and full development of minicomputer applications, the resistance of people in changing to new methods that are not so secure as the traditional ones must be overcome. But it must be remembered that the concept introduced with these new computers is opposed to the valuable experience that data processing people have built up through the years. The methods are also very new and have not had the crucial test of time.

Organizational or philosophical constraints. A very real and very important consideration when using minicomputers in a multiple-location large company is how they fit into the company's way of doing business. When computers are at many remote locations, there may be lack of control in the use of these systems. If these installations are not carefully audited, many of the users could start modifying their systems or developing new applications. This would result in loss of commonality of systems and possibly redundant or wasted development effort.

All the disadvantages discussed above are very real factors to be considered before a commitment for a system is made.

It has been emphasized that minicomputers are very capable machines. They can be used in many different applications, and are extremely important for cost-cutting applications. They are most important because they serve the user and bring him back into the data processing picture. But the user must also be concerned with service, program maintenance, backup considerations, and all the things required to produce an effective, ongoing system.

DISTRIBUTED PROCESSING SYSTEMS

It is evident that there is not one universally best way to perform the data processing function; instead, there are many. Data processing costs, benefits, and suitability depend upon the characteristics of the application, the company, and the environment.

The availability of low-cost data processing power in the form of microcomputers and minicomputers makes many alternatives possible and worthy of serious consideration in any company's data processing plan. There is now available a variety (in fact, just about a complete spectrum) of computer processing alternatives to solve business problems. These include methods that use programmable calculators, both programmable and nonintelligent terminals, and a variety of computer products from the microprocessor chip to the supercomputer.

A company need not choose just one of these methods as the sole way of processing data, but may, and usually does, employ a number of these techniques at one time. Intelligent terminals, possibly with a built-in microprocessor or minicomputer, may be used at remote locations for the entry and validation of data. A large computer may also be used at the same site or at the next hierarchical organizational level for traditional data processing. In addition, the company may use one or more large supercomputers that might share, even dynamically, the corporation's major data processing load. A combination of one or more of these and other data processing methodologies constitutes the activity now known as *distributed processing*.

Like many other terms and techniques involved in data processing, distributed processing, unfortunately, is often used to describe a number of related but somewhat different processing methods. As a result, a precise definition of what functions are being distributed and where processing is being performed should be made before any discussion of distributed processing is initiated.

Let us narrow the scope of the definitions. Distributed processing does not mean using a front-end processor to handle data communications from the central site; nor does it mean using several minicomputers located at the central site to replace one large computer, nor even using intelligent terminals at remote locations to preprocess data that is then transmitted to the central computer.

Distributed processing implies computers at a number of locations. This is the strict and traditional definition of a distributed processing system, although it does not necessarily coincide with the common usage of the term. With the recent advances in semiconductor technology, it is becoming quite common to replace computers with the almost invisible data processing of microprocessors at remote entry locations.

A distributed system also implies multiple processing locations tied together through a telecommunication network, but this, too, is not a strict requirement of such a system, since data can be distributed by ways other than a telecommunication network. Distributed systems are used with on-line communications and with batch transmission, as well as with mailing of data on floppy disks, tapes, cassettes, or punch cards. Some distributed systems exhibit all these modes of communications at once. While not usual, other systems have no intersite telecommunications at all and still can be considered distributed processing systems.

Types of Distributed Systems

Distributed Processing

The traditional and initial use of distributed processing originated with the large computer operations. For security reasons and to handle peak-load requirements more easily, it became desirable to distribute processing from one large computer to several other computers of the same company. This provided companies with the security of having alternate sites that could perform the same type of processing; so, in the event of a break in service, the company's data processing operations could continue at another site.

A second reason for distributing the processing was to reduce peak-load requirements. If a company had computer sites located throughout the country, the work loads on these computer locations were likely to vary by time of day. Considering time differences between different parts of our country, work-load peaking at one location could possibly occur while another location was lightly loaded. As a result, some of the work load could be shifted from the heavily loaded computer to the lightly loaded one on an un-scheduled arrangement as a means of satisfying the demands of the moment. Also, the same type of work-load shifting may occur when multiple computer sites do a variety of processing. One location might be occupied with an engineering problem, causing the waiting processing queue to be shifted to an alternate location. This procedure allows a company to reduce the amount of equipment needed to satisfy peak-load requirements.

In addition to a single company using this type of technology, computer utilities or associations of computer service companies have organized to provide this kind of facility for members of their organizations. When a company or an organization provides such a service, a network of similar or dissimilar computer centers and many data input locations are tied together by the communication network. Data flows from the terminals into the communication hubs. Minicomputers are used to direct the traffic and to decide to which processor the data entered at the terminal will be directed. The person entering the data does not know on what computer the processing takes place. The system delegates the task to an available processor, usually the closest and least loaded or the one supporting the particular feature needed. While not usually as complicated as the commercial network, the business organization frequently distributes processing in a similar manner.

The advantage of this type of system is that it reduces hardware costs by providing relief from peak-load requirements. However, this reduction in cost may not offset the additional cost for establishing such a network. But, in many cases, the transmission network is necessary for other reasons, thus helping to justify the distribution of processing. The main reason for such a method of processing is usually to provide backup and security of operations afforded by multiple processing locations.

Establishing such a distributed processing system requires an extreme amount of planning performed by a staff of high competence and technical level. For this reason, distributed processing in the pure sense is usually found in larger companies, with the minicomputer's primary role being that of controlling communications. The other types of distributed processing systems discussed in following sections are more likely to be used by smaller companies in our present environment, with the minicomputer used as the main processor.

Distributed Application Systems

Very closely related to the preceding type of distributed processing system is the type of processing whereby applications are distributed among numerous processing locations in a multilocation environment. Specific data processing centers are established as the sites for the processing of specific applications. For example, a company with several major processing centers might have one center specialize in accounting and related types of applications, while another center would be doing the processing for product inventory, production control, and similar functions, with a third specializing in engineering and development.

Similarly, other specific functions would be processed at other locations. Each of the locations, as well as any other data input points of the company, would either mail or transmit their data to these processing centers for performing the data processing work. Usually, these data processing centers are connected by a transmission network through which any input location could transmit data to any processing center. This type of distributed processing system also strongly implies that the development work is distributed as well. Each of these centers would usually have companywide responsibility for all analysis, development, programming, and installation of applications under its authority.

Distributed application processing is largely independent of the requirements of the minicomputer. All types of processing, whether using large computers or using minicomputers, can be distributed in this fashion. In the extreme case, when applications are very large, each configuration of this type of distributed system is similar to a traditional data processing system. As applications expand, more computer power in the form of additional CPUs or additional peripherals can be added to the computer system.

This type of arrangement, where specific functions are handled by stand-alone processors, has become common in many manufacturing companies as well as in banking. Several large banking organizations have installed separate minicomputers for demand deposit, for loan accounting, and for many other specific functions. Data to be processed on these systems is entered into a communication network from each bank location. The data is transmitted to the location of the processor for the application, where the function is performed on the the minicomputer.

Distributed Data Systems

The distributed data system type of processing arrangement is becoming more economical with the use of minicomputers and minicomputer peripherals. In these systems, a significant portion of the data files are maintained at the remote processing sites.

If the amount of data at all remote sites is at least as large as the remaining data stored at the central location, it is considered to be a distributed data system. In this type of system, remotely located data files allow processing to be accomplished without heavy volume demands on the communication networks. Since communication is a major or at least significant portion of the cost, any means to reduce the communication load can surely make an application more economical and easier to justify.

Distributed Function System

The most common type of distributed processing system, and the one that appears to be regularly referred to in the literature on minicomputers, is the distributed function system. In this system, which is illustrated in Figure 6–1, specific functions of one or more applications are performed at remote locations. The data entry portion of an order entry system is a common example of the remotely performed portion of a distributed processing system. Many output functions, such as printing reports or preparing checks, are also commonly performed remotely in a distributed function processing system. Of all distributed processing systems, these systems are the easiest to understand and implement. In addition, vendors have advanced their level of knowledge, technology, and experience, and can easily accommodate this type of system.

A system may include more than one type of distributed processing. In conjunction with the distributed function system, we frequently have the distributed data system. In this situation, when data is entered at the remote location, local files are used in editing and validating to assure that no errors are being introduced with the data. The main part of the processing may be accomplished at a large computer center, following transmission of the validated input data to that site. After processing, the data returned by the central computer may be stored by the remote files from which, at a convenient time, it can be drawn off for the completion of the processing, such as printing reports or preparing checks. Figure 6–2 shows a relatively common processing configuration where entire applications are distributed and other applications are distributed by function.

Figure 6–1. Distributed function configuration. Data entry (T) and printing functions (P) performed locally using local computers (B) and files (C), which are subsets of the central data base. The local files are also used to store data received from the central computer for off-line printing.

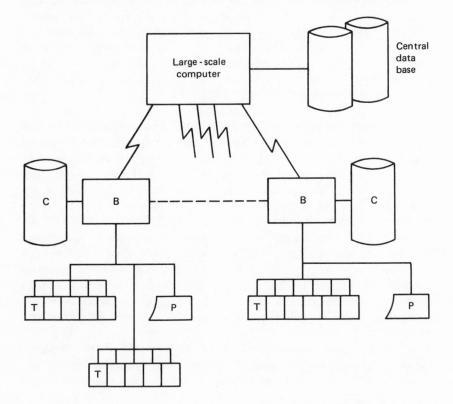

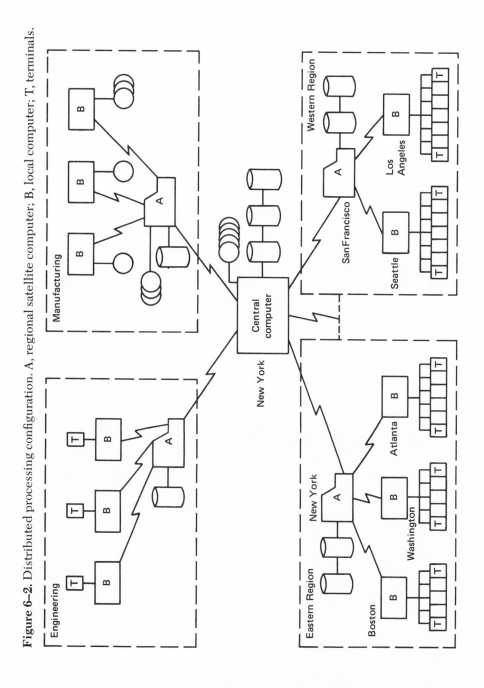

Figure 6-2. Distributed processing configuration. A, regional satellite computer; B, local computer; T, terminals.

Networking

Communication between processors, and between the processor and its user, in some form is an essential part of a distributed system. In almost all systems the various processing points are connected by communication lines. Communication lines and software make the difference between a cluster of computers that act independently and a group of these same computers integrated into a smoothly functioning, cost-effective distributed processing system.

Just as different buildings can be constructed from similar steel and bricks, a number of different communication networks can be configured from similar computer hardware to satisfy distributed processing requirements. Some basic network types described below provide insight into the operation of such distributed processing systems.

Networks can be simple or very complex. They can perform other functions besides distributing the data processing application. Many networks are used to provide redundancy and backup processing, thus providing added security to the organization. Since they are designed to suit the requirements of the organization, many different configurations are used in business today. However, even the most complex hybrid forms are built from the four basic types described below and illustrated in Figure 6–3.

Point to point. This type, the simplest of computer networks, employs a communication line to link two computers together. The two computers might share a processing load or might perform two different parts of the same application. In addition, if they are of suitable size, the computers might also serve as backup for each other.

Hierarchical, or tree. In this arrangement, many computers, each performing a dedicated function, are linked to another (usually larger) computer. This larger computer might perform a higher-level application function and could also serve as partial backup for the lower-level computers. There may be other, higher levels of processing in this hierarchical arrangement.

Star. The remote computers in the star network all communicate with the same central computer. This is a commonly used configuration when the main data base must be consolidated at one location for economic or control reasons. The remote computers do the local processing, using local files, but extract data as needed from the central data base for some functions.

Loop, or ring. Processors linked serially with all other processors form a loop, or ring, network. Data lines connect each processor only to adjacent ones. Since any communication to distant processors must follow a serial path, the computers in the pure ring network must be physically close together for economy reasons.

Because of such limitations, the ring network is seldom used in its pure form, but rather it serves as a foundation for hybrid type networks. The basic network types of Figure 6–3 can be combined to create a hybrid network as shown in Figure 6–4. Several central computers, for example, each surrounded by a separate star network of satellite processors, can also be connected together in a star of their own. Such a multistar configuration is an excellent alternative to the high-cost ring network if the main processors are at a distance from each other.

Use of the Minicomputer in Distributed Processing

The motivation for all distributed processing systems, as well as for any other innovative method of data processing, is to reduce costs without degrading service or performance of other parts of the company. It is evident there are many different ways to process data. The one that is right for a particular company may be entirely wrong for another company whose products and services appear to be similar. The situation that has lowest cost in one type of operation may be economically and operationally unfeasible for other companies.

Some measurements have indicated that minicomputer pure processing costs for a particular, special application may be one-tenth of the processing costs for the same application performed on larger computers. Despite the apparent hardware economies in some applications, however, companies have not universally found that minicomputers are the best way to go. When the costs of added support and controls are factored in, the savings diminish and sometimes disappear.

While lower cost is usually the motivating factor, there are many other factors—and some of them just as important as cost—to be evaluated. The time response to members of the organization and to its customers and clients must be considered. Technical support of the many locations as well as the associated security problems must be analyzed. Economies in other areas of the company can be

Figure 6–3. Communication networks for distributed processing systems. A, regional computer; B, local computer and communication controller; C, local data base; T, terminals and other data entry devices.

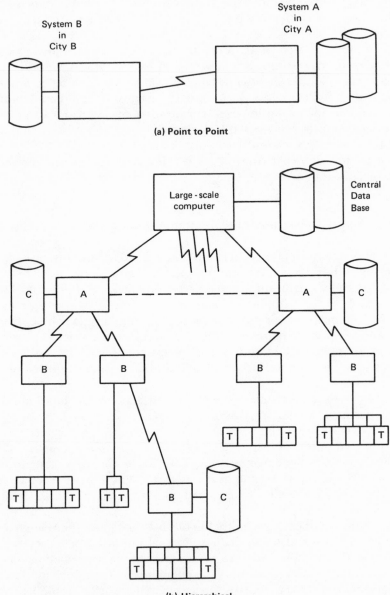

(a) Point to Point

(b) Hierarchical

Figure 6–3 (continued).

(c) Star

(d) Ring

Figure 6–4. Hybrid configuration. Large-scale computer and regional computers connected in a ring, each with its own star configuration.

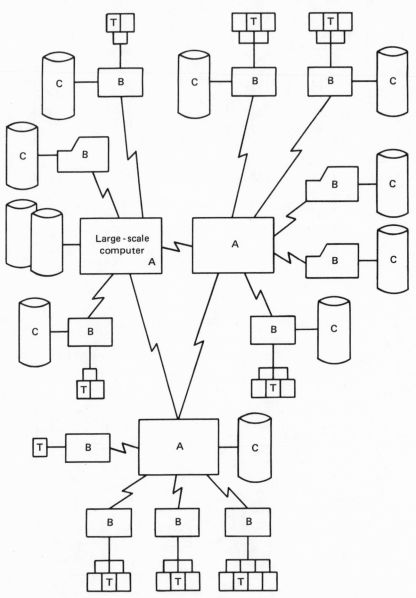

seriously reduced or enhanced by the data processing performance. Therefore, in considering cost, not only the data processing cost but also the total system cost—that is, the overall effect on the entire company—is to be considered. The lowest-cost minicomputer equipment makes many innovative processing methods appear attractive, but unless careful evaluation of the results is performed, considering all the factors that affect the cost, the low-priced data processing equipment might lead a company into a more expensive situation.

Today's minicomputer equipment manufacturers can best support distributed data and distributed function applications through their standard equipment and software. Other types of distribution, such as distributed processing, require a great amount of technical expertise that is beyond the easy reach of many of the minicomputer companies at this time. As a result, the primary use of distributed processing systems at present is in the distributed function mode of operation, and it is this use that will now be evaluated in detail.

The Distributed Processing Environment

Distributed processing is only relevant to the company that has more than one location—usually a company of significant size and with a certain amount of data processing experience. As a result, distributed processing techniques potentially replace other data processing methods or at least vie with existing alternative methods. In order to avoid having a description of the characteristics and benefits of distributed processing appear to be a one-sided copy of vendor sales material, the distributed processing approach should be put into proper perspective and compared with existing logical alternatives for performing the same operation.

Just about any computer is technically capable of performing an almost endless array of data processing chores, and when many computers are tied together, the capabilities become truly mind-boggling. But unless the costs of processing support, communication, control, and security are considered, the real world is being ignored. Distributed processing certainly is no different from any other processing method in this respect. In fact, because of the great potential distributed processing has for solving just about any single data processing problem, the detrimental aspects of this approach are often overlooked. And, because the benefits of cost reduction can be quantified more easily than can reduced support, reduced control, or added training, the lower economic course often presents the more salable argument. Solving one problem for the company may, however, introduce additional risks, higher costs, or other undesirable effects, and these offsets must be considered at least as seriously as the benefits.

At present the most common minicomputer distributed system approach is one in which data entry and output functions are performed at a remote location along with a part of the processing function. Data is entered through keyboard terminals at the source location where minicomputers control the entry and validation of data. The minicomputers also support large disk files of application data. Local files are used for validating the data key entered at the terminal. The validation files are subsets of the master files maintained at the central processing location. After validation and partial processing, the data is transmitted on line to the central processor for completion of processing and updating of the corporate data base.

Frequently, more than two levels of processing are involved. For example, in a national retail organization, each retail store will usually have numerous terminals controlled by one minicomputer (See Figure 6–5). Inventory will be checked for availability, and extension of the purchases and other calculations will be performed by the local-level minicomputer. The regional computer will maintain the regional credit file, against which each purchaser's credit will be verified. Each transaction processed will also be stored at this location until it is forwarded to the corporate location. At the end of each day a tape of all the day's transactions and other data is mailed to the central computer location for updating the corporate master data base.

An alternative to this method of processing could be an on-line operation where nonintelligent terminals communicate with a large central computer, which also maintains all files and performs all processing. Other alternatives include an intelligent data-entry terminal (a key-to-disk system, for example) performing only the entry and validation of data. The validated data is batched for later transmission to the computer center, where the remainder of the processing is performed.

Potential Economic Benefits of Distributed Processing Systems

Processing costs. Even when the general characteristics of the two alternative processing methods are known, it is difficult to determine if the processing costs of a distributed function system

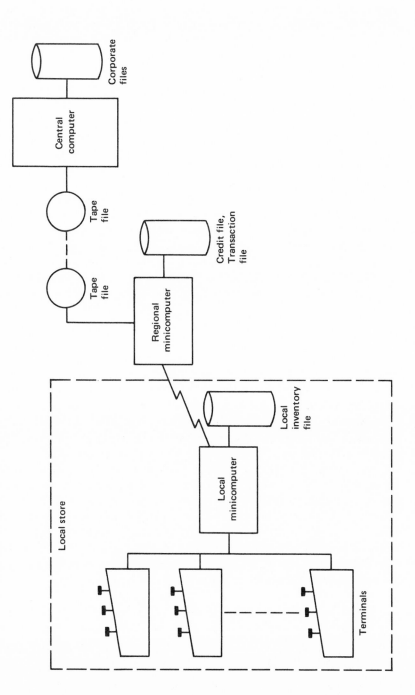

Figure 6–5. Distributed processing system for a retail organization.

will be less than those of a traditional central processing system. Additional details of the application alternatives must be known before this judgment can be made. The processing costs are highly dependent upon how the processing load is split between the remote and central site, as well as the type of data base and communication software necessary to support the system. Costs also depend upon the company's security, control, and accounting philosophy.

Potentially, the remote processor has the advantage of more processing power per dollar of cost for selected applications. But even this generally accepted guideline is not always true. If the essential central-site processing requires the same file information as that used for validation at the data entry stage, then duplicate and redundant accesses to the disk file as well as possible redundant processing are performed. The sum of the two parts of the required processing could be more than the amount required if all were done at the same central site. Frequently, performing all processing at the local site is not possible because of equipment limitations or because of a system requirement, such as the need to store and maintain all data at one location.

Communication costs. Performing some of the required application processing at the source of the input data will certainly decrease the amount of data to be transmitted to the central site. At times, the reduction is truly significant. Possibly as much as 90 percent of the screen format and application data that is transmitted back and forth between the remote location and central location of a centralized, interactive process could be eliminated in the distributed processing mode. Of course, in some applications the reduction would not be so great. There is also the possibility that the communication rate structure, which makes the cost independent of volume within certain limits, could result in identical cost regardless of the different data transmission volume. However, distributed processing will never require transmission of more data than the centralized process and, as a result, will usually result in lower communication costs.

Application customization. Having computer intelligence at remote locations allows the special needs of the user to be accommodated. These special needs could be the application characteristics that make this particular location different from all others, or they might be the added controls or productivity features requested by local management. With the presence of minicomputers or programmable terminals, these features can be easily added to only the specific input terminals at specific locations, thus satisfying local needs.

Elapsed processing time. A central processing system must adjust its processing schedule to optimize the overall company performance. As a result, the processing of a particular segment of an application may have to be performed together with similar jobs from other locations. This type of central processing constraint could extend the time needed to process an application to completion for any individual location.

Response time. An interactive application is performed by entering data into a formatted CRT screen, sending that data to the central processing unit, where some processing occurs and a new screen is returned to the input CRT for additional data entry. Between each step in the process there are several delays, each usually very small. These delays are associated with the two-way transmission of data between the terminal and the processor, with the retrieval of file data, and with the processing of the data in the computer.

The amount of this delay, or the response time, depends on many factors such as the type of terminal, the type and quality of lines, the level of use of the lines, and the amount and type of processing. Considering similar applications, the only difference between remote processing and central processing should be the added time required to communicate with the more distant central computer processor. Typically, for an efficient, relatively unloaded system, this additional time would be about 1 second for each transmission. A multiple-screen data entry operation could thus require 25 percent additional time for completion when transmission to a central location is required. Therefore, 25 percent more data entry personnel and equipment would be needed, even for an efficient system, because of the additional delay when processing is done by a remote processor.

Backup operation. When a processor in either the central or distributed processing arrangement is down, processing suffers. A centralized processing system is usually large enough to justify a backup processor, and as a result, the failure of one processor would not be catastrophic. In a distributed network other processors could conceivably take over the work load of the failed processor, but this is not always possible. Usually, when the processor is down, the file data cannot be delivered to the alternate processor, thus making backup processing capability meaningless. Therefore, one of the advantages of distributed processing, the availability of backup processors, can only be utilized if the implementers of the system incurred the additional ongoing expense of backup facilities.

All work is halted when a system fails, causing many dollars of waste because of the personnel who are idled. If a communication line or any other piece of equipment in the transmission path fails, transfer of processing to a remote site cannot be accomplished. To assure uninterrupted processing, backup communication facilities and equipment would be required at additional cost. Alternatively, the distributed system's on-site computer, given some costly and technically complex arrangements, could be used to perform some ongoing work. Through the use of special software the on-site computer could be arranged to allow the data entry operation to continue even though communication with other computers in the distributed network is cut off.

Flexible scheduling. Depending on the degree to which the remote location processor is independent of its associates in the network, the local processor has various degrees of freedom in scheduling its own operations. The remote location is not dependent on other corporate demands and can schedule the processing to best suit its individual requirements.

The Technical Problems

Data storage. Data base management systems are now being effectively used in many large central data processing centers after many painful and costly years spent in understanding their use. Data base systems can provide efficient storage of billions of character of data, and the associated software provides the means for extracting information from the file according to a multitude of possible attributes. Just as the industry is learning to economically use this technology, data processing facilities with the associated data files are being distributed to the user site to satisfy a collection of important but very different problems. As frequently happens in leading-edge technology areas, the attempt to solve one problem may impact on previously settled issues.

Even when most of the processing is done at a remote processing location, there are few business applications that do not require access to some of the data stored at another site (such as in the corporate data base). Maintaining a copy of such data at the remote site introduces inefficiencies. The redundant data requires space, and although the unit cost of storage is low, significant cost can be involved because of the voluminous data used in business applications. Redundant data also means that there is now more than one file that must be updated. As a result, procedures must be instituted to ensure that the two files do not get out of step, and correction procedures must be developed to rectify the problems when they do get out of step.

Merely transferring the data from the centralized data base to the remote location can involve unbelievable control and cost problems. Consider a distributed processing environment that has several locations and numerous business applications. Hundreds of draw-offs from master files must be executed, each followed by transmission of data to the proper location and updating of the local files. All these steps are costly, complex, extremely susceptible to error, and (because of the heavy volume) very time-consuming.

Equipment redundancy. The low-cost minicomputer equipment—the primary reason for even considering distributed processing—actually approaches the cost of a mid-size system when major peripherals, such as disks needed to store large volumes of data, are added. In addition, to ensure reliable operation, disks and other redundant equipment must be used. Equipment redundancy at each of the distributed processing locations greatly increases the cost of the original low-cost system. The remote user frequently must decide between the risk of interrupted service and cost of backup equipment. Central computer backup system costs can be spread over its many users, but the cost of redundant equipment at each site inflates the distributed processing cost for all locations.

Lack of uniformity. Economies in equipment costs can be attained through the significant quantity discounts provided by most manufacturers. This benefit is lost when each location can choose the terminal and computer equipment it wants. Application software costs are multiplied by the number of different versions of the same application that are developed. Moreover, application dissimilarities require special training and extra personnel, and nullify all advantages associated with commonality of use and economies of scale.

Software development. User options in computer programs and programmable terminals mean different systems for different users. More programs must be documented and maintained, and when a change common to all locations (for example, a change of a tax rate or addition of a new government report) must be made, the individual programmer's testing and training expense is multiplied by the number of locations involved.

To make matters worse, because each location has unique application requirements, programming experts crop up at each of these sites. This ultimately leads to attempts to modify the programs without bothering to obtain corporate approval or even notify the corporate site. Thus, corporate control of the application is lost.

Initial equipment investment. It frequently takes a significant period of time for an application to grow from an initial low volume to the expected full application volume, but the entire cost of the equipment must be carried from the very first step. This is repeated at each location, resulting in very high unit costs. These costs, of course, decrease to the expected value after a period of time when the volume reaches anticipated levels, but each location meanwhile has accumulated additional costs.

Vendor relations. When the user at each distributed location can select the equipment type and manufacturer, the pressure a company can bring to bear on a single vendor is lost. In addition, there are many more vendors the company has to deal with, thus making it more difficult to identify responsibility. Also, depending on the vendor, the maintenance of equipment and software can be very spotty, especially in remote areas. This can cause delays in arrival of service help at the processing location, and also consequent downtime of the equipment.

Technical support. A dilemma the remote manager must face concerns the need for technical assistance. Without technical support at the remote location, even diagnosis of a system malfunction could be extremely difficult and correction could be impossible. But when each site has its own hardware and software technical support, all anticipated savings can be lost. Therefore, it is preferable to have centralized facilities support the cost of various technical specialists, since one technical expert for each function can assist all locations.

Compatibility. Many computer vendors and their associated systems houses have developed and marketed hardware and software bundled in application-specific packages. These packages frequently offer limited flexibility for new application development. Moreover, many vendors lack complete application libraries, and thus the bundled systems are often incompatible among vendors. In too many cases the result has been separate processes, different software disciplines, and even parallel data networks to support the application needs of a single location.

Security and Control

Distributed processing provides greater opportunity for invasion of data security. People are fascinated by the creativity of the

thief in devising unusual and resourceful ways to violate the security of a data processing system. Security, however, is a complex problem. Auditors, accountants, and corporate executives are deeply involved in controlling and accounting for the physical and financial assets of a company. The accounting is done satisfactorily by data processing systems, but security measures, even in the centralized data processing environment, have not been impressively successful. The distributed concept adds significantly to the risk involved. Data is not only originated at the remote location, but may also be stored there, with only summaries sent to the corporate centralized data base. The opportunities for fraud and embezzlement are multiplied thereby, so that much tighter, less manipulable system controls are needed.

Among the many new uncertainties with regard to physical and data security in the distributed processing environment are the following:

• Problems related to maintaining the safety of hardware and vital computer information are obviously compounded when there are numerous processing sites to be made secure.

• Software tools to limit access of information to computer systems are generally not available and, when needed, must be developed at significant cost.

• Of the many links in the processing stream, the one most vulnerable to interception is in the communication of data. Having many remote processing sites that communicate regularly with the corporate data base increases the security problems.

• The replication of data bases between the central site and distributed sites adds significant system control and security problems.

• Centralized management control of the data base is weakened and the problem of the audit function, both for data processing and for management accounting, is increased substantially.

The Human Resource Issue

With both data processing and data files distributed, company management must take steps to organize operating management, particularly data processing management, in a different fashion. If hardware and applications are distributed, so must the data processing management function and its reporting relationships. The problems involved are very familiar, and the trade-offs are similar to those in any centralized/decentralized evaluation. Bringing management closer to the operating function makes the organization more responsive to the user. It also provides the manager with increased autonomy and supports the concepts of profit center and functional responsibility.

However, in transferring from a centralized control to a distributed processing concept, with its attendant responsibilities, many managers and professionals are uncertain of their proper roles. Difficulties, in the form of management and control problems, arise in this shift of business methodology. Remote managers accustomed to the authoritative characteristics of centralization are uncertain about how much to loosen the local controls and how much to ease standardization.

With a centralized system, the manager can view things from a single vantage point—the central organization with its central data processing facilities. This focus is no longer possible in a distributed approach. Instead of dealing with the computer experts in the computer room, not one but many individuals (at least one for each remote location) must be involved, and these individuals are clerical professionals rather than computer professionals.

A solution of this problem requires dedication, significant investment of resources, deep and costly involvement, and considerable patience. Well-conceived training programs are essential. Particular attention to good system design, exact documentation that is always up to date, and precise testing and auditing procedures are needed.

The most imposing challenge to successful distributed processing is not minimizing hardware and communication cost or any technical issue but the proper application of management and human resources to do the proper job. Learning to live in two mutually exclusive yet coexisting realities is perhaps a necessary attribute of today's data processing manager. It is necessary to have the right people properly trained under the proper degree of organizational control in order to have a distributed processing organization that can fulfill its promise of lower costs and greater responsiveness to the users.

Guidelines for Distributed Processing Systems

The technique of distributed processing has many benefits and is growing in popularity, but, as with all new developments, it has disadvantages that detract from its glowing attributes. It has to be investigated thoroughly with a careful eye on all costs. Even when it is decided that distributed systems are valid and cost effective, it must be determined whether they are adaptable to the company and its specific situation.

The effectiveness of a distributed processing system depends to a very large extent on the location of the data relative to the processing. The degree to which data needed at the central location is independent of the data needed at the remote processing location is the single most important factor in determining the suitability of distributed processing. If the information needed by the remote location to perform its function is the same data needed by the central or corporate application, then it is not likely that distributed processing will be effective. However, if the remote location can function with only its local data, sending only summary data to the corporate center, an effective distributed processing application would likely result.

Distributed processing is usually very effective in environments such as manufacturing, where central data is largely irrelevant to smooth operations. There is no need for a manufacturing application to send production data, parts inventories, in-process data, vendor files, and production control information to a central location. Only summary information on the results of the manufacturing operation need be sent to the corporate center. By contrast, accounting applications rely heavily on central data and therefore do not usually lend themselves to effective distributive processing.

It is possible and likely that different modes of processing could be used effectively within a single company. Even a manufacturing company that uses the distributed approach in its main application might centralize its accounting, payroll, and other similar operations.

Some additional recommendations on the optimum use of distributive processing follow:

- Centralize batch data processing functions to obtain economies of scale of the computer hardware.
- Centralize to achieve efficiency and effectiveness in software and talent.
- Centralize the development and design of systems to maintain a high-level professional staff that will have all the necessary services and facilities needed for efficient development work.
- Centralize control, coordination, and cost accounting.

- Centralize critical functions, accounting, and control to enhance and improve the security of the computer operation.
- Centralize large companywide files to maximize the use of magnetic storage and data management software.
- Decentralize data input to detect errors at the source and to return error correction to the people who entered the data.
- Decentralize output to place information in the hands of the user in as short a period as possible.
- Decentralize selected processing functions to reduce the accesses to the central data bases and to reduce communication requirement and cost.
- Decentralize some computer intelligence into the terminals and data input devices for local validation and preprocessing.
- Decentralize for easier tailoring of applications to user needs.
- Decentralize for lower overhead, greater responsiveness, and less contention.

SOFTWARE—
THE MAJOR COST AREA

Software is a general term used to indicate computer programs of all types. Any desired computer functions not built into the computer hardware must be performed by software. Programs give direction to the hardware for executing the problem in the computer.

Great strides have been made in the development of low-cost, high-performance hardware, and costs have been reduced by a factor of 6 in the past ten years. These reductions in cost and upgrading of performance brought about the acceptance and use of devices such as the microcomputer and the minicomputer.

On the other hand, programs are developed and written by people—highly trained people. Therefore, the cost of programming has not decreased, and as long as highly trained personnel are required to write programs, the cost of software development will not get any lower.

Programming Problems

The present state of software development is far from being acceptable. Although manufacturers of computers are producing sophisticated equipment, using the latest technological advances and modern production techniques, software is still being produced in a handcrafted, individualized manner dependent upon the skills and whims of the programmer. In no other field has management had so little control of the resources needed to achieve projected objectives! Development of the software takes longer than anticipated and the costs are almost always more than expected. At times the finished product does not perform as expected, and there have been times when it didn't perform at all.

Since software systems are essentially handcrafted, great care must be taken to define the job precisely before it is started. Most programming difficulties stem from the lack of definition of the problem and the objectives at initiation. Consequently, the user must define the job he wants done. Unless these specifications are understood and properly translated in the program, there is little chance that a usable product will be developed. However, definition can never be conclusive at the start of the program because the real scope of the problem is not completely understood until software development is well under way. Agreements must be reached at each decision point, and the decisions must be documented.

The universal problems associated with software are many. The major ones are costs, development, time, revisions, compatibility, and control.

Costs. Costs are high. Software development costs normally exceed hardware costs. In addition, software expenses are getting higher while hardware costs are decreasing.

System development. Development takes months even for the smallest jobs, and several years for large commercial systems; up to five years for real-time networks is not uncommon. Debugging usually continues until well after installation. Development time is extended and chances for success decrease as a result of programmer turnover during the long development period.

System changes. Changes are time-consuming and costly. Large staffs of programmers are required just to maintain the system. Maintenance is hindered by the usual lack of understandable documentation.

Language incompatibility. Very often systems contain programs written in a number of different programming languages or versions of languages because of changes in computer hardware generations or the availability of more efficient languages. This results in an inefficient or inflexible system.

User control. The user has little control over the system design and no real control once development starts. He has to wait through the long development time, paying the bills and hoping the system will deliver what was promised.

These are the problems that have been experienced in the

development of systems. Experience has taught users and developers how to minimize the risks and costs in programming, but until the basic method of software development changes, the problems and uncertainties will continue to exist.

Present Software Costs

Despite the fact that it is a highly visible, high-technology industry and is used to automate many operations, data processing is essentially a labor-intensive activity. Costs in the form of salaries to programmers, analysts, operators, schedulers, control clerks, and many other people engaged in data processing now far exceed the cost of hardware. In the initial days of computer use, hardware costs made up more than 80 percent of the EDP budget, but this percentage decreased to 50 percent in the late 1960s and is now less than 40 percent, as illustrated in Figure 7–1. With continuously decreasing hardware costs, improved processing power per dollar, higher costs for training personnel, increased benefits, and the development of more costly and complicated systems, this trend is not likely to change. It is expected that microprocessor code will be commonly used in the future as a more economical replacement for software functions, but even if this expectation comes true, software

Figure 7–1. Personnel costs as a fraction of total EDP costs.

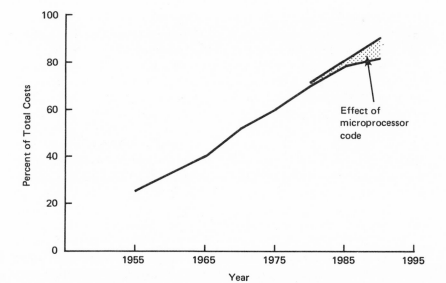

Figure 7–2. Costs of a small disk-based minicomputer system.

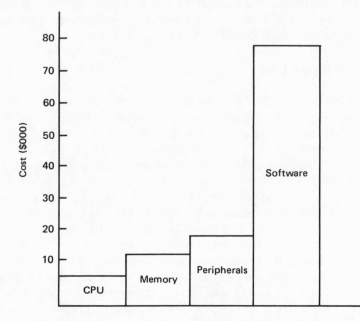

costs are still likely to be about 80 percent of the total electronic data processing costs through the late 1980s.

With the advent of the low-cost minicomputer systems, the high cost of software becomes the major item in the application budget. While software cost is about half of the large-system cost, it could possibly be 90 percent of the cost of a minicomputer system. The computer—CPU and memory—represents the lowest-cost part of the system. The peripherals usually required with a business system generally are more expensive than the computer. The software developed is dependent on the application, but it is common for its cost to run to twice the total hardware cost. Figure 7–2 shows the costs of a disk-oriented application system, assumed to be a new software development effort. The availability of software from the vendor or elsewhere can reduce costs significantly.

Function and Components of System Software

The function of software is to make the computer usable. System software is the general term given to the programs that, when loaded into the computer, are used for handling many recurring operating problems, leaving the programmer free to solve his application problem.

A computer cannot function without software. The performance of a computer is at least as dependent upon the quality of the software as it is upon the hardware. Superior software often compensates for poorly performing hardware, but even the most efficient hardware cannot compensate for poorly performing software. Whether a company buys a computer and develops its own system or buys a complete turnkey system from the computer manufacturer or a third party, it is important that the system have proper and competent system software.

Two major categories of computer software, particularly important in minicomputer use, are the operating system and utility routines.

Operating systems. An operating system is a group of programs or program modules that takes care of all functions essential for the operation of the computer system. The operating system is often called the "executive," "monitor," or "control" system in small machines. As a minimum, the system takes care of input and output control, provides the software for the computer to communicate with a variety of input and output devices, and provides the means for loading and linking programs for execution.

Operation systems include disk operating system (DOS), tape operating system, virtual operating systems, and a variety of a real-time, time-sharing, and special-purpose operating systems. Different systems require different features. The type and quality of the operating system features are very important, as is the amount of memory the system requires. If there is any doubt about the quality of the operating system, expert help in evaluating it will be of great value.

Utility routines. Besides the fundamental software items that make the computer operable, there are also some indispensable items that enable the programmer to correct and edit the program, to diagnose hardware malfunctions, and to reconfigure the system software when adding or changing peripherals.

As a minimum, the manufacturer should supply the following types of utility routines with the system:

1. Dynamic debugging (program correction) software.
2. Input/output diagnostics.
3. Memory and register diagnostics and dumps.
4. System generator.

5. Library routines, including numerous math functions, fixed and floating-point multiply and divide.
6. Editing routines with both character- and statement-editing features.

In addition there are the following utilities, essential in most business systems, which would be extremely expensive to develop:

7. Sort-merge: Although the type of sort that can be used in a minicomputer system might be inefficient by traditional data processing standards, some kind of sort is essential in a business-oriented system.
8. File management system: An appropriate access method or file management system is essential in large random-access disk file systems such as those used in many business applications.

System software that is comprehensive, well-designed, and proven is essential to get the most out of the system, but if it is insufficient or faulty, continuing successful operation is practically impossible.

Computer Languages

Assembler versus Compiler

It is possible to write programs in binary machine language, but no one would think of doing it today, for it is time-consuming, error-prone, and difficult to change or correct. In present practice, language translators in the form of compilers and assemblers are used to translate into machine language the instructions given to the computer by a programmer.

A high-level language, or compiler language, such as FORTRAN or COBOL, has the advantage of being in a form resembling written English. Assembler language uses easy-to-remember mnemonics, which are translated on a one-for-one basis into machine language. The Assembler language is still far removed from normal English and requires the programmer to work out each operation the computer must execute. Furthermore, the program can be used only on the one type of machine for which it is written. The compiler, or higher-level, languages overcome these objections. They are generally machine independent, can generate many machine instructions from one compiler language statement, and are easy to read, resulting in self-documenting programs.

Figure 7–3 illustrates a simple program written in machine, assembler, and compiler languages. The example gives an idea of the relative simplicity of the compiler languages. Figure 7–3 also lists the advantages and disadvantages of each type.

The advantages of high-level languages can be translated into dollar savings. These languages are easier to learn (thus reducing training expenses), and they produce programs that are easier to change and document. As a rule of thumb, Assembler language programs cost about four times as much as a program written in a higher-level language, with estimates ranging from three to ten times as much, depending on the specific application. Despite this economic advantage, much programming is done in the Assembler language. This is done to provide a more efficient program and to reduce program size. A high-level, or compiler, language has to provide flexibility of expression for the user. The resulting program uses more instructions, and therefore more machine time, than if the programmer had set out to solve each problem in the program in Assembler language.

The additional running time needed for compiler language is not usually important in the application program, but is obviously very important in system software programs. System software should not be conspicuous in operation. It should not detract from the performance of the system. Therefore, these systems programs, which are used constantly to move large amounts of data between parts of the computer and between the computer and peripherals, are always written in Assembler language.

Higher-level languages result in programs that require larger amounts of internal memory. Because of the relative costs of programming and computer memory, the economies resulting from the easier-to-learn, easier-to-use, higher-level computer language should be chosen. There are some exceptions, of course, and judgment should be used. If a program is to be written for a system that is to be duplicated in many locations, the $3,000 that additional memory could cost per system, multiplied by the number of installations, would likely be more than the additional programming expense. If no updating of the programs were needed and maintenance of the Assembler language programs could be handled, then forsaking the high-level language might be more economical.

Figure 7–3. Comparison of machine, assembler, and compiler languages.

WRITING A PROGRAM IN MACHINE LANGUAGE

It is possible to write a program in machine (absolute) language. This is accomplished by writing *in binary* the operation to be performed, as well as the address where the data is located.

Example:

```
Oper-
ation       Address
0110000111110 1000
0100000111110 1001
0100000111110 1010
0100000111110 1011
0100000111110 1100
0100000111110 1101
0100000111110 1110
0100000111110 1111
0100000111111 0000
0001101111000 0001
0111001111110 0010
```

$$X = \sum_{i=1}^{10} R_i/10$$

SYMBOLIC PROGRAMMING (Making Programming Easier)

Since the machine language programming has more disadvantages than advantages, assemblers are used. With an assembler, the programmer represents machine addresses by arbitrary alphanumeric symbols, and machine operations by assembler operation codes. This type of programming requires translation by an assembly program into machine language before it can be accepted by the computer for execution.

Example:

Opera-tion Code	Oper-and Ad-dress	Remarks
LDA	R1	Get R1
ADA	R2	Produce sum = R1+R2
ADA	R3	Produce sum = R1+R2+R3
ADA	R4	
ADA	R5	
ADA	R6	
ADA	R7	
ADA	R8	
ADA	R9	
ADA	R10	Produce sum = R1+R2....R10
JSB	DIV	Produce sum/10
STA	AVE	Save average in AVE

$$X = \sum_{i=1}^{10} R_i/10$$

PROGRAMMING USING COMPILERS (Man-Oriented Programming Languages)

Languages that allow man to communicate with computers in an English-like or mathematics-like manner are provided by compilers. Programming at this level is accomplished by using statements to define computer operations to be performed. Statements such as READ, WRITE, GO TO, IF, DO, are typical of a compiler

Example (Using FORTRAN language):

SUM = R1+R2+R3+R4+R5+R6+R7+R8
+R9+R10
AVE = SUM/10.

$$X = \sum_{i=1}^{10} R_i/10$$

Figure 7–3 (continued).

Advantages:

(a) Allows the programmer to communicate with the computer in its native tongue, and thus take full advantage of any hardware capabilities.
(b) Gives the programmer complete control over the coding.

Disadvantages:

(a) Programming is time-consuming.
(b) Programming errors are easily introduced, and difficult to find.
(c) Requires intimate knowledge of the hardware and its operations.
(d) There is no capability to enter comments to document the program.
(e) Once written it is difficult to change.
(f) A simple addition of one more computation becomes a major task.
(g) Makes it difficult to divide the coding of a problem among several people.

Advantages:

(a) Reduces programming time.
(b) Uses codes for machine instructions, and these are easy to learn.
(c) Eliminates the need for assigning and keeping track of memory locations.
(d) Debugging is easier.
(e) Comments to document the program may be provided in each line of coding.
(f) Efficient coding can be generated.

Disadvantages:

(a) Assembler level instructions are on a one-to-one relationship with machine language coding.
(b) The problem to be solved must be broken down into detailed operations to be coded.
(c) Coding complicated problems at the assembler level is still a time-consuming proposition.
(d) Programmer errors are still easy to introduce.
(e) Programs written at the assembler level are machine dependent, therefore not transferable from one computer to another.

Advantages:

(a) Compiler languages are much easier to learn than machine or assembler languages.
(b) Compiler languages are generally machine independent, allowing the source program to be compiled and executed on different computers.
(c) Compilers reduce programming effort. A single statement generates several machine language instructions.
(d) Programs are easy to read and are self-documenting.
(e) Programs are easy to modify.

Disadvantages:

(a) Compilers may generate inefficient coding.
(b) Compilation times may be long and therefore compiler use could be expensive (Not usually a disadvantage in small machines.)

(*From "An Introduction to HP Computers," Hewlett-Packard, April 1970.*)

Higher-Level Languages

As a general method of operation, the high-level languages are recommended because hardware costs are getting lower all the time while programming costs are going higher; evidently the trend will continue. Also, the self-documentation feature of the high-level language eases the problem of enforcing documentation standards in multiple remote installations. Programmer training and program maintenance problems are also eased when high-level programming languages are used. The full cost of the use of Assembler language is difficult to determine. Unless the quantifiable economic benefits of Assembler language programming are large and irrefutable, then the high-level language should be used.

FORTRAN. This language is a mathematically oriented language. FORTRAN (FORmula TRANslation) has widespread use in engineering and scientific applications. Most minicomputer manufacturers have FORTRAN compilers. However, the language is not particularly suited to business-oriented problems.

COBOL. On the other hand, COBOL is well suited to business problems, but is not suited to the memory limitations of the small machine. COBOL (COmmon Business-Oriented Language) is designed for business application and has powerful file-handling ability. COBOL statements are easy to read. Few people would read a statement like IF HOURS GREATER THAN FORTY GO TO OVERTIME-CALC and fail to comprehend its meaning. However, to be effective, a large memory is needed to compile COBOL. Minicomputers, in general, do not have this capacity. As a result, *standard* COBOL is not available for minicomputers, but many *subsets* of COBOL are available.

Although limited in overall capabilities when compared to those available for large computers, existing COBOL compilers have a high degree of sophistication and can be used for highly complex problems. If a problem-solving procedure can be defined in English, it can be stated in COBOL for the computer.

Freedom from memory-size limitations is being attained, to some extent, through program segmentation. The compilers that provide for segmentation operate upon the COBOL programs as collections of logical program subsegments. This means that COBOL programs can be written with only moderate consideration of the computer's memory size.

Since COBOL is by far the most common language used on large computers, COBOL programs provide a direct, inexpensive bridge to larger data processing systems. The ability to move existing programs to another system, with little of the reprogramming effort or cost usually associated with conversion, offers long-term protection for the programming investment and means that future projects can be planned with confidence.

RPG. Rather than use a fairly complex COBOL-like language, many users (particularly first-time users) prefer the simplicity of RPG (Report Program Generator). Despite its simplicity and functional limitations, users find it can generally satisfy all their needs.

RPG uses a "fill-in-the-blanks" procedure and is written on printed programming forms. It is self-documenting and requires memorizing of very few rules and conventions. The standard procedures and forms increase the efficiency of programmers and decrease the cost of program implementation at the expense of flexibility of program design. It is a convenient low-cost programming tool that, because of its eager acceptance by minicomputer users, has frequently been enhanced. Segmented programs, disk systems, and communication systems are now possible with RPG.

RPG is less complicated than COBOL, and therefore training time and expenses are much less. Also, RPG II, an advanced version of the language, is becoming almost a standard in the small-business computer industry, allowing easy upgrading and transferring of programs from one computer to another.

Vendor-developed languages. Nonstandard languages designed for use by people with little programming knowledge have been introduced by several of the minicomputer manufacturers for use with their equipment only. These languages often combine the English-language characteristics of COBOL with the easy-to-use formatted procedures of RPG to produce an effective low-cost method of implementing programs. While suitable for many applications, use of these languages limits the user's flexibility in upgrading the system to accommodate new equipment technology or to move to another computer.

BASIC. The use of time sharing brought many nonprogramming people in direct contact with the computer. To stimulate use and to provide an easy means for writing programs, the BASIC language was developed. An objective of BASIC, which has been fulfilled, was to implement its use with a minimum of training. A nontechnical user can learn to write a simple BASIC language program in a matter of hours.

Consistent with the minicomputer philosophy of bringing the computer to the user, a growing number of minicomputer manufacturers support an improved version of BASIC. For example, to solve the problem listed in Figure 7–3 ($X = \sum_{i=1}^{10} R_i/10$), the BASIC program would be written as follows:

```
DIM   R(10)
SUM = 0
INPUT   N
FOR I = I TO N
INPUT   X(1)
SUM = SUM + X(I)
NEXT I
AVG = SUM/N
PRINT AVG
```

Cross Assemblers and Cross Compilers

Developing programs in a small minicomputer that has limited input and output gear is, at best, tedious. The assembler or compiler operations should be done in a computer that has relatively fast card readers and printers as a minimum. This equipment is not always available, but cross assemblers, which use larger minicomputers or standard data processors to prepare programs, have been developed to overcome this limitation. The user can program his application in the language he knows best. He can use the superior input and output facilities of the large computer to facilitate program development. In addition, a more efficient compiler—one that generates a number of lines of program code for a single input statement—can be used, owing to the large storage capacity of the large machine. When this method is used, the large machine must also be available whenever maintenance is performed on the application.

Application Programs

When the small businessman's record-keeping problems have expanded to the point where they must be automated, he is faced with a major problem: he must make an important, almost irrevocable decision on how to handle his first automatic data processing application. He lacks the in-house expertise to confidently determine the best way to handle his problem, and is probably reluctant to put the problem totally in the hands of a vendor. And he probably realizes that his staff is not large enough to allow training some employees to program a data processing application, no matter how small.

Although application software is far from being the strongest support area of minicomputer suppliers, several alternatives are available to the first-time user. These include industry application programs, customized manufacturer packages, turnkey systems, and so on.

Industry Application Programs

As an aid in marketing the computer systems, the small-business computer manufacturers and several minicomputer manufacturers supply basic industry application programs. These are programs that can perform the main functions for companies in a number of specific industries. The packages include applications such as insurance billing, distribution, civil engineering, doctor's billing, pharmacy, education, and many others.

Vendor support of the installed packages varies. Some companies, including IBM at this time, will not make modifications. Other vendors, and almost all systems houses, acknowledge that additional programming might be necessary and offer the option of providing assistance, either from the vendor or from an outside source.

Many systems houses specialize in the support of a limited number of industries; as a result, they frequently include industry-oriented packages as part of the system being supplied.

Accounting Packages

Most suppliers of small-business computers provide programs for standard accounting applications. These packages include general ledger, accounts payable, accounts receivable, payroll, and many others. Provided the standard packages suit the new user's requirements, this facility provides the means for operating his system and handling the basic business functions without having to train technical personnel.

Some companies have a library of several hundred accounting packages available to potential users. The supplier of the package usually charges either a single one-time fee or a monthly rental charge. However, some packages are available from user organizations at no charge.

Turnkey Systems

Another alternative for the new computer user is to have a systems house provide the entire system software as well as hardware. This is called the turnkey system. The systems house will either use a standard application package or modify a standard package to meet the user's distinct requirements. The application is then installed and tested, with the hardware, and delivered to the user as a unit.

Value of the Packaged-Software Approach

The different methods using software application packages are all intended to accomplish the same results. This approach helps the inexperienced user to get an important application on the computer in a short time, at relatively low cost, and with virtual assurance of success. A further advantage is that it removes the communication difficulties that frequently exist between the businessman, who is not familiar with the computer, and the person who has to program the application. Finally, by providing a reasonable known cost for the complete service, a significant part of the pre-installation cost is fixed and known in advance. This minimizes uncertainty and the vulnerability to excessive cost that might otherwise exist.

The disadvantages of the package approach center on the inflexibility of the product:

• The packages are standard programs designed by the manufacturer. Even after modification, the program package usually does not precisely follow the user's way of doing business. As a result, either the user has to modify his procedures or a new application must be developed from the beginning.

• These applications are available for only a limited number of specific industries and applications.

• The user is dependent on the vendor or supplier of the system for future upgrading or modification needs. Frequently, much more skill is required to change a system than to institute it. Thus, while technical skill may not be required at initiation, that skill usually must be acquired before long.

• The system cannot be changed readily; even when the vendor packages are capable of being modified, the changes cannot be accomplished easily. Only minor changes can be made without distorting the application package and making it invalid.

Programming and Minicomputer Design

Not everyone wants to program a minicomputer and not everyone should. In fact, probably as few people as possible should program it. But some facts about programming are useful to anyone who decides to get a minicomputer and to everyone who decides what computer to get. Buying a minicomputer could be like buying a used car. The salesman tells the purchaser only about the good points of the product. Negative features have to be discovered by the user.

There are many designs of minicomputers. All are different, yet all have some similarities. Among comparably priced machines, it is not likely that one computer stands far ahead of all others in clear superiority of all technical features. There are always trade-offs made in design, and these trade-offs affect the use. It is important for the user to know a little about how the program works so that he can determine if the computer he is considering has made the design trade-off that favors his situation.

Hardware-Software Trade-Offs

Instructions telling the computer hardware what to do are provided by the program. Most computers can add automatically, but it is the program that instructs the computer when to add, supplies the numbers, and stores the result. Any function can be performed in hardware or in software. Many operations, including the multiply and divide functions, may be included in the computer hardware or may be available only as an extra-charge option. If not supplied in hardware, these functions could be programmed and handled in software.

The cost of the computer would be less without these hardware features, but performance could be poorer. It might take ten times longer to multiply two numbers in software than in hardware, but the time of the software multiplication might be on the order of one-thousandth of a second. Unless the machine were extended to do a large amount of multiplying, the user might opt for the lower-cost route and program the multiply function.

There are two items to be considered. When comparing different models of computers, the user should realize that there can be differences in the hardware composition of similarly priced computers. Also, the design trade-offs may favor the application by providing hardware features needed, excluding those unnecessary for the specific application, with compensating price reductions. The user should be aware that all functions can be performed in hardware, providing higher performance at a higher cost, or in software that is cheaper but less effective. The user should make the choice that is best for him.

Instruction Set

The most frequently quoted statistic pertaining to the minicomputer performance is its basic cycle time. The minicomputer cycle time, typically less than one-millionth of a second (1 microsecond, or 10^{-6} second), compares favorably with the large data processors. But to determine how long it will take to perform a specific function, the number of instructions and the instructions per cycle should be known. Usually, an average of two computer cycles will be required to execute each instruction, but this could vary and should be checked. However, the number of instructions required may vary greatly. Some machines have powerful instructions that are comparable to two or three instructions of another machine. Clearly, then, it pays to program some small but pertinent routine critical to the application in question so as to determine the relative capability of the machine. The routine need not be executed in order to provide the necessary timing, for the program steps and use of the manufacturer's reference manual readily provide the required timings.

Word Size

The computer's basic internal unit is the *word*. A "16-bit computer" means that the word is 16 binary digits (or bits) long (a bit is either 0 or 1). The word unit can be used to represent data or an instruction. Assuming that it is 16 bits long, the word can represent 2^{16}, or almost 65K, different numbers, letters, or characters.

Minicomputers normally have word lengths from 8 to 32 bits. A machine with a longer word costs more, but because of its longer size, each word stores more information and can be used for more powerful instructions. Any cost advantage of the 8- or 12-bit word lengths may be lost in anything but the simplest applications. There is also an inherent advantage in buying a minicomputer with a word length that is a multiple of 8, since industry has established communication and computer standards using the 8-bit unit (or byte). The 16-bit minicomputer, as a result of these factors, is the most popular size.

Addressing

The basic 16-bit word may contain data or may be an instruction. When used as an instruction, it must contain two kinds of information: (1) the action to be performed by the computer hardware (this is called the *instruction code* or *operation code*); (2) the location of data on which the action is to be performed (this is called the *address*).

If the machine is to have a large number of different types of instruction codes, it would have to use a large number of the bits of the instruction word to identify the instruction types, leaving very few bits for the address. On the other hand, if a large portion of memory is to be addressed without intermediate operations, then there would be very few bits left for the instruction segment. This would mean that the computer could have only a very few instructions. A machine with only a few basic instructions could still be used, but would require a large amount of programming and would have long-running programs.

Naturally, a compromise is made. Usually 5 or 6 bits are used for the instruction code, which provides for 32 to 64 distinct instructions unless some other special tricks are used (such as taking another address bit only in special cases) to extend the instruction set. Double-word instructions are also used in some computers to

Figure 7–4. Instruction word format.

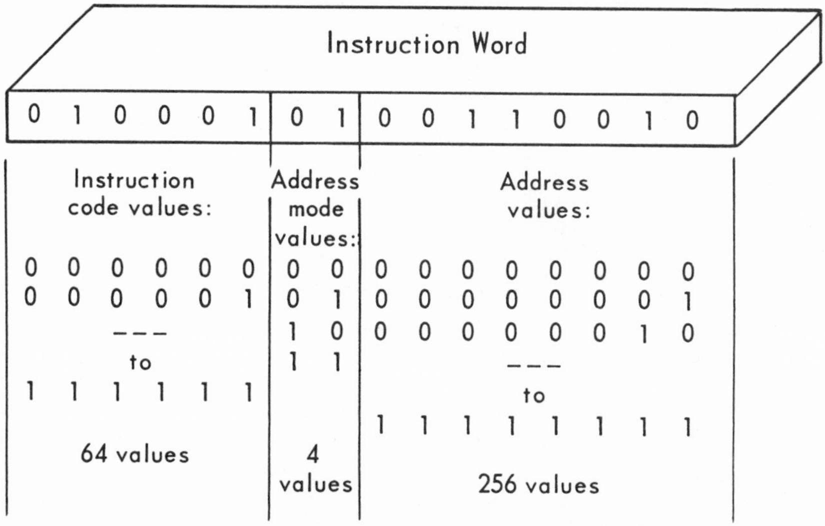

extend the instruction repertoire and addressing capability. If 6 bits are used for the instruction code, then only 10 are available for the address. This allows 2^{10} (or 1,024) locations to be addressed. But since the minicomputer is built to address over 32,000 locations, a smaller address field used in conjunction with a one- or two-word address mode indicator is used to allow the computer to address, indirectly, the additional memory areas.

Figure 7–4 illustrates a typical construction of the instruction word format. The address area is 8 bits long. This allows 256 distinct address locations to be designated. To go beyond this takes an extra step (and increased program running time). The field labeled "address mode" tells the computer how to go beyond the 256 words.

A computer always has a direct mode of addressing. This means that the address shown is precisely the location where the data is located. Relative addressing, which would be indicated by a particular value in the addresss mode area, allows access to a movable

Figure 7–5. Comparison of 12- and 16-bit instructions.

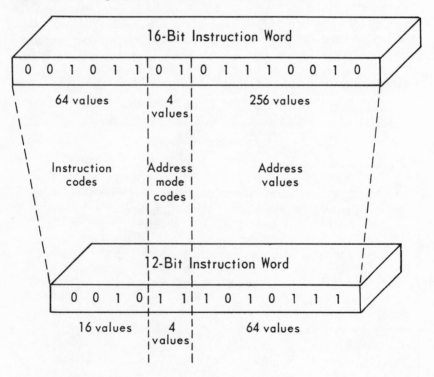

block of locations some distance ahead and behind the location of the current or last address. Any other methods of addressing take longer to execute.

It is important to have relative addressing. It is also important to have a large direct address area and a large movable block for relative addressing. Even the 256 words of directly accessible memory shown in Figure 7–4 is small, but to get more the instruction code area has to be limited. This is one of the basic trade-offs that minicomputer designers make. There have been a number of clever methods used to get around this problem in some addressing, but special tricks often make complicated programming. With a 12-bit minicomputer, the problem is more severe. Unless special tricks are employed, fewer instructions and fewer addresses can be handled. A similar conclusion results from comparing the 16-bit word to a 24- or 32-bit word. See Figure 7–5 for the comparison of 12- and 16-bit instructions.

A potential user should be aware of these trade-offs so that the choice will not be a minicomputer that has a design criterion unfavorable to the planned application. The close relations among design, performance, and programming strongly suggest that the person who does the programming should assist in evaluating the computers.

Least-Cost Programming Method

The primary justification for the use of minicomputers, especially at this time, is their low cost. Their use is a departure from traditional means of processing, and their newness and lack of maturity in the marketplace suggest less security in the area of service, support, and training. Therefore, the economies of their use have to be clear-cut and irrefutable. Improper handling of software development could dissipate the reduction in expenses anticipated by the adoption of the minicomputer system.

The use of cost-saving techniques in application software development will reduce not only development expenses but also the problems and resulting expenses due to difficult program maintenance, programmer training, and divergence and duplication of efforts within the company. This approach offers a very valuable benefit: by reducing costs through a standardized development method and by providing control over the important but nonquantifiable expense areas, applications that previously seemed impossible to automate can be economically justified.

The approach and techniques described below for cost reduction apply whether development is done in the user's organization or by a supplier or systems house.

Requirements for Cost-Effective Software Development

Planning and common sense. The potential user should have a good idea of where he wants to go. Applications that are particular problems, and therefore candidates for automation, should be identified. Volume increases in existing processes, which make automation of manual operations desirable, should be anticipated.

Single hardware supplier. The key to minimum software cost is the ability to re-use developed software. But much of the software already developed is Assembler language programs and system software that can work only on a particular make of computer. Therefore, the selection of the computer line and the supplier that will best suit the user's needs (and staying with that line, if at all possible) is essential.

Level of support at each location. The user must decide whether he will train an in-house programming staff. The approach selected depends upon many factors, particularly company size and data processing philosophy. It is suggested that a small company depend completely on a reliable manufacturer or systems house for all its development and support. Large companies will probably find it best to develop a centralized in-house development unit that will serve as the systems development and maintenance house for the entire organization. These decisions can be changed, but it is important to develop a point of view or objective in this important area in order to select the lowest-cost and most effective system development. The developer must decide on the extent to which the programming will be done by in-house personnel and then work to maximize the benefits of that approach.

Decision on language approach. An economic analysis of the entire system will help decide on the type of user-computer communication required. The preferred approach is to interact directly with the computer in an on-line fashion whenever possible. This requires little expertise at the user's site, but it does need more at the development location, which is usually a desirable trade-off.

Recognize common system types. We all can recognize duplicate systems and know that planning for them can save money, but recognizing that important and costly features of different types of systems could be quite similar is important. The segments of program that are difficult, time-consuming, and costly to develop are the data management system associated with random-access files, information retrieval logic modules, and real-time interactive programs. If it is recognized that systems whose functions are as different as personnel retrieval and order entry can have these program modules in common, some large development costs can be saved.

Realistic design requirements. Systems developers tend to design for maximum performance of the equipment. Overdesigning might be very expensive. Capacity for expansion should be provided, but response requirements, backup requirements, and user interactions must be realistic.

Development control. Regardless of whether development is done in a company by its personnel or by an outside firm, strict control over the development of the system must be exercised. All expected benefits may be dissipated by allowing frequent changes of specifications or by allowing someone such as the programmer to make the design decisions.

Techniques for Reducing Software Expenses

The reproducible system. For a system in which similar functions in many localities may be used, the obvious way to reduce software expense is to design at the top of the line. It may not cost much more to develop the software for a system capable of handling 16 data-input stations than it would for a 4-station system. In addition, it provides for a great deal of expansion.

Multiple similar systems. In order to accommodate local ways of doing business, a company's procedures in the same application might vary in each location. A properly designed system can accommodate these variations at low cost. Minimal requirements include:

1. A good operating system to handle all possible peripherals needed.
2. A general-purpose file management system to handle large data bases, designed so it will be common to all systems.
3. A carefully designed modular program.

By proper design, no more than 25 percent of the total lines of software need be changed for additional systems, and that 25 percent is almost always the least complicated coding. Over half of the changed software relates to editing and formatting output reports and to the testing of input data.

Generic system. Although the external applications are different, many important computer system functions in these systems are the same. This is particularly true for information retrieval systems. Information retrieval is used for personnel and manpower retrieval systems, inventory control systems, order-entry systems, production control systems, and data-entry systems.

System requirements are similar to the multiple application system; that is, they must provide a good operating system, complete general file management and updating system, and well-planned modular programming. For an information retrieval system, the first software development costs could be approximately $100,000. The software for the second and subsequent systems would likely cost about $20,000.

Additional advantages. In addition to lower development costs, there are the following expected advantages of the suggested approach toward application programming:

Better support from hardware supplier.
Easier maintenance.
No duplication of effort.
Development of professional staff, or better support by a systems house aware of user's needs.
Specialized software packages (such as simulator or cross-compiler) more easily justified.
Built-in control over development.
Greater likelihood of user acceptance because of low cost.
Justification for applications that could not otherwise be automated.

User-Oriented Systems

The ability to dedicate the minicomputer to a single application decreases the need for an operator. Even when the computer is used in a true data processing environment (such as where punch cards are used in a batched input mode), an operator would be idle much of the time if only one application string were processed. This leads to the completely user-oriented system, where the computer is an integral part of the complete system, operating as an extension of the human beings running the business operation.

Systems have been developed for nontechnical users, uniniti-ated in the techniques of data processing, who have been able to run and maintain the computer operation. This kind of computer operation is the forerunner of the future normal mode of small operations. These types of systems have certain characteristics:

1. Data is entered in an on-line fashion as it is received by the organization.
2. Application programs are called into operation automatically by the nature of the input instruction.
3. Random-access disk files are required for data and program storage.
4. Built into the application program are the instructions for the entry of the business data. The clerk is stepped through the data-input operation, assuring that all procedures are followed.
5. Data is validated for accuracy as it enters the system.

There are significant benefits offered by such a system. The system can be used by employees with a minimum of training. Since the computer steps the input clerk through the procedure and checks each step, the clerk requires even less training than for an entirely manual operation. In addition, the data entered is more accurate. The computer is programmed to check the data for logic values and reject invalid data.

This approach is more difficult to program and therefore is more costly, but the benefits can be large. Furthermore, if the input routines are programmed in a well-planned modular design, as discussed in the preceding section, succeeding applications will not be any more costly than in the noninteractive systems. It usu-ally pays off to invest in the development of a user-oriented system to save the data-entry expenses in multiple installations. This tech-nique, as well as all other cost-reduction programming methods discussed in this chapter, is applicable whether the system is de-veloped in house or by a third party such as a systems house.

SYSTEMS ANALYSIS
AND ECONOMIC EVALUATION

The installation of a computer system starts with the recognition of a problem and with the realization of a possible method of solution. Systems, therefore, start out with requirements that are to be satisfied, and end with a solution that is designed to satisfy those needs. However, before a solution can be selected, a careful analysis of the problem must be made. This analysis starts with a study of the existing system, an analysis of costs and benefits, a review of alternatives, and a determination of economic, technical, and organizational feasibility.

The System Study

The system analysis is the starting point. The more accurately the analysis and documentation are performed, the more likely the user is to have a system that truly satisfies his requirements. The solution may take one of many forms, depending upon the size and nature of the problem. The first step in the analysis is to define specifically the problem area.

Scope of the System

Many systems studies expand to cover ever-increasing areas as the analysis progresses. A constantly changing scope will tend to produce a long and expensive study, a system with fuzzy or even diverse objectives, or a large expensive system that is difficult to install and whose economic benefits are questionable or nonexistent.

The area in which the greatest benefit can be obtained at the least cost is to be concentrated upon. In general, the system need not encompass any more than this area. Increasing the system to include additional processing areas or functions reduces the average return on the system development dollar and delays achieving the benefits of the system. The system, however limited in scope, must include the capability for expansion, particularly in the software.

It is usually easy to expand hardware modularly within a fairly wide range, but unless the software is designed properly, expansion of the system could mean discarding all existing programs and starting over again from the beginning. Characteristics of a good, expandable software design are (1) modular programs and routines, and (2) file and record layouts designed with sufficient capacity in each record so that the addition of new fields and new data does not require restructuring.

It is rather easy to determine the high-cost, high-benefit area of the system. It is usually where all the people are, or it is at the location of the problem that caused the user to consider an automated approach. There is normally a great, sometimes uncontrollable, urge to expand the suggested automated system to include all related functions. There is really no end to such a plan; all systems are related at some level. Many times it appears that the existing system is a continuous process that cannot be broken into manageable and meaningful segments. Although this is sometimes true, careful and diligent analysis will indicate that, in almost all situations, the process can be divided logically and installed segmentally.

Modular Design

Modular installation has many benefits. By installing only parts of the system at a time, the economic benefits and the return on the development dollar are increased. Even though it might be possible to justify the automation of the entire system, it will always be found that certain segments of the system provide much larger proportional benefits. Coupled with more than proportionately lower costs (since development costs increase exponentially with the size of the system), the return on investment for small systems or for small portions of a major system could be very large. Implementing a system in segments requires that each segment be cost-justified; this practice greatly improves the economic benefits of the total effort by not automating certain low-benefit functions unless absolutely essential for integrated operation.

For example, a company recognized the increasing difficulty in obtaining order-taking personnel at what it considered to be a reasonable salary, and decided to change its system approach. After a study, it was decided that a comprehensive system to include order entry, inventory accounting, invoicing, and accounting was needed. It was also found out that the system could be cost-justified, since there were significant clerical savings to be achieved. However, a post-audit of the completed installation indicated that a more modest approach would have solved the primary problem with a much lower investment. If only the order-entry function had been automated, the system would have cost slightly over half as much, 75 percent of the total system savings would have been achieved, and the system would have been installed five months sooner.

The maxim is, "Plan big but implement small." Plan big so that expansion will be easy if it becomes necessary. Implement small so that the installation is more manageable, costs are lower, and benefits are achieved sooner.

Design of the System

Input/Output Requirements

A method that provides almost all information required for many systems and is a good starting point in most computer studies is an input/output analysis. The parameters needed are the form and volume per unit time of each type of input and output data.

Input data forms include manual input such as for order information taken over a phone, printed information such as for an address change when adding a new customer on file, a punch card if the information has come from another automated system. The form of the output should be determined on the basis of its use rather than the form in which it is presently delivered. Output forms include data processing media such as punch cards or magnetic tape, printed reports, or printed forms such as invoices.

In the determination of volumes, data down to the detail of the number of characters of input and output is usually required. The characters per line of the output forms, such as the invoice and the number of lines of printing on the invoice, as well as the number of invoices, are necessary to plan the proper system. Input volumes of the same detail level are also required. Consideration of peak loads as well as total or average loads is necessary for adequate design of the system. The number of transactions input to the system over the peak half-hour and the resulting data rates in characters per second are an example of the time-dependent volumes required for designing for input and output requirements.

File Storage Requirements

The amount of data that has to be stored in the files is a very important consideration and has great effect on the price of the resulting system. The number of different files that must be maintained must be determined first. There are permanent files such as a customer file and product file for an order-entry system or an employee master file for a payroll system; and there are temporary files such as a back-order file or a payroll transaction file. The data maintained on each file is grouped in logic segments called *records;* very often one record comprises each logical set of data. Complete information details about a single customer—name, address, customer identification number, credit status, discount, payment method, amount due, discounts—are typical contents of a record. The number of characters of information on each record must be known, and an additional 20 to 30 percent is often allocated to provide easy expansion, except in the very massive files. In determining the number of these records required, possible increases during the life of the system must be considered. Again, some factor is applied to this number for safety and easy expansion.

The same routine is followed to determine the number of records and the number of characters for each record of the temporary or in-process files. If, for example, the system is to store all invoices over the day to be printed at a single run, or a file of change transactions that are batched over a short period of time, maximum storage requirements have to be included in the design for these files. Consideration should also be given to historical and backup files, those that are not customarily needed for the processing but which would be essential in case of an audit of the system, an investigation of a particular problem account, or a destructive system failure.

Processing Requirements

With input/output and storage requirements defined, the analysis requires that the procedure or rules that get the information from the input to the output must be set down. This involves indicating the means by which a piece of information is identified and the procedure involved in passing that data through the system in a manner that follows the procedures of the company. A statement like IF THE CUSTOMER NUMBER STARTS WITH 9 (commercial customer), THEN DISCOUNT SCHEDULE B APPLIES is an example of a company procedure that must be included in the new system processing. These procedural statements are the heart of the system. They make the system work and respond to the needs of the user. This is what makes a system successful. The procedures followed are the standard business procedures of the company. Documentation of these processes very often can be done most conveniently by using a flowchart.

It is very often found that when the company procedures are studied and documented in detail, a number of inconsistencies in processing or some illogical steps are detected. A major value of the system study is to uncover these errors. Many times, the resulting modifications to manual procedures have been of greater value to the company than the installation of the new system, and in some cases the automated system was not needed after these areas of improvements were implemented.

The time requirement for a study of one of these small systems may vary from two man-weeks to three or four man-months. The output of the study is an understanding of the system by the people who are expected to perform or direct the implementation and proper documentation upon which the new system can be based. Improvements to the system should be planned at this time. The system study information, when modified by the suggested processing improvements and updated for future volume increases, is sufficient for designing the proposed system. With this information, several new systems or system approaches can be priced to see if changing the system is still economically feasible.

At this point, before any additional work is performed, the problem of operational feasibility should be addressed. Many systems have been technically successful and have also promised very substantial economical benefits, but have failed dismally because of operational or political opposition. A system can fail because it is too complex for the users to maintain or because low-level opposition to the new system cannot be overcome by positive motivation. Before going any further in the study, it should be confirmed beyond reasonable doubt that the company environment (level of competence, degree of acceptance, method of operation) is such that if the functional and economic aspects of the system are assured, then the system will have a good chance for success.

Data Validation

Frequently, special programs must be written to validate the data that is to be put on the file. Handwritten records that have been updated many times over many years usually have numerous errors in them. When working a manual system, the clerk who transcribes this data can make logical assumptions in the case of unclear data or make corrections based on the context of the rest of the information. However, the data required for the computer system is used by the computer without interpretation and must be correct. Therefore, it is usually desirable to write a special program that performs logic tests on this input data. In addition, the file conversions process, because of the time constraint in requiring a large data file to be installed in a relatively short time, is usually done by someone not familiar with the application. The timing is such that the people familiar with the data and the system must keep the existing system running; therefore, the job of converting the data is usually delegated to a service bureau or to temporary help. To maximize the use of these people, they are asked not to make any interpretations and are required to transcribe the information literally from the document. Any incorrect or illegible data will be transcribed as best as possible. As a result, unless special precautions are taken, incorrect data will get into the file of the new system. It is important to correct any erroneous data and to isolate those that may be loaded into the new system.

In the continuous and regular operation of the new system there must be some means to assure that data required for the system is properly inserted. For example, as an added feature or function of the new system, suppose large mailings of advertising material will be sent out to selected customers who are maintained on the master customer file. To conform to postal requirements, the mailings should be supplied in zip-code order. Although the original file contained zip code, no serious problems would have existed if this information happened to be missing. But in the new system, the zip code is a key field and must be entered on every customer record.

When the new system is operating, the programs that accept new customer file information should check for the presence of the zip code, and if one is not present or has an illogical value (too many digits or nonnumeric data), that fact should be reported to the person entering the data.

A program developed for this purpose, to validate data for regular use in the production system, can and should be used to validate the data in the conversion process. The only problem with this approach is in the timing of the development work. Frequently, the data conversion effort is a large one, requiring a long lead time. In order to use the production programs for input data validation, priority should be given to writing those programs. The validation programs should perform the following three types of tests and functions.

Test for missing or incomplete information. Several approaches to handling missing information are taken, depending upon the requirements. Input transactions that are missing information necessary for the smooth running of the system should not be passed on by the validating program. If the data is not essential, the validation program could accept all the information submitted and report the fact that desirable information is missing.

Test for logical values. Wherever single fields can be tested to assure that the values they contain are logical values, it should be done. Many of the tests are possible because of characteristics of the company's method of doing business and the numbers and codes used. Others depend upon common sense. For example, a company might use a purchase-order code consisting of a prefix letter and five digits. The computer program should make these specific tests and reject the input item if the data is not in this form. In another case, an age field might be tested for specific values if the business requirements indicate that only persons between specific ages could use the service. The program would not only test for the allowable range, but would also test for the presence of only numeric information.

Computer-generated codes. In some situations, the values of a particular field of information may be assigned on the basis of information contained elsewhere in the record. The system should be designed so that it makes the assignment of the code whenever possible. This type of logic should be written into the data validation programs. It will reduce input costs and produce a more accurate, more trouble-free system.

A product code a company uses might contain a six-digit number

followed by a two-digit suffix indicating the type of product, followed by a check digit. A one-character "how packaged" field
might also be required on the file to indicate whether the product is
carried in bulk or packaged form. The manual information input
should be limited to the six-digit number and the two-digit suffix.
The computer system should be programmed to the following
operations:

Testing for the proper number of input characters.
Testing for all numeric input characters.
Calculating the check digit.
From the type of product suffix of the product code, generating
the field to indicate how the product was packaged.

These are just examples of the type of logic that should be contained in the program that handles input data in the file conversion
effort and in the regular production system. Anything that can be
done to maintain accurate data in the file should be done by the
computer system. This is important in any system, but especially so
in small installations. The smaller the installation, the less likely a
need for heavily controlled manual procedures and formal training
programs. But with the dependence of the small company on the
automated system, error-free operation becomes more important.
Programming the system to maintain the accuracy of the data is an
extremely important procedure that will compensate its costs many
times over.

Determining System Operating Costs

Most analyses include cost, and while the decision regarding
installation of a new system is based on many factors, cost is the
primary one. Almost all users know or can find out what their
present system is costing them. This cost must be compared against
the cost of the proposed system before deciding on the direction to
be taken.

Cost will be the basis for deciding between two or more alternatives. The costs for each system may be determined independently or
relative to the existing system. At times, the total cost of the existing
system is difficult to obtain because it is so interrelated with other

existing systems. Use of shared facilities, equipment, or personnel could make an accurate determination of discrete costs impossible to attain in a reasonable time. But, since it is the difference in costs between two systems that is pertinent, the approach that takes into account only these variations is easier, probably more accurate, and in almost all instances just as useful.

The most obvious cost is personnel expense. This is determined by multiplying the number of people required in each system by their salary rate plus benefits. Determining the differences in personnel costs between two systems must be done on a pragmatic rather than on a theoretical basis. If the calculations indicate that, say, 7¼ keypunch operators are required in the new system, as opposed to 9 in the existing system, the saving is only one person unless other conditions are brought in. In fact, company policy usually dictates reassignment of personnel; therefore, the actual personnel savings would be zero until normal attrition reduced the number.

Equipment savings are calculated in a similar manner. Only savings that affect the actual out-of-pocket expenses are to be credited. If a system uses a small amount of time on an existing internal large computer, the savings due to eliminating this processing is limited to the change in the company's billed expense, which often is zero. Rented equipment that can be eliminated is a true saving. The savings due to replacement of leased equipment must be handled according to the individual contract. It is possible that savings can be credited only after the expiration of the lease term, and any lease-termination charges must be considered as a reduction of savings. Displaced purchased equipment (items such as desks, cabinets, and other office equipment as well as adding machines and keypunchers) can be credited as a saving only if there is a resale value and it is the intention to sell the equipment.

A saving often overlooked pertains to the time value of money. If a new system allows the company to deliver its bills a week earlier than the customary billing date, there is very likely a real saving to the company as a result of the reduction of the company's receivables. If, after careful analysis, producing statements earlier is expected to reduce the time lag for payment by four days, then a real saving equal to a standard interest rate on a four days' billing amount is a justified saving.

Other items to be considered in the financial analysis include cost of floor space and supplies such as punch cards and various forms.

One-Time Costs

The items previously discussed are those that pertain to the operation of the system and to the difference between the operating cost of the existing method and that of a proposed system. There are also other costs, those incurred in starting up the system, which must be taken into account when evaluating system alternatives. Many alternatives that have otherwise looked very attractive had to be discarded because of high startup costs. Common costs include special construction, wiring, or other type of site preparation. Some computer alternatives also require air conditioning or special ventilation. Training of operators and programmers would be included as a startup cost, but it may also be a continuing cost in a large installation. The largest startup cost is the expense of converting the existing files (hard-copy customer files, product files) to the form needed for the new system.

File Conversion

The major preinstallation cost—and it has been large enough to forestall many an installation—is the file conversion cost. If the company is changing to a computerized system from a manual system, a major outlay is made in converting the data to computer form. In large systems this cost is typically 20 percent of the total expenditure for the purchased system. Many techniques and methods are used to convert existing file data to data processing form. The method to be chosen depends upon the data form and the equipment on which it will eventually be used. Typically, the new master file information will be maintained on a disk file. If the data of the existing system is on hard copy such as ledger cards, which are typed, the conversion process may be very expensive if files are voluminous. The process will have to include transcribing the ledger card data, usually by keypunching or a similar method, verifying and correcting keying errors, validating and editing the data, making corrections to the data, and setting up the data in a logical layout and format in the proper organization on the computer system master file. If this file is maintained on a random-access device, a considerable amount of thought and effort must be put into the organization of the data and the access method best suited for the application.

Special programs frequently have to be written to set up the data on the file. These programs must tie together logical segments of the data records and must include a method of updating individual records, purging selected records, and rearranging the file. The vendor may have some conversion program available from previous installations, but very often, because of the unique nature of each company's data, special programs must be written. At the minimum, a fairly large amount of adjustment to existing programs will be necessary.

Financial Evaluation

The most important part of the study that decides among several alternative plans is the financial analysis. Almost all computer system decisions have used financial considerations as a major factor in reaching conclusions, but in many instances no more than the system purchase price has been used as a criterion. A recent survey of medium-size and small companies showed that a majority made a feasibility study before the equipment was selected. Almost all responses indicated that the study was related almost entirely to economic matters. Despite this high percentage, no firm stated that it used any of the accepted methods in evaluating financial expenditures, such as rate of return or present value. Even the most elementary financial measurement method, computing a payback period, was not mentioned. This leads to the assumption that although the respondents claimed that an economic evaluation was practically the entire feasibility study, that evaluation was possibly nothing more than a comparison between total system prices. Analyses of this simple type are often erroneous.

Example. Consider the situation when a company wants to install a system for a very definite two-year period, after which it plans to consolidate with another branch and install an entirely new system. The purchase price of the equipment is $65,000 and monthly maintenance costs $180. The estimated value of the system in two years is $36,000. Rental, including maintenance, costs $1,500 per month. This simple analysis, as was probably done by the companies in the survey, would suggest that it would be cheaper to purchase than to rent. This conclusion is reached by computing

$$(\$65,000 + \$4,320) - \$36,000 = \$33,320 \text{ (purchase)}$$

as compared with

$$\$1,500 \times 24 = \$36,000 \text{ (rental)}$$

Unfortunately, the conclusion that purchase is cheaper may be incorrect. A dollar spent some time in the future is worth less than a dollar spent now. In the preceding computation, dissimilar dollars have been added together and may have resulted in an erroneous conclusion. All expenditures should be put on common terms. Relating all expenditures to the present is one way of doing this. The analysis must include all expenses and incomes (capital investment, depreciation, rentals, and so forth) and must relate all these elements to the same period in time to determine their proper effect.

Present Value

In all situations, goods and services in the present are considered preferable to equivalent amounts in the future. Two factors account for this: risk aversion and time preference. A dollar now is certain, as is the existence of its owner, whereas the future dollar rests on promise and is less than certain. This can be expressed in more practical terms: A dollar obtained today will be worth more than a dollar to be paid two years from now. If 88 cents is deposited at 6 percent annual interest, it will be worth about $1.00 two years from now. In other words, at this typical rate of exchange, 88 cents now is equivalent to $1.00 two years from now. Or, 88 cents is the present value of $1.00 when calculated at a 6 percent annual rate of interest. At other rates of interest, 76 cents or even 60 cents today might be equivalent to $1.00 two years from now. Seventy-five cents is the present value of $1.00 two years from now if the assumed interest rate is 15½ percent. At 20 percent, the present value of $1.00 two years from now is about 70 cents. At the same rate the present value of $1.00 ten years from now is only 16 cents. The concept of present value is the key to understanding adequate methods of financial comparisons.

In performing the present-value analysis, the net amount of money (that is, the benefits less the costs) accrued each year over the life of the project is discounted at a specified interest rate for each year and is summed for the entire project. The result is the net present value (NPV) of the project. The alternative with the highest net present value is the more desirable solution. An example of this method, and of others covered in this section, is shown in Tables 8–1 through 8–6.

The appropriate interest rates can be obtained from a financial handbook or a financial organization. The interest rate used in project evaluation depends upon the company's sources and uses of capital funds and the current interest rate. A 9 percent after-tax rate of return is a commonly used value in projects of this type.

Rate of return. As we have shown, an appropriate method for evaluating alternative courses is to calculate the net present value of the flows of cash over time. According to our rule, the alternative with the greater NPV is preferable. In the cash-flow calculations, we start with an assumed rate of interest. An alternative method evaluates the alternatives by determining the interest rate or rate of return of the monies invested in the new system. In determining the rate of return, a consistent interest rate is applied to each year's cash-flow amounts until, with the proper rate, the present value becomes zero. This interest rate is then the rate of return of the project.

The concept of rate of return provides a useful and familiar rule for decision making. Some companies require a minimum rate of return before any project can be initiated, and this calculation allows the rule to be equitably applied. In some cases the rate-of-return calculation provides two possible results, and it may not always produce the alternative that satisfies the present-value decision rule, but these limitations are rarely important. Once the user is aware of the limitations, he finds the rate-of-return concept useful and meaningful.

Breakeven analysis. Despite the fact that breakeven analysis is not completely accurate, it is used frequently as an economic evaluation technique, either by itself or in conjunction with another method. Its virtues are its ease of use and the clear manner in which the important matter of capital recovery is expressed. In this method, cumulative expenditures are compared with cumulative benefits over the project life.

It is normal to have high expenditures at the beginning of the project because of the preinstallation development, the file conversion effort, and equipment payments. After the first year, the benefits are consistent and much greater than the costs. The point at which the total amount of benefits equals or exceeds the total expenditures is called the *breakeven point*. At this point, all development and installation expenses have been recovered; from that point on, benefits will constantly accrue.

The breakeven point is usually expressed in time units such as years and months. The results of the analysis are frequently shown graphically. Although this technique is not completely accurate, since it fails to consider the time value of money, it is quite useful because it is easy to use and indicates an important point very lucidly.

In the following section a simplified economic evaluation is displayed to illustrate the three different methods of analysis: present value, rate of return, and breakeven.

Example of Economic Evaluation

The problem. The situation to be evaluated concerns two possible alternatives for solving an operating problem. Alternative A requires a large new development and a fairly large investment in equipment, but will greatly reduce the manpower requirements. Alternative B is more modest in terms of investment, but will not produce the benefits that the more expensive system will deliver.

This example shows simplified economic evaluations. Depreciation, some taxes, and other miscellaneous items are not included. A 50 percent tax rate is assumed. The expenses and some pertinent facts of the two potential alternatives of the present system are shown in Tables 8–2 through 8–4. The expenses of the present system (see Table 8–1) are considered the base case, and the costs and benefits of the potential alternatives are calculated relative to this system.

Present value. This method of economic evaluation compares the alternatives on the basis of the present value of the benefits less the costs. Unless additional criteria such as maximum amount of investment or risk are included, presumably the alternative with the greatest net present value is chosen. The present-value calculation in Table 8–5 demonstrates the process for both alternatives. The benefits, less the costs of operating the system over the life of the project, are discounted at an appropriate interest rate for each year and are summed for the entire project. A 9 percent after-tax interest rate is used in this example.

This example indicates that both alternatives have almost equal net present values (A=$34,000; B=$33,000). Because of the higher investment required for Alternative A and the associated greater risk, it is intuitively felt that Alternative B is preferable. However, the next step in economic evaluation—the rate of return—may produce quantitative evidence to reinforce this initial judgment.

Rate of return. To determine the rate of return of the investment in the new system, successive trial calculations are made with different interest rates, as in the present-value calculation.

When the present value is equal to zero, then the interest rate

used in the calculation is the rate of return. This means that the
future benefits, when discounted at that particular interest rate, are
exactly equal to the initial cost. In ·other words, the investment
represented by the initial cost will return monies "invested" in the
system at the indicated interest rate over the life of the project.
These calculations are shown in Table 8–6.

Table 8–1. Present system: annual operating expenses, years 0–5.

Expense	Yr. 0	Yr. 1	Yr. 2	Yr. 3	Yr. 4	Yr. 5
Personnel	$80,000	$84,000	$88,000	$101,000	$111,000	$115,000
Equipment	8,000	8,000	8,000	11,000	11,000	11,000
Supplies	2,000	2,000	2,000	2,000	2,000	2,000
Total	$90,000	$94,000	$98,000	$114,000	$124,000	$128,000
After tax (50%)	$45,000	$47,000	$49,000	$ 57,000	$ 62,000	$ 64,000

Note: Volume increase expected yearly. In the third year an increase in equipment
to $11,000 will be necessary. Personnel will also increase. One additional person
will probably be added in both third and fourth years. Also, pay rates are projected to
increase at 5% per year beginning in year 1.

Table 8–2. Evaluation of alternatives: initial costs for Alternatives A and B.

Alternative A		*Alternative B*	
Time to installation	1 year	Time to installation	6 months
Purchase price of equipment	$125,000	Software development	$ 12,000
Software development	$ 75,000	Installation and conversion	$ 15,000
Installation and conversion	$ 35,000	Supplies	$ 2,000
Annual operating expense:		Analyst time (6 months)	$ 7,000
Personnel	$ 25,000	Annual operating expense:	
Maintenance of equipment	$ 3,000	Equipment rental	$ 24,000
Supplies	$ 5,000	Personnel	$ 48,000
Total costs, Year 1	$268,000	Supplies	$ 1,000
		Total costs, Year 1	$ 85,000

Note: Future operating expenses:
Personnel costs will increase by 5% annually. Equipment will handle anticipated future volumes. Resale value of equipment of the end of its six-year life is conservatively estimated at 12.5% of the initial hardware cost.

Note: Future operating expenses: Personnel costs will increase by 5% annually. An additional person will be needed starting in year 4. Equipment will handle anticipated future volume increases.

Table 8–3. Six-year expenses for Alternative A (in thousands of dollars).

Expense	Year 0 Existing System	Alternative A	Total	0	1	2	3	4	5
Personnel	$80	$ 25	$105	$105	$24	$26	$28	$30	$32
Equipment	8	128	136	136	3	3	3	3	3
Supplies	2	5	7	7	1	1	1	1	1
Development	—	75	75	75	—	—	—	—	—
Installation	—	35	35	35	—	—	—	—	—
Total	$90	$268	$358	$358	$28	$30	$32	$34	$36
After-tax cost (50%)	—	—	179	179	14	15	16	17	18
Investment tax credit	—	—	(10)	(10)	—	—	—	—	—
Resale value	—	—	—	—	—	—	—	—	(8)
Net expense after tax	—	—	169	169	14	15	16	17	10

Note: Since one year is required for the development of the Alternative A system, the existing system will continue to operate for the entire year. The expenses in year 0 are therefore the sum of development costs and the present system operating cost.

Table 8–4. Six-year expenses for Alternative B (in thousands of dollars).

Expense	Existing System, 6 Mos.	New System, Development	New System, 6 Mos.	Total	0	1	2	3	4	5
Personnel	$40	$ 7	$24	$ 71	$ 71	$51	$53	$55	$65	$69
Equipment	4	12	12	28	28	24	24	24	24	24
Supplies	1	2	1	4	4	1	1	1	1	1
Development	—	12	—	12	12	—	—	—	—	—
Installation	—	15	—	15	15	—	—	—	—	—
Total	$45	$48	$37	$130	$130	$76	$78	$80	$90	$94
Net expense after tax (50%)	—	—	—	65	65	38	39	40	45	47

Note: The Alternative B system is developed in six months. Therefore, the existing system is operating during the first half of year zero while development of the new system is proceeding. At midyear, the new system becomes operative.

Table 8–5. Present value calculation for Alternatives A and B, Years 0–5 (in thousands of dollars).

Factor	0 A	0 B	1 A	1 B	2 A	2 B	3 A	3 B	4 A	4 B	5 A	5 B
Expenses												
Present system	45	45	47	47	49	49	57	57	62	62	64	64
New system	169	65	14	38	15	39	16	40	17	45	10	47
Benefits (new system less old system)	(124)	(20)	33	9	34	10	41	17	45	17	54	17
Discount @ 9%	1.000	1.000	0.917	0.917	0.842	0.842	0.772	0.772	0.708	0.708	0.650	0.650
Net present value by year	(124)	(20)	30	8.3	29	8.4	32	13	32	12	35	11
Net present value total	34	33										

Table 8–6. Rate-of-return calculation: Alternatives A and B, Years 0–5 (in thousands of dollars).

Factor	0 A	0 B	1 A	1 B	2 A	2 B	3 A	3 B	4 A	4 B	5 A	5 B
Benefits	(124)	(20)	33	9	34	10	41	17	45	17	54	17
Discount @ 9%	1.00	1.00	0.917	0.917	0.82	0.842	0.772	0.772	0.708	0.708	0.650	0.650
NPV	(124)	(20)	30	8.3	29	8.4	32	13	32	12	35	11
Total	34	33	—	—	—	—	—	—	—	—	—	—
Discount @ 12%	1.00	—	0.893	0.769	0.797	—	0.712	—	0.636	—	0.613	—
NPV	(124)	—	29	—	27	—	29	—	29	—	33	—
Total	23	—	—	—	—	—	—	—	—	—	—	—
Discount @ 18%	1.00	—	0.848	—	0.718	—	0.609	—	0.516	—	0.437	—
NPV	(124)	—	28	—	24	—	25	—	23	—	24	—
Total	0	—	—	—	—	—	—	—	—	—	—	—
Discount @ 20%	1.00	1.00	0.833	0.833	0.694	0.694	0.579	0.579	0.482	0.482	0.402	0.402
NPV	(124)	(20)	27	7.5	24	6.9	24	9.8	22	8.2	22	6.8
Total	(5)	19.2	—	—	—	—	—	—	—	—	—	—
Discount @ 30%	—	1.00	—	0.769	—	0.592	—	0.455	—	0.350	—	0.269
NPV	—	(20)	—	6.9	—	5.9	—	7.7	—	6.0	—	4.6
Total	—	11	—	—	—	—	—	—	—	—	—	—
Discount @ 50%	—	1.00	—	0.667	—	0.444	—	0.296	—	0.198	—	0.132
NPV	—	(20)	—	6.0	—	4.4	—	5.0	—	3.4	—	2.2
Total	—	1	—	—	—	—	—	—	—	—	—	—

The present value of Alternative A, using the 9 percent interest rate, was positive by a large amount, indicating a rate of return much higher than 9 percent. An interest rate of 12 percent was tried and was also found to be too low, and the use of a 20 percent rate provided a negative present value, indicating a too high interest rate. Of all the rates used, only the 18 percent rate produced the desired result, a zero net present value (NPV), indicating that 18 percent would be the correct rate of return for Alternative A. As was expected, because Alternative B showed a much higher rate of return, over 50 percent, it would be the preferred system in this example.

Figure 8–1. Breakeven analysis for Alternatives A and B.

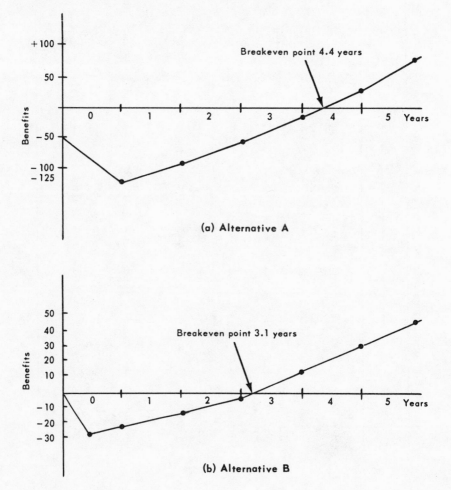

Table 8–7. Breakeven comparison of Alternatives A and B ($000).

System	(½)	0	1	2	3	4	5
				Year			
Alternative A							
Annual	—	$(124)	$33	$34	$41	$45	$54
Cumulative	—	(124)	(91)	(57)	(16)	29	83
Alternative B							
Annual	—	(20)	9	10	17	17	17
Cumulative	(24)	(20)	(11)	(1)	16	33	50

Breakeven analysis. The breakeven technique provides an easy and descriptive method for showing how long it takes to recover, in equal value dollars, the initial cost of the system. Every new system has an initial expense, but it is expected to produce benefits comparable to, or in excess of, this expense. The point at which the accumulated savings are equal to the investment in the new system is called the *breakeven point.* Beyond this point, the system becomes profitable and pays a return on the investment.

Figure 8–1 shows this relationship graphically for the two proposed alternatives. Table 8–7 gives the cost comparison of Alternatives A and B. As can be seen from both Figure 8–1 and Table 8–7, the breakeven point occurs in year 4 for Alternative A and in year 3 for Alternative B.

CASE STUDIES IN SELECTING MINICOMPUTER SYSTEMS

The choice of a system that satisfies the needs of a company is not always guided primarily by technical considerations or by economic attractiveness. Very often, despite many obvious technical and economic advantages of a particular system, it will not be chosen because it does not fit in with the company's way of doing business and with the level of technical competence available. This important aspect of minicomputer selection must be considered from the viewpoints of relevance and interaction of the various decision criteria as they apply to the organization's operating philosophy and personnel capabilities. Therefore, this chapter explores applicable criteria and illustrates them by presenting two typical applications—the general business system and the order-entry system.

For these two cases, specific problems are described, potential solutions are developed, and recommended actions (with the reasons for these actions) are discussed. Through an in-depth discussion of the problem and the proposed solutions, the interaction of the economic, technical, and organizational considerations in making a decision are graphically illustrated.

The problems and the solutions are real and are typical of those frequently encountered. As a result, the equipment configurations proposed are those that could be used in satisfying decision criteria. Sufficient information is provided for modeling a proposed system based on information determined through the study of its applicability to a particular business. Each study describes and illustrates (1) what the problem is, (2) how it can be solved, (3) how the system is configured, (4) what the best solution is, and (5) why that solution is chosen.

A General Business (Case 1)

This application was chosen for detailed coverage because it represents a typical problem for the small businessman or for the remote-profit-center manager of the large company. The manager has realized, because of difficulties in obtaining dependable people and because of the increased work load, that his clerical operation must be automated. Two solutions have been proposed. The first one is a limited approach that will adequately satisfy his primary needs, but which will not do the things that the manager always felt a data processing system should do. Things like providing instant information on any account, or providing rapid analysis of sales and other functions of a predictive nature to help him in planning and managing his business, cannot be accomplished with this low-key approach.

The second approach is more comprehensive and will accomplish all desired functions, but it involves a "space age" system (using the words of the manager) that awes him and impresses him, but which also frightens him to some extent. If he accepts this system, he will be totally dependent upon something he does not fully understand. This exotic, complex system will be handling the functions that are the center of his business. Undoubtedly, without a full grasp of the system, the manager would choose the smaller, limited system. Even when he gained more experience and developed more confidence in automated business operations, it would be very likely that the smaller system, which takes care of the basic problem, would be the more desirable solution.

In addition to this philosophical problem, this case illustrates two alternative methods for handling the basic business functions of a small business, and shows the equipment configuration necessary for each. The first, or smaller, approach handles each application as a separate, discrete process. The larger system is an integrated system that acknowledges and uses to best advantage the interrelated nature of the business data. For example, when an order for a product is recorded by either system, that order will generate an invoice item. However, in the integrated system, that order item will also generate transactions to update the product inventory file, the salesmen's commission file, and the in-process file. It will also provide information for sales analyses and forecasting subsystems.

Hard economics—the costs and benefits of the new system—are only a part of the decision and in this case are probably a less significant part. More important is the relationship to the method of doing business and the level of competence with data processing that exists within the company. A knowledge of computers and programming is not always essential, but without an understanding of data processing concepts and philosophy a sophisticated system would probably never be successfully installed. After some experience with the smaller system, the user can move up to the more powerful, integrated system.

The Problem

A small organization requires a system to handle a number of functions. The organization does about $20 million gross sales at that one location each year. All business functions are performed at the single location. A number of office workers perform all clerical operations, which include the basic business applications such as accounts payable, accounts receivable, general ledger, and invoicing. The amount of work that the office staff performs is increasing each year and this increase is only partly due to the increase in business. In fact, the major improvement in business volume pertains to the volume of products ordered at one time, the quantity of a particular product, or the number of line items per order. This type of increase does not add to the overall work load to any noticeable extent. What does increase the work load is the burgeoning number of reports and statistics that must be prepared for the various levels of government, the resulting amount of paperwork, and the special variation in packing, shipping, and invoicing insisted upon by the large industrial customers.

The staff, which now numbers ten people, is finding it difficult to keep up with the added work load. Additional clerical help is not the solution because it is difficult to obtain competent and experienced clerical help. It takes a long time for new employees to become familiar with all operations, and during this time the new clerk and the person doing the training are working at much less than maximum efficiency. Moreover, because of the conflicts in accessing the hard-copy ledgers and files, additional personnel are rapidly becoming counterproductive. As a result, the manager recognizes that automation of his procedures is essential.

Existing System

Orders are received through the mail and occasionally by phone. The phone orders are recorded and, except for their more frequent urgency, are handled exactly like mail orders. Clerks pull the customer record and check for poor credit risks and delinquent payers. These are referred to the manager, who decides how to handle them.

The customer record is updated manually, and an entry is made in the receivables ledger. An invoice and a bill of lading are made up, and the latter is sent to the warehouse for assembly of the order. The products are picked from the inventory and product cards are changed to reflect the change in inventory. If a product is not in stock, the office is notified and the invoice is adjusted. This is a complicated, time-consuming, and error-prone procedure, since out-of-stock products can be either back-ordered or canceled by the customer, resulting in possible changes in the quantity discounts.

The return of a copy of the bill of lading to the office is both advice that the order has been filled and is authorization for sending the invoice to the customer.

Volume of orders. An average of 250 orders per day are received and each order may be for one or many products. Five products or line items per order is the average. Approximately 1,600 invoices are prepared each month, half in the first week of the month. The numbers of orders and invoices are relatively constant, but the number of items ordered increases by about 10 percent per year. There are approximately 4,000 customers for whom a record is kept. There are also 400 different products for which a product ledger card is maintained.

Functions performed. The company performs a number of identifiable applications that are basic to any business. Typical of these operations are:

1. Order entry: Includes taking orders, determining product availability, verifying credit, establishing back-order and future-order files.
2. Inventory accounting: This is done at the warehouse location, where a product card is updated for all additions and

issues. Product re-orders are initiated manually as a result of withdrawing the product.

3. Invoicing: This includes preparation of an invoice, a bill of lading, a stock-picking list, and packing slips.
4. General ledger.
5. Accounts payable.
6. Accounts receivable.
7. Payroll.
8. Salesmen's commissions.

Proposed System Design

Application objectives. The proposed system must be able to handle in a simplified manner the existing order-entry and invoicing applications and an improved inventory control function. It would also be desirable if some of the other basic functions could also be handled. In addition, it would be very desirable if a sales analysis function, which could indicate what items were selling well, were included.

Operational objectives. The system must be designed to operate without a team of computer-oriented personnel. No in-house programming or operation talent is available, and training such a staff is not planned. No provision for in-house computer system skills will be made, and it is felt that economic justification of the application cannot support additions to staff. Because of this approach, and also for easy design and maintenance assurance, all components of the system are to be supplied by a single vendor.

Proposed Solutions

Electronic accounting machine. After a study of the system requirements and potential benefits, two different system designs are proposed. One approach is to use a small-business computer system that handles the several applications. The applications are handled sequentially, and no internal processing connection is needed between applications. All essential functions can be handled, although some cannot be handled as completely as desired by the company. The back- and future-order functions, for example, cannot be satisfactorily handled automatically, and so will be maintained manually. Commissions and accounts payable will not be handled initially. Also there is no possibility of handling sales analysis requirements of the company.

The equipment vendor provides fully developed application packages that are programmed only for his machine. These application packages have to be modified to accommodate the company's method of business, an adjustment that can be done by the vendor's staff at a reasonable fee.

The integrated system minicomputer. The second method uses a minicomputer with a random-access disk file in an advanced processing method. Orders are entered into the system by a series of keyboard CRT display units. The order-entry transaction is processed as each part of it enters the system. When the customer identification is entered, the system will immediately check the customer's credit. The existence of the proper amount of product is verified at the time information is entered. Notification is made to the input clerk if special action has to be taken.

Invoicing for all deliverable items is performed automatically, as is the preparation of shipping documents. The same transactions initiate other functions, such as inventory control and salesmen's commissions. The sales analysis function can be handled in exactly the way the company desires, providing practically instantaneously a listing of all items that meet criteria established to identify them as current fast movers. Accounts payable and payroll, being largely unrelated to the rest of the application, will not be handled by the system.

All of the preceding applications are to be designed and programmed specifically for this company, and by this procedure it will get the system that performs all of the desired operations. But in obtaining such a system, the user will have to bear the high cost of programming and debugging as well as the risk of unproven programs.

New System Configuration

Electronic accounting machine. Magnetic ledger cards are used as the storage medium in this system. These cards may contain as many as 600 digits of information and may be processed in the computer two at a time.

The computer is programmed internally for each application and updates the magnetic ledger cards. There is a magnetic ledger card for each product and for each customer. The customer card is used in order-entry, invoicing, and accounts receivable programs. The product card is used in order-entry, invoicing, and inventory programs. There is also a magnetic ledger card for each employee and salesman; these are used in payroll and commission runs.

Processing is performed one application at a time. When the accounts payable program is loaded into the computer, only that application can be run. Input to the program is provided by the magnetic ledger cards and by typing in the variable information at the keyboard. Output is produced on the printer as the magnetic ledger card for each customer is updated.

Other applications work in a similar manner. There is no automatic linking between applications. When the next application is to be run, the new program is read into the computer. The application is then run, using the proper set of magnetic ledger cards and typing in the variable information at the keyboard. A diagram of the equipment is shown in Figure 9–1(*a*).

The integrated system. A diagram of the equipment used in the integrated system is shown in Figure 9–1(*b*). This system maintains the necessary files on a random-access disk storage device. Permanent files, such as the customer file, product file, and the salesman file, are maintained on the disk. The disk is also used for in-process and temporary storage of transactions, back orders, future orders, adjustments, and unresolved errors.

Processing is initiated by the input of orders, which is done at the terminal keyboard, and proceeds through the preparation of invoices. These processes are shown in Figure 9–2. After these functions have been completed, the salesmen's commission file is updated by the same orders. Other processes are handled in a similar manner, starting with a manual input and following through in automated sequence.

Output determination. A potential program regarding the ability of the output printer to handle the anticipated volume of printed output has to be resolved. The accounting machine system has two printer options. The smaller printer operates at ten characters per second. Another printer, available for less than $3,000 additional, has an average speed for this application of 40 characters per second. (The printer moves across spaces at about eight times its actual character printing rate; therefore, the average print rate is dependent upon the application.)

The minicomputer equipment supplier for the integrated system can provide either a ten-character-per-second printer or a computer type of line printer that costs $10,000 more than the character printer. The 10- or 15-character-per-second printer cannot do the job, but the 40-character-per-second printer is adequate, as the following calculations indicate.

Given. The system must produce, on the peak day each month, 250 bills of lading having an average of 12 lines of printing and 350 invoices having an average of 8 lines of printing. The printer and forms are 72 characters wide. Therefore one line of printing takes approximately 7 seconds on the 10-character-per-second printer and 2 seconds on the 40-character-per-second printer.

The total printing time requirements for each of the two printers may then be calculated as shown in the table on p. 187.

Figure 9–1. Two alternative systems: *(a)* a small-business system, *(b)* an integrated minicomputer system.

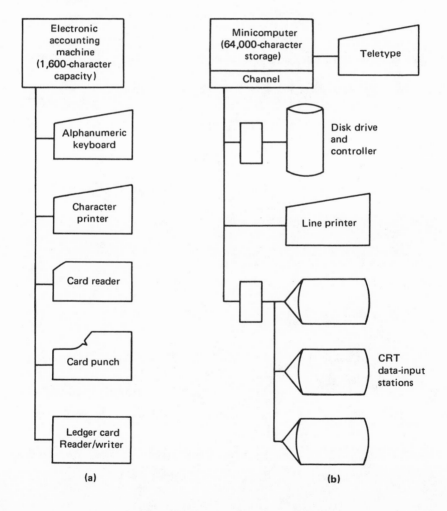

(a)   (b)

Figure 9–2. System processing.

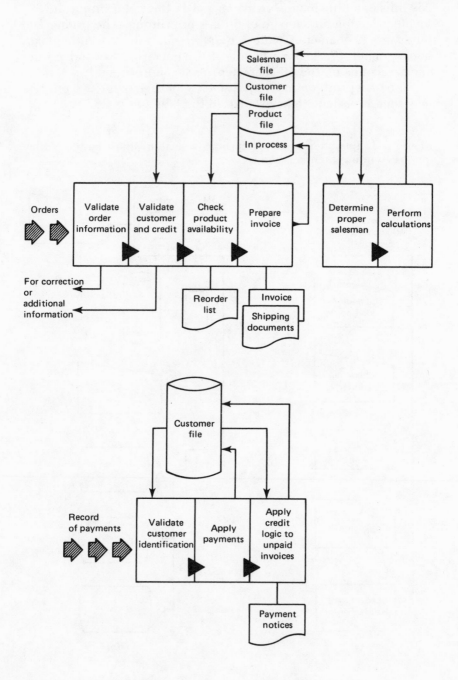

	10 character/sec printer	40 character/sec printer
Bills of	$250 \times 12 \times 7 =$	$250 \times 12 \times 2 =$
Lading	21,000 sec. = 5.8 hr.	6,000 sec. = 1.7 hr.
Invoices	$350 \times 8 \times 7 =$	$350 \times 8 \times 2 =$
	19,600 sec. = 5.4 hr.	5,600 sec. = 1.6 hr.
Total	11.2 hr.	3.3 hr.
	Not Acceptable	*Acceptable*

Thus, if the minicomputer system is chosen, the expensive line printer will have to be used, whereas an inexpensive printer is available if the small business system is selected.

System costs. The accounting machine and the integrated systems provide management with very different alternatives with regard to the processing method. The different methods also present costs that are quite different.

Choosing the Best Solution

Electronic accounting machine. The supplier provides developed basic business programs with this machine. As a result, the user incurs a programming cost only if he requires deviations from the standard program. The vendor supplies the programming at approximately $3.00 per instruction.

Modifications to the order-entry, invoicing, inventory accounting, and accounts receivable programs are desired. These modifications will cost about $6,500. The general ledger and payroll programs will be used without change. The user company will modify its internal procedures slightly so that there will be no deviations from the standard procedures that are provided through the vendor program.

The hardware configuration shown in Figure 9–1(a) has a purchase price of $32,450. On a five-year monthly lease, the monthly payments are $725. Monthly maintenance will be additional. Installation can be accomplished in three months. The vendor will supply four more weeks of programmer training for the user at any time he desires. In the future, the user may perform his own programming for changes or new development, or may rely on the vendor.

Integrated minicomputer system. The major difference in costs between the two approaches is the result of the high software development costs for the integrated system. The hardware, which costs about $36,000, is only slightly higher than the more limited system. The system hardware will cost $790 per month on a five-year lease. Maintenance will be $280 per month. Application software will have to be developed in its entirety to make the integrated approach work.

Programming cost is estimated at $75,000, despite the use of much of the manufacturer's system software. Not only is this approach costly, but it also presents some risks. Any new software development has associated with it a probability, surely a very low probability, of not working. Any large, newly developed program has to be run for an extended period of time before it is judged to be in minimal failure condition. In some extremely large and complicated programs such as a large-computer operating system, minimal failure status is not usually achieved before years of service, despite the large number of users who are running the program continuously and detecting bugs that the large, experienced manufacturer's staff would ordinarily correct.

If the user of this system decides to have it developed for his use exclusively, he should be aware of the possibility that the system will not be ready on time and that it will not perform all the functions that the user expected it to perform. He should also be aware of the likelihood that in the first months after installation the system will have downtime of a considerable number of hours (possibly days) while programmers analyze, correct, and test program bugs. Furthermore, a number of program modifications will have to be made in order (1) to get the system working in the way the user thought it would work and (2) to correct oversights in the original design. More than just considering these contingencies, the user should allow for them in his planning of the system. Since he will be dependent upon this system for the continuing operation of his business, he must have a contingency plan available. This, too, is expensive in terms of people, time and expenses.

Implementation. The time to installation is estimated at three months for the smaller system and nine months for the large integrated system. In addition to being shorter, the estimate for the small system is undoubtedly more accurate. During this time, equipment is checked out and programs are written and tested. The larger requirements of the integrated approach necessitate more expert and thorough project management and documentation.

Since the files are not large, data conversion costs are not high and are roughly equal for the two systems. The manufacturer of the small-business system provides, at a charge, the means to convert a company's customer and product files to the magnetic ledger card medium. For the large integrated system, the programs developed for updating the files in production will be used to put the data, which will first have to be keypunched, onto the disk files.

Benefits. The integrated system offers the user more benefits, both tangible and intangible, than the smaller system. For instance, if the small-business system is installed, the user will not reduce any clerical help but will thus avoid the necessity of hiring more in the near future. Whenever employee replacements have to be found, the levels of experience, dedication, and talent previously required to fill their jobs are unnecessary. Also, overtime expense will be immediately reduced as a result of a reduction in errors and the consequent adjustments expected. The business will no longer be dependent upon the knowledge of one or two people, the head clerks, for successful operation of the clerical functions.

Even with this smaller system, the company will be able to better serve its customers and, more important, service will not continue along the deteriorating course it had been going for the past year. Deliveries will be made on time more often. Customer relations can be expected to improve because of fewer errors and adjustments and the ability of the company to inform the customer of out-of-stock products before the shipment is scheduled. Overall, the small system allows the company to perform its business in an ordered, professional manner for years to come. Although the immediate dollar benefits are limited to reduction in overtime, other less tangible benefits are real and very important.

The larger, integrated system matches the efficiency of the smaller system and also provides other immediate tangible and intangible benefits; for example, fewer errors, lower training costs, less overtime, and the immediate displacement of at least two people. By providing information on the customer's credit at the time of order, by producing invoices earlier, and by using a systematic past-due account review and collection procedure, a reduction in the company's accounts receivable and bad-debt write-off can be expected.

Product inventory is also expected to be substantially reduced, owing to two major improvements brought about by the new system.

1.. More accurate inventory accounting system:
    Available stock is known at the time of order.
    An automatic back-order system is activated.

Automatic allocation for future orders is scheduled.
Automatic inventory alerts give better stock control.
2. Better knowledge of what is selling:
The sales analysis program will report to management the
rapid-selling and slow-selling items. This will allow reduction of inventory by clearing out and not producing
the slow-selling items.

Another area in which large benefits are provided by the integrated
system and not by the smaller system is in accounting for salesmen's commissions. In a nonautomated system, many people check
the geographic assignments of the salesman against the location of
the sales for proper assignment of his commission. This function is
not included in the smaller system and will have to be performed
manually if that system is installed. However, it will be handled
very well by the larger system, which will designate sales assignments on the basis of address zip codes and perform the commission calculations automatically. Only in special cases, such as a
commission split more than two ways, is human intervention
necessary.

A summary and comparison of the benefits of the two systems
are given in Table 9–1. As the table shows, the integrated system
will provide a company with the means to operate an efficient and
orderly system for many years into the future. It costs more than the
smaller business system, but provides many more benefits.

Final Choice of System

In Case 1 the decision was made to obtain the smaller business
system. The decision was based on the user's lack of confidence in
his ability to direct and control the development of a large system
that appeared to be novel in concept and operation. The decision
was a correct one. Without any experience in data processing practices or philosophy, the user was in no position to monitor the
development of the system properly. In a small business, as in this
case, the data processing system performs all basic accounting functions that are essential to operation of the company. The potential
danger to the business, if the system were to develop a malfunction
or to take an unduly long time to install, outweighed all other
factors considered in this decision. This uncertainty, this risk, was
the reason the user should, and did, choose the smaller, more

Table 9-1. Comparison of systems.

Application	Electronic Accounting Machine	Integrated Minicomputer System
Personnel	Lower-paid personnel can be used Overtime expense reduced due to fewer errors and adjustments Training easier	The same
		Fewer people required in office More equitable, accurate, and rapid salesmen commission payments
Receivables	No change	Decreased accounts receivable because of more rapid billing, more accurate billing, regular past-due analysis, and credit letters
Service	Faster service to user Ability to inform user of nondeliverable items at time of orders Fewer errors	The same or better
Inventory	Improved inventory accounting	Inventory control with automatic out-of-stock alerts
Business planning	No reports or data supplied	Sales analysis prepared regularly; data available on request

conservative approach of the small-business system over the larger integrated system.

The Order-Entry System (Case 2)

This second case illustrates the use of a minicomputer in a large, on-line, order-entry application. This application has a number of important features: It is a large and expensive system; it is an interactive, on-line system; and it is an application frequently performed on a large-computer system. Despite the system cost and size, the principle and philosophy of minicomputer use apply more directly in this type of system than in many other smaller ones.

This system features on-line date entry. This approach can easily be economically justified when a low-priced processor is used. In fact, this mode of operation appears to be the most natural one when human factors are properly considered, one that has been largely developed in minicomputer systems.

The order-entry application of a minicomputer allows the system to step the operator through the processing, and tests and validates the data as it enters the system. This helps to assure the validity and accuracy of the data. In addition, the iterative, conversational technique reduces the amount of training that the entry clerks require, and in fact allows a lower-paid clerk to be used in the job. Thus, many operational and economic advantages are realized.

A second very important feature of this system is that it interfaces with a large-scale, third-generation business computer. The processing on the large computer is kept unchanged. It performs the same functions it did in the previous system, which include accounts receivable, inventory control, and sales analysis. These functions are performed daily or weekly as a batch process. Very few modifications have to be made to the existing large data processing system, and all are minor.

The input to the large system from the minicomputer order-entry front-end system is made to look like the edited punch card input from the existing methods. The interface connects the minicomputer system directly into the data channel of the large machine. In fact, the interface supplied with the minicomputer is designed to look like a magnetic tape to the large computer. Therefore, interfacing can be accomplished easily and with no risk, since no change needs to be made to the operating system or software of the large system.

The Problem

A system is proposed to handle the entry of orders in a mail-order application. The proposed system is to utilize CRT terminals for the preparation of data related to customers' orders. The system will edit and validate all data where possible. For example, product and customer information will be tested for logical values to assure the validity of all data. Also, product information will be automatically located in the file through either an alphabetic or numeric key.

The system will bypass the need for manually coding each order and for subsequent keypunching of data. Also, the system will eliminate certain time-consuming steps currently performed by the order-editing department (for example, researching a product code for each item ordered) and will decrease the number of customer complaints due to erroneous input. It is expected that the proposed system will reduce costs and increase the accuracy of data.

Existing System

The existing order-entry system consists of a series of manual steps that results in the completion of a number of keypunch coding forms. Cards are then keypunched from the coding forms and are entered at night into the large computer system for processing. The processing produces invoices, packing slips, and other necessary documents. Some orders, including rush orders, are processed during the day on "rush" accounting machines, which prepare the packing slips and other documents. This allows the early processing of rush orders.

Processing steps. All orders are checked to determine that all information required for processing is present. Certain information such as "ship to" addresses is highlighted. All orders to be sent to the rush operation are segregated and other orders are segregated by type such as mail order and general account. If any irregularities are present (for example, discounts beyond accepted limits), the order is directed to a supervisor for approval.

After the pre-edit step, orders are sorted by state and distributed to the edit clerks. The edit clerks follow a series of procedures that provide for the entering of proper shipping information on coding sheets, called order-data forms. Product-data forms, additional coding sheets, are also prepared. The procedures that provide for the completion of the coding forms require the entry of "constants" into particular fields if certain conditions are met. These values are, of course, ultimately punched, verified, and converted to tape.

The order-data forms and the product-data forms are checked against the orders to see that all necessary information has been coded. These forms are the source-coding sheets from which keypunching is performed. After the computer processing, the invoices are checked for keypunch errors or omissions. This completes the processing in the existing order-entry system.

Personnel. The existing process involves 31 employees, plus an estimate of at least 14 keypunch operators. The functions of the 31 employees are allocated as follows:

Pre-edit	6
Edit: General accounts	7
Wholesale	7
Export	2
Mail order	2
Quality control	7

Keypunching is performed by a keypunch pool, and the number of people involved in this operation is not constant. An estimate of six million cards per year was provided as a guide to the keypunch time. This indicates that more than 14 people are involved in keypunch alone, not including any that might be required for verification. This example is an estimate of keypunch time and personnel requirements for a specific job.

Given:

$$6,000,000 \text{ cards/year} = 115,000 \text{ cards/week}$$

processed at 30 characters punched per card produces

$$115,000 \times 30 = 3,450,000 \text{ characters/week}$$

This activity is performed at 6,000 key strokes per hour. Thus,

$$\frac{3,450,000}{6,000} = 575 \text{ hours/week}$$

Assuming a 40-hour week, then

$$\frac{575}{40} = 14 \text{ operators (approximately)}$$

Volume of orders. The number of orders is estimated as 35,000 per month. This is subdivided as follows:

Wholesale	8,000
General account	8,000
Mail order	15,000
Export	1,000
Rush	3,000

Proposed System Description and Operation

The proposed system is an on-line dedicated computer system in which orders are entered by clerks through CRT data-entry terminals. The clerk enters the order information by means of a keyboard and the information is displayed on the screen. The clerk is led through the order-entry procedure by an interactive, conversational computer program, assuring a high degree of accuracy in the entered data.

Orders are stored on a disk file as they are prepared at the terminal. They are formulated to resemble the image of the punch card that results from the card-to-tape conversion in the existing system. This is provided to minimize or eliminate any change in the programs of the existing large-computer billing operation.

A customer file and a product file are available on line on random-access disk drives. The customer's account number and the product code number are entered into the output record when the disk is accessed, using a customer-name key word or an abbreviated product-title key word. The completed orders are stored on the disk file until it is desired to start the invoice operation on the IBM 370 system. This can be done as frequently as desired. Through a command given at the console, the completed orders can be transferred from the disk through the computer interface into the large-computer system. The interface simulates the tape drive normally accepted by the large system.

Equipment configuration. The minicomputer order-entry system consists of the following hardware:

Sixteen CRT data-entry terminals.
One minicomputer with 56K characters of memory.
One head-per-track disk, 500,000-character capacity.
One movable-head disk, similar to IBM 2314.
One interface for direct transfer of data between computers.
One console printer (Teletype or similar).

Order entry. The pre-edit function in the old system will continue to exist, but will have some of its present functions eliminated. The pre-edit clerks will continue to review all orders to assure that they contain all information needed for completion. Clerks will still be expected to resolve any irregularities, but they will no longer be required to highlight information or segregate orders according to type or for rush status. The pre-edit clerk will also assign an appropriate invoice number to each order. The number is to be put on each order form and will be keyed into the system by the edit clerk. All orders will be delivered to the order-entry clerks without segregation or sorting. An estimated four pre-edit clerks will be required.

Files. Two main files, the customer master and the product files, are required for this system. Four additional directory files are to be used for determination of product identification. All six files are described as follows:

Customer Master File (indexed)
Record size   138 bytes or characters
Number of records   80,000
Approximate total size   12 million bytes
Product File (indexed)
Record size   100 bytes
Number of records   20,000
Approximate total size   2 million bytes
Key Files (sequential)
Record size   20 bytes
Number of records   45,000
Approximate total size   1 million bytes
Transaction Files (sequential)
Record size   100 bytes
Number of records   10,000 (daily maximum)
Approximate total size   1 million bytes
Customer Key Name File
(sequential)
Record size   20 bytes
Number of records   160,000 maximum
Approximate total size   3.2 million bytes
Supplementary Files for Statistics
(negligible size)

Processing. Order entry is accomplished through CRT data-input terminals in a conversational, interactive manner. An example of the order-entry processing is given below. The procedure is ordered according to whether the operator performs a function (left side of page) or the computer performs the operation (right side).

Order-Entry Processing Procedure

Operator	*System*
1. Keys in invoice number.	
	2. Performs logic test on numbers, such as sequence and test for all numerics. (If incorrect, CRT screen signals by blinking the numbers. A correct number would then be entered.) Stores number on output record.

Order-Entry Processing Procedure (*Continued*)

Operator	System
	3. "Regular Account?"
4. *Yes* or *No*.	
	5. If *No*, go to step 40. If *Yes*, "Customer?"
6. Customer key name.	
	7. Searches file. If no hit, searches customer key-name file. Returns to operator a series of possible customer names.
8. Operator selects proper name.	
	9. Selects proper customer account. Displays full name and part of address for operator verification.
10. Operator verifies proper customer.	
	11. Customer number stored on output record.
	12. System stores certain constants such as 1 in invoice type, and special handling in message. All information put in output record.
	13. "Special discount?"
14. *Yes* or *No*.	
	15. If *Yes*, special discount alternative module is displayed on screen for operator to make proper choice.
16. Operator makes selection.	
	17. "Ship to address?"
18. Keys in address or "No."	
	19. "How to ship?"
20. Operator enters value.	
	21. Sets up array on screen with heading for product name, code, quantity, and price.
22. Enters abbreviated name or code of product or product type.	
	23. Displays array of products.

Order-Entry Processing Procedure (*Continued*)

Operator	*System*
24. Enters quantity and price, if required, in array.	
	25. Enters price if not entered by operator. Stores item in output record.
26. Enters continue or end signal.	
	27. If continue signal entered, processing returns to step 22. If end signal is entered, processing continues to close out order, accumulate totals, and otherwise complete the order.

As shown in this operator-system sequence, the operator is stepped through the procedure by the use of displayed requests for information. As the information is put into the system by the operator, small program modules check the data for validity and logic values. After the data is entered and validated, it is stored on the disk file in a format similar to the present card layout.

The proposed system operates in a time-sharing mode. The operating system shares the time among all terminals entering orders, so that each terminal seems to have the use of the entire computer. The number of input stations required depends on the amount of input volume, and can be estimated on that basis. For example, say that the business discussed in this Case 2 has an order volume of 35,000 each month. These orders generate about 170,000 items (or lines) to be processed monthly. To estimate the number of work stations needed for input of order-entry data, assume that two minutes input time is required to enter information relating to customer, shipping, and other information. Four items (or lines) of products can be entered per minute. Then

$$35,000 \times 2 \text{ minutes} = 70,000 \text{ minutes/month}$$

and

$$170,000 \times \text{¼ minute} = 43,000 \text{ minutes/month}$$

Thus, the total time of processing is 113,000 minutes per month, or 1,884 hours per month. By averaging four weeks to the month and 40 hours per week per operator, with 10 percent reduction in efficiency for personal needs, the processing time is computed as

$$4 \times 40 \times 0.9 = 144 \text{ hours/month/person}$$

From this it is seen that the number of input stations should be

$$\frac{1,884}{144} = 13.1$$

or approximately 13 to 14. This number is effectual only when operators have completed an initial familiarization period on the job. If only a single-shift (day or night) operation is scheduled, an increase to 16 stations is suggested so as to provide for a margin of safety.

Other procedures. Other procedures that relate to the order-entry function and should be included in the system are log-in/log-out and statistical or totaling routines. These can be as detailed as desired. The following is proposed:

1. The operator logs in her code (initials), a start code, and the time of day when she starts.
2. To log out, she enters a log-out code, the time of day, and her identification code.
3. Every time any one operator logs out, the complete status of the 16 entry stations is logged on the console printer; that is, the identification of each operator is listed with the time of day.
4. The operator identification code can be printed on each order so that data-entry complaints can be quickly identified with an operator.
5. Statistics on the number of orders may be maintained in any way desired. It is proposed that daily totals be kept for the number of orders by operator, by station, and by type of order. These measures of operator efficiency will be printed out daily at the end of processing or at any time on request.

Output. As each order is processed, the information keyed in or developed is stored on the transaction area of the disk file. It is edited into a format that the large computer system will find most compatible. This will probably be in the design of the output of the present card-to-tape conversion program.

The transfer of the order information to the large computer is accomplished through an interface under the control of the large computer. To the large computer, it appears that the interface is a tape drive and can be appended to the multiplexor or selector channel.

New System Costs

Hardware costs. Costs of the equipment include not only the purchase price but also monthly maintenance. Table 9-2 lists the amounts applicable in each case for associated components of the system.

Acquisition is normally via a payback lease, with the transfer of ownership at the end of the lease. The monthly costs of a five-year lease can be calculated by using a factor of about 2.2 percent of the purchase price ($150,000). This results in a monthly payment of $3,300. When maintenance is a separate expense ($900, as shown in Table 9-2), the total monthly payment would be about $4,200. It should be noted that outright purchase or rental options are also available, but are not as frequently used. An exact calculation will require consultation with appropriate company tax authorities to determine the factors now being used by the company.

Software. The software required for the system is categorized in the following manner:

1. Operating system: This is the software system that controls all of the processing and which also has the software drivers required for interfacing with the required peripherals. This package is supplied by the computer manufacturer. There is no charge for these programs.

2. Application programs: These programs for the basic order-entry processing are a series of small modules. The number of instructions needed is estimated as

$$50 \text{ instructions/module} \times 40 \text{ modules/processing path}$$
$$\times 4 \text{ processing paths} = 8{,}000 \text{ instructions}$$

with an additional 300 instructions for CRT special reading and display macros. *Estimated cost for application program = $45,000.*

3. File management software: The software establishes directories and provides for file organization according to proper access method. *Estimated cost = $40,000.*

4. Interface software: This provides any necessary modification to any of the supplied interface software or drivers (if any) and for contingency. *Estimated cost = $15,000.*

5. *Total software cost estimate = $100,000.* This estimate is based on the number of instructions and a rate of $4 to $10 per instruction, depending on the language used. As such, the cost is the same, whether it is done in house or by a systems house. The price includes the complete programming and testing, starting when the

specifications have been established, through the installation of the debugged program.

Table 9-2. Hardware costs.

Quantity	Item	Approximate Purchase Price ($000)	Approximate Monthly Maintenance
1	Computer, with 64K of 16-bit words, real-time clock, bootstrap loader, all hardware, power supply, cabinet, and console printer	$ 30	$250
1	250 million 16-bit word, head-per-track disk, and interface	15	75
1	Disk drive and interface	45	125
1	Direct computer transfer interface (hardware and software package)	10	50
16	CRT terminals, 72 × 20 characters, 1,200 bauds	50	400
		$150	$900

Implementation

Implementation will require about 9 to 12 months for software development and startup. This time estimate assumes that the systems analysis effort has been performed so that a complete, detailed set of specifications is available. The required effort may be divided between the professional staff and a qualified systems house. Two general divisions of tasks and responsibility are recommended.

Professional staff. The in-house staff works with the systems house to develop operating software, develops application programs, and appropriately modifies any large-computer programs necessary (not included in estimate).

Systems house. Responsibility for overall hardware integration and system effectiveness lies with the systems house staff. These people provide working hardware configuration for program development until equipment is delivered. (This is essential because delivery of some components may require a number of months.) They also must develop operating software and train the professional staff.

Benefits

It is obvious that two major displaceable costs will result from the reduction of operators from 45 to 20 and the elimination of the rush-order equipment. An additional, but less obvious, saving will result when six million punched cards will no longer be required. At $1.50 per thousand, this represents a saving of about $9,000 per year.

Less quantitative but important benefits are expected because of greater customer satisfaction when fewer errors are made and delivery is faster.

SYSTEM
SELECTION TECHNIQUES

A most commonly asked question is: How do I choose the best computer to do the job? The proper answer should get across the point that it is seldom necessary and very often wasteful to choose the *best* computer. It is proper to choose the least costly computer, with expansion capability that will exceed the requirements of the job, even though it is not the best computer for the application.

There is a tendency to take the technician's approach—to evaluate all hardware features of the computer and to choose the best technical model. The procedure that should be employed is the one which eliminates computers that cannot do the job and then judges those remaining on their cost-benefit characteristics. Depending on the nature of the job and resources available, the selection may be made based on either of the following methods:

1. The lowest-cost system that meets the performance requirements.
2. The system that satisfies cost and performance standards and has the greatest performance-to-cost ratio.

Variable Factors

Many variables affect the selection criteria. The selection method and criteria are totally dependent upon the use to which the computer is being put. For example, selection criteria for a

small batch-processing system would be very different from those
for a communications processor.

The point of view and method of operation of the user company
also affect the choice of pertinent criteria. Factors that affect the
selection process include items such as the level of computer experience within the company. If the company has no programming
experience, its choice would be either to hire or train competent
programmers or to buy a complete turnkey system from a vendor
who will select the hardware, develop the software, integrate the
system, install it, and train the workers. The criteria for selecting
the proper system are very sensitive with regard to the degree to
which management wants its technical personnel involved in the
development and running of the system. Another consideration is
whether the system is one of a kind or one of very similar types
within the company. Also to be taken in account as an effect on
selection criteria is the important question of where the system will
be installed. Its geographic location as well as the working environment must be known so that proper criteria can be established,
and proximity of the installation to the vendor's service center is an
important aspect of this requirement.

The environment in which the system is to operate must be
precisely known in order to establish a proper basis for selection. If
the computer were to be used in an out-of-doors location subjected
to extreme variations in temperature, or in a factory where there is
heavy vibration or other detrimental environmental effects, the
criteria that reflect these facts could be the most important ones in
the selection process.

Summing up, the variable factors that must be considered in
establishing the selection criteria include:

System use.
Degree of intended involvement of company personnel.
Number of similar systems to be installed in the future.
Environmental factors.
Geographic location.

Universal Factors

In addition to the factors that cause the selection procedure to
vary with each system, a number of very important items must
always be considered. The most important factor that must be

entered into the evaluation is the nature of the vendor—his experience, his competence, and (most important) his financial stability. As noted previously, several hundred minicomputer manufacturers have been active in this field. Many are no longer in business. A user will not want to buy a computer from a manufacturer unless he is certain that the manufacturer will be around in the future to supply service, upgrading, and spare parts. By far the most important consideration in the selection of the system is the financial stability of the manufacturer.

In the selection procedure, avoid the strictly technical evaluations. Avoid starting the evaluation with the benchmark tests in which sample routines or programs are written for a number of computers so that their performances can be compared. These procedures are very expensive and should be used only when deciding between the last few contenders. However, it is best to determine first if the benchmark results really matter. It is frequently very evident that the capabilities of these machines far exceed their requirements. These tests should be used only if acceptable performance is questionable, and the analyst should not be swayed by the technician's approach. He should apply normal business judgment such as he might apply to selection of a new machine.

It is also very important to look for a company with a full line of equipment, since the system should preferably contain only equipment from a single manufacturer. If the manufacturer is a stable one, he will stand behind the performance and assist in the repair when things go wrong. This service adds a high degree of security, even if a third party such as a systems house developed, assembled, programmed, and installed the system. If the systems house is committed to only one vendor's equipment, the system and the user company are not vulnerable if that systems house should go out of business, change its business, or lose some of its key people in the future. Upward mobility is also assured when a company with a full line of compatible equipment is selected.

Many people insist that it does not make sense to spend $30,000 to evaluate a $30,000 computer, and to those who examine the argument superficially, this appears to be true. To others, a comparison on this basis neglects long-term benefits translated in terms of dollar values. Even though, in general, a small computer system will require less evaluation time and money than a large system, in any case sufficient evaluation must be performed, keeping in mind the importance of minimizing evaluation expenditures. Actually, what we are looking at is not a $30,000 computer—although this may be what the hardware costs—but a continuing operation. Involved with that computer are time, people, and other company resources. The people include those who studied the system, programmed the system, wrote procedures, and operate the system. Hopefully, the system will be used for five years, maybe ten years, in which its operation will contribute to the profitability of the company. The cost differential between a good system and a poor system might then be many hundreds of thousands of dollars. It might make sense, then, to spend $30,000, $50,000, or possibly more to be certain that the system selected is the right one.

Defining the System

When relatively sure of the type of system that will suit the company's needs, the analyst should check with a number of vendors to locate similar system installations. Then inquiries to managers in these companies will ascertain which vendors have supplied good systems and reliable service. Or, preferably, a consultant who is independent of a manufacturer but is knowledgeable and experienced in the minicomputer field should be contacted. Such a person can aid tremendously in computer selection. This investment in time and money could be the wisest one made by the analyst in the entire development and installation of the system.

The user defines the specification for the system in his own terms. He states what has to be performed, not how to perform it. He does not try to translate these into computer or technical terms, but leaves this to the people who are developing the system. This practice will actually provide better understanding and give much greater assurance of obtaining the precise system desired.

The external characteristics of the systems should be specified. For example, in a conversational real-time system the worst-case response time should be stated (that is, the maximum tolerable delay time for the computer to respond to the user). Would it be one second? Would it be three seconds? Rarely would it be as much as five seconds. Comparable systems or simulated system performance should be viewed to obtain realistic values and then these values should be stated in the analyst's terms.

The volumes for which the system should be designed are also specified. These volumes are not today's volumes but are design volumes that must take into consideration the anticipated growth during the system life. If great increases in volumes are expected, two sets of volumes are given, one that provides for sufficient growth for the next couple of years and the other for large future anticipations. A separate quote may be requested for the changes required to get from the first system size to the ultimate size. This will provide a good method to judge the expansion capability of the system.

The description of the company output must include volume, data fields, the order or sequence of data, and all facts pertinent to its method of doing business. Sample input and output forms are drawn up and the same information is supplied to each of the vendors.

Vendors work in preparing the bids, but the company must provide them with accurate information, respond effectively to their questions, and maintain an open avenue of discourse with them. Complete understanding is essential. Unless there is good communication, the analyst may find after the system is developed that he and the vendor were talking about two systems with significantly different requirements.

If the technical limitations of the computer are in doubt, the vendor should be asked to supply some computer timings on the performance of a sample function. The function should be one that is an important and recurring one in the processing, and which is suspected to be particularly taxing on the computer. This type of problem might be the multiplication of two numbers representing a quantity and a unit price. By providing each vendor with the characteristics of this problem, such as the number of digits to which the unit price must be carried out, or how large a number of the quantity might be, he will be able to provide the programming instructions to perform this and also estimate the length of time required by the computer for performing it. By comparing the results of performing the same problem, a rough comparison of each vendor's computer can be obtained. Vendors will work with the analyst as long as he is cooperative and sincere about obtaining a system that will fulfill company objectives.

A Method for Selection*

Development of specifications. It is assumed that the problem has been analyzed and a general solution has been decided upon.

---

*The Additional Readings section lists a number of publications suggesting valuable alternative evaluation techniques; however, most are more technical and more complicated than the one proposed here.

Then the minimum performance characteristics of the desired system are to be developed. Performance requirements and design volumes are to be detailed. The more care taken with this step the better. Accurate, detailed specifications will save time and expense and assure getting what is really wanted.

Selection of competent vendors. A list of qualified vendors is developed. This list is based on the company analyst's experience or knowledge or the knowledge of someone who is competent in the field. If no better means are available, a letter may be broadcast to all possible suppliers, asking them for a statement of their interest and their competence. This should be done well in advance of requesting the bids.

Solicitation of bids. Specifications are mailed to the qualified suppliers, and three to five weeks are allowed for their return bid. A vendor will require at least two weeks for a proper bid on even small jobs, but no more than four weeks is usually necessary for even larger types of systems. With an additional week for mailing, all bids should be returned in five weeks.

Development of evaluation criteria. The evaluation criteria are developed before bids are returned. All relevant factors are listed. Weights are assigned to each factor, depending on the relative importance of the factors. The Bid Evaluation Sheet (see Appendix) shows such a list. Each factor is rated on a scale of 0 to 10. The rating is multiplied by a weighting factor to put the criteria in proper perspective. Some factors are critical. As shown in the Bid Evaluation Sheet, a rating of zero for certain criteria may result in disqualification. This is a commonly used technique, and the Appendix example is an actual application developed and used by an existing company. The factors and weights can be adjusted for use in other applications and other environments. In addition to its primary use, such an evaluation sheet has value simply as a checklist.

Evaluation of performance. The evaluation proceeds by rating each bid according to the established criteria. Annotations are usually added to the evaluation sheets to document key differences. The rating is multiplied by the factor weight and then all weighted factors are summed to obtain the total score of the bid.

Price determination. Prices are always supplied with bids. However, the bids supplied are almost never equivalent. Additions and modifications in price must be made to arrive at equivalent systems. For example, for vendor A's system, additional software may have to be developed and added to his bid, whereas vendor B

Table 10–1. Ranking of bids.

Vendor	Equivalent Price	Score
Minimum allowable rating		500
C	$ 67,600	628
G	72,100	725
F	75,330	800
A	87,350	625*
B	89,000	820
E	97,200	800*
Maximum allowable price	100,000	
D	103,250	870*

*Eliminated.

may have included it in his bid; or some additional interfacing or equipment might have to be added to a bidded system so that both bids are comparable and both systems are equivalent. Thus, in the comparison of the bids, it becomes necessary to adjust the quoted costs when comparing them so that the costs reflect equivalent systems. The system price used in the evaluation is this equivalent price. If payments or costs are spread over a period of time, the time value of money should (ideally) be entered into consideration. If this is done, the present value of the equivalent price should be used in the comparison.

Cost versus system capability. Bids are ranked and listed according to ascending equivalent price, with their score noted. A bid lower on the list (higher price) and with a lower score can be eliminated (see Table 10–1). From this point on, the selection is entirely subjective unless it has been established that the lowest-cost bid that exceeds the minimum standard will be selected, in which case the job is done. If this is not the case, it must be decided if the additional capability is worth the additional price. This can be done only subjectively, although referring to the annotated evaluation sheets will be valuable.

This is not the only method by which a bid can be evaluated, but it is an effective and presumably complete one.

The Continuing System

The system is a dynamic entity—the process is not over once the choice has been made. The company will live with and work with the system for many years to come. The costs that really matter are the full life-cycle costs of the system. This includes development, operation, maintenance, system changes, and system downtime. In making the decision, initial price is not so important as the anticipated lifetime cost of the system because the objective of the company is to buy and install not only an economical and effective system, but also one that delivers continuing value. Careful evaluation, careful selection, and placing more importance on the quality of the vendor than on the technology of the hardware will help a company attain this long-term, effective solution.

Reliability

The minicomputer, in its most frequent and most desirable type of use, requires extremely high reliability. It is common to use the minicomputer in a real-time environment, but the failure of a real-time system means that the entire operation halts—thus idling people and possibly losing information. The minicomputer system is usually a free-standing configuration, dedicated to a single application. In these situations it is not usual to have backup equipment like that in a large data processing center. Fortunately, the reduced complexity of both associated hardware and software makes minicomputer systems more reliable than their large-system counterparts. Reliability depends on the application. In some applications, reliability means that the system will operate continuously; in others, it means no prolonged periods of unavailability ("prolonged" is defined differently by different users).

Software reliability. Studies of downtime in large-computer systems indicate that about 75 percent of the diagnosed causes of system failure are due to software problems. Some of these problems were due to program bugs, but most were due to failures of the operating system in allocating and scheduling internal memory and other resources, particularly in a multiprogramming environment. The minicomputer system software is less complex and therefore more likely to have fewer errors. However, since the minicomputer system software is used by fewer people for fewer hours than large-computer software, these bugs go undetected longer. Application bugs in real-time programs are difficult to locate, difficult to correct, and cause much damage; however, problems tend to increase exponentially with program size, and the smaller minicomputer programs should be more error-free than those used on the larger computer systems.

Hardware reliability. Reliability considerations start with the design. To an extent, reliability can be built into the system. Techniques such as microprogramming, in addition to being functionally valuable, also increase the reliability of the system. Furthermore, modifying the configuration has a large effect on reliability and must be a major factor in system selection.

A system that is down or malfunctioning costs a large amount of money. Interruption of operations means a period when workers are underutilized or not utilized at all. Then there is the cost of repair such as new parts and new equipment, and possibly special personnel will be needed. When the system is again running, extra effort is needed to catch up on the work backlog. This usually results temporarily in inefficient operation as well as overtime pay to people during the catch-up period.

The minicomputer, like all other modern computers, is a very reliable device. The intense use of integrated circuits (IC) reduces the number of components used. The intrinsic reliability of the IC is much greater than the reliability of the discrete components it replaces. The simpler logic, construction, and data paths further reduce the number of components required. Reliability is improved tremendously by the drastic reduction in the number of components and the corresponding reduction in wiring and circuit connections. This elimination of many thousands of external circuit-to-circuit interconnections removes the chief cause of failure in electronic systems.

The modular construction of all parts of these machines allows easy and rapid maintenance. Plug-in modules can be readily replaced, reducing the mean time to repair, which is just as important as the mean time to failure. With a supply of spare modules and the manufacturer's diagnostic programs, repairs can be made rapidly.

The reliability of the peripheral equipment is much more of a problem than the computer. Disk devices, printers, tape devices, and so forth, being electromechanical devices with moving parts, have significantly lower reliability.

Table 10–2 gives some conservative but typical figures for the average or mean time before failure (MTBF) and mean time to repair (MTTR) of minicomputer equipment. It can be seen that the mechanical devices, such as disk and tape drives, have a relatively low MTBF. High peripheral reliability and therefore high system reliability are usually attained by redundancy. In critical installations, extra tape drives or disk devices are employed to back up the system. In very critical installations, entire dual systems, including the computer, are used.

Table 10–2. Mean time to failure and repair of minicomputer equipment.

Unit	MTBF (hr)*	MTTR (hr)*
Moving-head disk drive	1,000	1
Fixed-head disk drive	1,500	1
Disk controller	14,000	2
Tape drive	1,000	2
Tape controller	20,000	3
Processor and console	7,700	1.5
4K core memory	34,700	1.5
8K core memory	25,000	1.5
Real-time clock	200,000	1
Multiplexer	40,000	1
Bus switch	20,000	1
Arithmetic unit	200,000	1
CRT terminals	2,000	2
Computer with 28K memory	3,500	2

*Figures have been adjusted in a conservative way from manufacturer-quoted data.

Consider a computer system that has 28,000 (28K) words of memory, a moving-head disk and controller, a fixed-head disk with its controller, and a large number of CRT terminals connected through a multiplexer. Any number of the CRT terminals may fail without affecting the system, but if any of the other components fail, the system becomes inoperative. The MTBF of one such system can

Table 10–3. Mean time to failure.

		Months to Failure					Failures per Year (7 days, 24 hr/ day)
	MTBF (hr)	7 Days (24 hr/ day)	6 Days (24 hr/ day)	6 Days (16 hr/ day)	6 Days (8 hr/ day)	5 Days (8 hr/ day)	
Computer with 28K memory	3,500	4.8	5.6	8.4	16.8	20.1	2.5
Computer system (no redundancy)	476	0.65	0.76	1.1	2.2	2.7	18.4
Computer system with redundant disks	2,210	3.0	3.5	5.3	10.6	12.7	4.0

be calculated to be 476 hours. This means that in a one-shift day, five-day-week operation, it would be expected to run an average of 2.7 months between failures. Doubling up the lower-reliability disks results in a threefold increase in the system reliability. This is very often worth the $20,000 or more additional expenditure.

Table 10–3 shows the average number of months to failure for the computer, the original system, and the system improved with redundant disks. The high computer reliability and the importance of redundancy for high system reliability are obvious.

CONTRACTS
AND VENDOR RELATIONS

A mistake frequently made by the computer user is to accept all terms established by the vendor. This may happen if a user who has arduously and extensively studied the question of whether to get a computer, and what computer to get, becomes very impatient at the important installation phase. When he has finally obtained his management's approval, he may rush through all succeeding phases to get the system installed as soon as possible. The expenditure of time and effort in working with the vendor is a worthwhile investment, and almost always saves time and money in the long run. It could mean the difference between getting the system he wants and getting a system that will cause more problems than it solves.

Before development work proceeds, two steps must be completed: negotiations and contracting. Negotiations with the vendor are conducted to assure that there is complete understanding between the user and supplier. This will help assure that the user obtains precisely the system he wants. Through discussions regarding the precise and final specifications for the system, the user and vendor will arrive at the approximate costs of many system features and options. This allows the user to estimate whether the value of a particular feature is worth its price. These discussions enable him to maximize his benefit at lowest cost while minimizing risk.

The contract is a legal agreement that specifies the rights and obligation of the buyer and seller or, in this case, the user and the vendor. It would be erroneous to assume that, after many meetings and months of discussions, the terms of the agreement are so well understood and the proposed system is so well defined that no contract is necessary. Regardless of such an understanding and the degree of confidence the user has in the vendor, there is no substitute, in terms of protection to the user, for a carefully considered contract.

Many items in the delivered system are subject to negotiation. The contract will eliminate later problems by specifying the responsibilities of each party. It will, to some small extent, help to protect the user against financial loss due to delivery delay of the product desired. The contract will also bind the vendor to supply the system at the price negotiated and agreed upon. A good contract defines each party's responsibility, helps in producing the proper environment, and assures (or, at least, greatly improves) the chances for successfully installing the desired system.

In order to install a computer system a company has to work with and through a group whose main concern and main area of knowledge is their equipment or system and not the company's business. There is always a vendor involved, and in many cases more than one. Whether the user is doing most of the work or obtaining a turnkey system, he must deal with the vendors. In fact, the organization that is confident enough to assemble its own system may frequently, in an effort to minimize hardware costs, buy equipment from several different suppliers and end up dealing with many vendors.

The following comments regarding contracts and negotiations apply almost universally to all users who are installing a computer system. If a systems house or computer manufacturer supplies the complete system—hardware and software—it is obvious that negotiations and a contract are essential. It is also essential to have a contract with the suppliers of the major pieces of hardware when the user is taking on the responsibility of putting the entire system together. In this case, the user obtains a measure of protection in assuring that the hardware specified will work properly as a system.

The key point in the entire procurement procedure is to concentrate on, recognize, and stipulate exactly what is wanted from a *system*. A collection of pieces of hardware is of no value if the software that is expected to make the system work is not functioning. The negotiations and contract must zero in at this point—the deliverable item must be a working system, not merely a piece of equipment.

Negotiating with the Vendor

Contrary to what many people think, vendors do not treat everyone alike. Although vendors operate under legal restrictions (such as the Robinson-Patman Act) and procedural rules that encourage fair and equal treatment, users can obtain benefits and considerations beyond the standard amount simply by maintaining constructive communications. If a company happens to be in a situation that can provide long-range benefits to the vendor, it may be able to negotiate some substantial cost reductions. For example, if the application planned for installation is one that the vendor believes to have a substantial market, he might very likely fund part of the development to gain the experience or to be able to market the same application with other companies. Also, depending on the work load of the vendor, he may be in a position to supply additional services to improve his customer relations. Sometimes, special favorable treatment can be obtained just by asking for it, particularly when the situation is competitive.

Special treatment can be realized indirectly in a number of ways. Potential users should be aware of at least the following:

1. The vendor may supply significant amounts of systems analysis without charge.
2. Programming of special routines may be supplied by the vendor under the guise of supplying system or utility software.
3. The vendor may buy back the application program for re-use in other installations.
4. Lower price can be negotiated for the use of the system as a demonstration location.
5. Lower price can be negotiated to meet competition.
6. Various amounts of training, above the normal amount, can be supplied.
7. A development system, or time on the vendor's system, might be supplied to save the user several months' rental payments.
8. Free consulting services might be supplied.
9. Data conversion and other types of installation help could be provided.

Additional items that must be worked out with the vendor are the system specifications, the definition of system acceptance, and checkpoints or milestones in the development of the system. These items are extremely important and will be covered individually in the subsequent sections.

After negotiating with the vendor and defining the desired system and the additional benefits he will supply, the user must retain these benefits by documenting the agreement. Skillfully negotiated benefits can be lost if they are not put in writing. These agreements must cover all mutually accepted points and must do so in language that the people performing the job can understand and which can be also used by nontechnical people who may be called upon to adjudicate disputes. Points hammered out in negotiations are often difficult to write, but they must be documented. Some aspects of the oral agreement may seem so clear to the participants that documentation appears to be redundant. And with the pressures and time restrictions due to the ongoing development effort, documentation of these agreements could be overlooked. Procurement, development, and negotiation involve so many details that little time may be retained for documenting the agreements. The result could be a belated realization that the fine print of a standard set of terms of conditions has been accepted, that these terms are highly favorable to the vendor, and that many requirements and concessions favorable to the user have not been included. Applicable written sources of agreements, such as specification sheets and memoranda of conversations with vendor personnel, should all be dated, retained in a central file, and finally included with the contract. Simplicity of the statements in the agreements has many virtues. They should be written in the words of the layman, avoiding both the tight legalistic terminology and the buzzword-loaded technical jargon. Technical terms should be defined. Agreements can then be used for the purpose intended—for guidance of the development people in their day-to-day actions—rather than to settle disputes.

System Specifications

Specifications for the system were developed when proposals and bids from the vendors were selected. After the vendor's selection, through discussions with him and because of additions or modifications, these specifications change somewhat. Before the actual development work is started, the vendor and user agree on a firm set of design specifications. System specifications are of two types: They may show how the system is composed, in which case they are called *design* specifications. Vendors usually prefer to define the system in these terms. The user should provide only *performance* specifications. These describe how the system works.

Defining the system by using performance specifications has two advantages:

1. It allows the nontechnical user to define the system in his terms. This makes him completely capable of determining acceptable system performance.
2. It allows the vendor to choose the components and design the system as he sees fit, which is his speciality. The user is less interested in how the item is made up as long as it performs and produces the desired results.

Without adequate performance specifications, precise definition of system acceptance will not be possible.

Accepting the System

The negotiations should establish the means for determining whether each item meets its performance standard before payment is due. The criteria for system acceptance should be carefully defined, not only to assure that the specifications are met but also so their fulfillment can be objectively and unequivocally judged, even by an outsider.

It must be kept in mind that an entire system is being acquired. Acceptance must be related to performance of the system. Performance of a printer or system peripheral is meaningless unless integrated with the entire system. This approach, by definition, includes the performance of software. To do otherwise, such as listing only equipment components, would be to overlook the most important and vulnerable part of the system. Vendors may assume that a computer system is ready for use when it is shipped to the user's location, and may call for payments to start at that time. Such a condition should never be accepted, since it makes no provision for installation time, faults in the equipment and in vendor-supplied software, or acceptance tests. Instead, suitable on-site tests of hardware and software should be agreed upon in the negotiations. Acceptance is to be made dependent upon the successful completion of these tests. Failure to pass should automatically call for correction of faults and their verification by repeating the entire test procedure. Thus an acceptance date should be set after this preliminary test of performance.

Preparation of specifications and acceptance test routines for large-computer systems are laborious, expensive, and time-consuming. Nevertheless, these matters are considered critical and should always be performed. With the minicomputer, because of the simpler application, computer system, and software usually involved, these important items are much simpler to prepare. But, from the point of view of the organization, the successful installation of the computer system might be more critical in the small company. Therefore, these crucial steps—development of written specifications and definition of acceptance—should never be omitted.

Deliverable Items

Having defined the system and the performance required by the system, the user might think he has completely nailed down the agreements with the vendor. Usually, this is not so. An explicit list and description of the items and services to be delivered by the vendor is necessary. The number one item is, of course, the computer system. Although a list of components of the computer system is of value to the user in many ways (to the installer of the system, to the person responsible for receiving the equipment, and to the purchasing agent), the important deliverable item is the working system. To receive the proper collection of computer hardware, printers, disk drives, and so forth, matters little if the combined system does not function properly.

The description of the deliverable system should be closely related to the acceptance criteria. The system to be delivered is not accepted when it is received at the loading dock. Neither is it accepted immediately after installing and running. Acceptance is a time-dependent condition. Systems, particularly the software portion, may not show any evidence of malfunction until a particular, unusual set of circumstances occurs. Thorough program debugging is extremely difficult. Complete accuracy is practically impossible to guarantee. As the size of the system increases, the likelihood that problems and errors will continue to show up long after acceptance also increases. Despite frequent assurances from salesmen to the contrary, people do not have the ability to anticipate the wide range of possible circumstances that must be provided for when designing, programming, and testing large systems.

Although it is true that computer users literally never have the assurance that their system is completely trouble free, a 30-day period to determine initial acceptance is usually satisfactory. However, during this 30-day period, the system should be run fairly frequently (two to three hours per day). This condition should always be described as *initial* acceptance. To the user, two criteria are important: the performance of the system in accomplishing its purpose in servicing the user; and the availability of the system to the user in terms of frequency and duration of failure.

The user is concerned about the following items pertaining to system malfunctions: frequency of failure; total inoperative time; and maximum length of time the system will be inoperative on a single failure. These items should be covered in the maintenance agreement, but should also be stated as a condition for acceptance. Actual values vary according to system complexity and the redundancy built into it. Strictly as an example: A typical downtime specification might be an average of one hour per week, and 20 hours per month with no single failure to last longer than 24 clock hours. Penalties would be invoked if these limitations were exceeded. In addition, the vendor's warranty would state that he is required to fix all malfunctions for a year to two years.

In addition to the main deliverable item—the working system—other items and services promised by the vendor should be explicitly described. These include documentation, training, installation assistance, programming and system assistance, and consultation. If the vendor has a standard list of support items that fulfill the user's needs, then there is no need to rewrite these items. However, usually the vendor's list is not sufficiently descriptive to be completely satisfactory, so the user should complete the description of the items. Some of the items that may be overlooked are described below.

Software. The software that the vendor is to supply should be listed. If there is specific utility software, such as a code conversion routine or a sort program that is important to the application, it should be explicitly listed.

It is also advisable to specify not only the names of the items but also the form and support for that software, such as flow diagrams, printouts, punched-card decks, magnetic tapes, diagnostic instructions, and interfacing instructions.

Training. Specify the number of training days, the type of training, the number of people to be trained without cost, and the schedule. Also determine and include as part of the agreement the cost, if any, for training additional people at a later date.

Documentation. Several sets of hardware and software documentation should be delivered.

Support. If systems analysis, programming, or particularly installation support is expected, it should be considered as another item upon which acceptance is based.

Evaluation Checkpoints

The vendor and user should, at the outset, establish a series of checkpoints at which progress is to be formally evaluated. It is always good procedure to do this, regardless of the size of the project. Although a system can be physically rather small, its importance to the user may be quite large. If the new system is not functioning as it should and when it should, some amount of financial loss is likely to result. Establishing milestones or checkpoints prevents surprises.

The vendor and user should establish a schedule for the completion of the job. Included in this schedule should be dates for the completion of discrete and important activities within the small job. At these predesignated dates, progress should be reviewed and appropriate action taken if the job is not on schedule.

Typical review points or milestones include:

Final agreement on the system specifications.
Inspection of the assembled hardware system. This is usually
    first assembled and tested at the vendor's location.
Installation of the hardware at the user's location.
Complete conversion of user's data and file records.
Design system acceptance test.
Initiation of training.
Performance acceptance test.
Cutover to new system.

Contracting with the Vendor

A written contract should be the culmination of the negotiations and developments that the user and vendor have completed. The contract for the computer should cover the entire hardware and software system to be provided by the vendor. It should be based on a clear description of the functions to be performed by the operating system rather than lists of components, however complete.

Ideally, different types of specialists should be involved in the preparation or review of the contract. In addition to the computer specialist, assistance should be provided by the purchasing agent, a financial adviser, and a legal consultant, just as in any other major purchase. Some basic facts should be understood by all involved in developing the contract. Computer systems frequently constitute a more integral part of a company's operation than do other types of machines, and the user quickly becomes completely dependent on their scheduled availability, continued functioning, and easy expandability. Even though delivery and performance guarantees, as well as penalties, may be included in the contract, the user never makes money by collecting damages and penalties. Including these in the contract merely shows evidence of the vendor's confidence that he will be able to keep his promises and provides him with some extra incentive to do so.

Financial Considerations

The primary financial consideration is, of course, the purchase price of the entire system. However, while this total price payable to the vendor might be the most important consideration, it is only the starting point in the financial analysis.

Types of agreements: buy, rent, lease. Vendors of computer systems usually prefer to sell their equipment outright. However, this is not always the best approach for the user. A rental or lease contract with the vendor spaces the payments over a considerable period of time and, in addition to the straight financial benefits, provides the user additional bargaining power to obtain concessions or improved service from the vendors. Rental agreements call for monthly payments and are cancelable by the customer on short notice without penalty after a minimum period. The minimum period varies with the vendor and can range from three months to two years.

Lease arrangements are always possible even if the vendor does not provide leasing directly. Many companies specialize in this function and will buy the system from either the vendor or the user and lease it back for monthly payments over a fixed period of time. Lease agreements entail lower monthly charges than rent, but require a longer commitment (usually three to seven years). The longer the lease term, the lower the monthly rate. A typical lease rate would be 2.2 percent of the purchase price, payable each month for five years.

Equity, or payback, leases are common and quite useful. When the lease term is completed, the payment of an additional sum (sometimes only a nominal amount is charged to satisfy legal considerations) allows the user to obtain ownership.

Termination or conversion. Termination charges and the method of conversion from one plan to another should be explored and evaluated at the start. Particularly important are the conversion terms. Usually, provisions included in the lease or rental plan will allow the user to apply some portion of his monthly payments toward the purchase of the equipment. If eventual possession of the equipment is at least a possibility (and it is difficult to conceive of any situation where it is not at least a possibility), then this item should be included in the contract and factored into the economic evaluation. There are two reasons for this: The equipment usually has residual value, and a minicomputer system normally has a very long life, since its use is relatively immune to technological innovations. The cost for analysis, design, and installation outweighs any economic advantages brought about by using the latest and hottest version of the computer that results in rather long-term system uses.

When a lease contract does not provide for ownership by the lessee at completion, a reduced rate should be quoted for renewal of the lease. One-half of the original lease would be considered a typical renewal rate for a five-year lease. The lessee is under no obligation to renew and can negotiate other terms at the renewal time. However, a renewal clause gives some protection by providing a guaranteed maximum rate and should be included in the original contract.

Schedule of payments. Because of the time value of money, it is obvious that deferring a payment is equivalent to saving money. In addition, if the vendor has money coming to him, he is more likely to respond to your needs than otherwise. However, it is important to treat the vendor fairly and he should be paid promptly for the services he supplies. Therefore, just as it is important to tie acceptance of the system to performance, the payments to the vendor should also be related to performance, with system acceptance by the user as the key item in the payment schedule.

Payments to a vendor for a total system development— hardware and software—are normally made in installments called *progress payments*. The timing of each installment is best tied to the milestones that were developed at contract time. The amount paid at each milestone is negotiable and should be also included in the contract on that basis.

Payments for software may be, and should be, separated from hardware payments. The payment for the software should never be completed before the system is totally accepted. Payments for the hardware are negotiated separately. Payments may be started when the hardware configuration is delivered or, if the user has negotiated hard enough and has contracted for a complete system, payments for the hardware may start at the time of acceptance of the system. In no case should the payments for hardware start before all the equipment has passed its functional tests at the user location. This applies to hardware-only procurements as well as the hardware portion of the complete system. Payments are not made unless the hardware in the system is usable.

Cost of additional systems. When having a complete system developed, the maximum costs for future systems should also be stated in the same contract. The software developed, documentation prepared, and the experience gained by the vendor in putting in the first system are valuable. If additional identical systems are planned, the software charge should be dropped after the first system. Since hardware costs continue to decrease each year, the contract should indicate that future decreases in the equipment price will be passed along to the user.

Many minicomputer manufacturers provide quantity discounts on the equipment they manufacture, as a matter of course. These price reductions start at a very low quantity and may amount to important dollars. Some minicomputer manufacturers provide discounts such as 5 percent on their own hardware when as few as three or four systems are installed or purchased in a single year. This discount is stipulated as part of the standard contract provisions. Other companies even include under one discount schedule all equipment purchased over a four-year span. In any event, even if reduction in price for multiple systems is not part of the vendor's standard contract, discounts for quantity is a properly negotiable item and should be included in the initial contract.

Taxes and tax credits. Sales and value-added taxes are separate items and are paid by the user. Investment tax credits are usually applicable and can be taken by the lessee. The contract should reflect this by requiring the vendor to take all steps required to obtain these credits for the user.

Maintenance Service and Charges

Maintenance is normally provided by the hardware supplier, even when the system is under a third-party lease or has been developed by a systems house, but there are many other servicing arrangements available. A number of large manufacturers of electronic equipment have large, nationwide service organizations that will service any company's equipment. Included in this group are the service organizations of Honeywell, RCA, and Raytheon. Other organizations, for example, Serviss, are totally dedicated to service as their only business and provide another alternative to service by the original manufacturer. All these organizations provide nationwide coverage. They are especially useful when the hardware system is composed of equipment made by a number of different vendors. Service of a mixed equipment system by one of these organizations removes the often unrealistic fear of having each manufacturer's representative blame each other's equipment when the system goes down. By having the system serviced by one organization, the responsibility for repairing and maintaining the system is defined.

Several types of maintenance can be arranged. Most common is the contract that provides for service calls during only the normal weekday working hours, with afterhour calls at extra charge. Another common and frequently used plan is the on-call-only plan. This plan merely guarantees that service personnel will be available at stated hourly charges, which will likely vary between normal and overtime calls. In all cases, the maintenance contract should state if spare parts cost or stocking responsibilities are to be borne by the user.

Contracts for purchase, or with a purchase option, should include a statement of the vendor's warranties and guarantees covering all parts of the system. This normally provides for no-charge replacement of any portions that fail within one or two years after acceptance.

Since both cost and promptness of response in emergencies may be affected, the contract should specify where spare parts and maintenance personnel will be located and whether travel or expenses or minimum-per-call charges are to be made.

Software Contracts

Many of the most costly problems that frequently plague new computer users involve the computer software. Typically, the hardware performance of the computer system is specified in a machine services contract, but the software guarantees often tend to be vague and are frequently specified in oral agreements or sometimes overlooked entirely. Problems can arise and costs incurred when the software is not completed on time, does not perform in the prescribed manner, is not properly debugged, or requires excessive computer resources in running.

Investments in outside software are increasing dramatically through the purchase of software packages, the use of outside development facilities, and the purchase of turnkey systems. The importance of software to the user and the large proportion of system cost incurred by software increase the risk to the purchaser. Not only is the cost of the product in jeopardy, but since software is intrinsic to the application and to the business, the business of the user is in fact also put in jeopardy. This, of course, requires the purchaser to place greater emphasis on an effective contractual relationship with the vendor. The contract becomes particularly important with respect to software when it is recognized that software is by no means as tangible or as well defined as hardware. Hence, operating characteristics are not so clear-cut as those of the hardware part of the system.

Contract components. The software contract, like the hardware contract, can be divided into specific and general clauses. Software contracts must deal with performance and must define the product to be delivered. In addition, the financial terms, warranty, staffing, installation, and support must be covered. All these features to be included in software contracts are quite similar to those discussed earlier for hardware contracts. In addition to the risks that apply to all computer systems, there are a number of risks that apply specifically to the purchase of software, all of which should be covered in the software contract.

1. *Nonperformance.* A package that does not work is easy to identify, and of course this risk must be covered in the contract. However, the more difficult situation is a package that may take too much time or excessive computer resources to process the application. A developed application involves the same risks; it may not perform the required functions or may fail to meet specifications. Development of the application may take too much time, and its cost may be considerably higher than the anticipated budget allotment.

2. *Excessive resource use.* Most software development contracts call for the purchaser to supply some resources. This may include machine time, keypunching, and other facilities that are usually only needed in the final testing stages of development. It is possible that the supplier may use far more of these than contemplated, perhaps partly as compensation for underestimating the development job.

3. *Staffing*. At the time the contract is signed, it should be determined who is to work on the project and what rules are to be followed. Workers assigned may not report full-time, may be transferred to other projects, or may not get along with workers of the user organization. All the caveats in dealing with internal personnel apply equally to those of vendors, who are under less control by the purchaser and who may indeed operate under totally different rules.

4. *Staff qualifications*. People assigned to the project are important and should be either referenced by name or by experience. Information should be made available on each person's background, such as education, data processing experience, tenure with the vendor, and application experience.

5. *Vendor bankruptcy*. Software companies are often not as stable financially as other companies in the business environment. They are frequently undercapitalized and often small. Their failure to perform may well result in an actionable case by the purchaser, but if they have no significant assets, winning a case is meaningless. If the vendor goes out of business, the users' only recourse, in addition to holding back the financial payments, may be to hire some of the bankrupt vendor's employees who are knowledgeable in the application area. The original contract with the vendor should give the right to access these people upon business termination so that, as a minimum, their information can be transferred to the purchaser.

6. *Infringement*. Software packages, even those tailored to a specific application, may not have a clear title belonging to the seller. A third party may thus assert rights against the purchaser on a totally unexpected basis if the seller did not own the code being used. To prevent infringement, clear title should be warranted. The vendor must document his sole ownership of the package and certify his full power and authority to grant the use of the package without the consent of any other claimant. Also, the vendor should agree to indemnify and hold the user free from any loss or liability arising out of any breach of the warranty.

Legal assistance. There is no substitute for a thoughtful and effective contract produced by the appropriate technical and legal talent. Professional help should be sought and used. The vendor always has the support of his legal staff at his disposal, and it is important that the user have similar resources. This is essential protection that should not be overlooked. Despite other priorities of the company's law and controllers departments, matters dealing with contracts require prompt review by a professional staff. The user is inexperienced in writing contracts, but the vendor does it every day. The user should attempt to even the score by using professional assistance.

Recommended Approach

Single vendor for hardware. Although there are many arguments to the contrary, as a general rule it is preferable to use a single vendor for supplying all system hardware components. This applies even if the user is contracting with a systems house or other type of third party for the system. A single hardware supplier provides an added degree of security. Not only can the systems house be held responsible, but also it is usual for the original manufacturer to stand behind his equipment and provide assistance and maintenance, if necessary.

Using the equipment of a single vendor will also eliminate a multitude of interfacing problems. Regardless of the user's degree of expertise in assembling systems, the job can be difficult. Interfacing major components could be a job that would take so long that any proposed benefits suggested by the approach would be lost.

Using a single supplier's equipment also eliminates much time and effort in developing, defining, and running acceptance tests. These matters, which appear to be simple, are actually very time-consuming when done well—and running acceptance tests has to be done well if they are to be meaningful.

Single vendor responsiblity. When dealing through a systems house for development of software, the responsibility for delivering a complete system should be specifically and explicitly assigned to one group. It may not matter what group is responsible as long as the assignment is made. Even if the user provides programming assistance, the responsibility for a total system should still lie with the vendor.

Available maintenance. Maintenance coverage varies greatly by locations throughout the country and throughout the world. A vendor or service organization might have hundreds of locations, but there might not be one within a thousand miles of the user location. Not only should the location of the maintenance facilities be checked, but also the level of experience and the location of spare parts should be established. The area should also be checked to find the number of other users of the maintenance service. If there are a number of users, then it is likely that the maintenance organization has a qualified local staff and a supply of spare parts. These considerations are important to reduce the time of response to calls for repair and to get the system up and running again.

Use of a consultant. Unless the user has highly competent personnel who have had experience with small computers, a consultant should be enlisted to assist in many matters, but particularly in the selection of the system and the vendor. For the smaller, inexperienced company this step is essential. This consultant, of course, should be independent of any vendor or supplier and should have experience working with dedicated computer systems. The benefits of an experienced and independent consultant in obtaining a system that is best for the user, by independent analysis and by deflating the claims of extravagant suppliers, will far outweigh the costs of his services.

A Contract Checklist

The following items are important enough to be considered for inclusion in the contract:

1. Payments: type (purchase, rental); frequency; discounts for multiple systems; price of future identical systems; progress payment schedule; start of payments.
2. Rent-lease provisions: length of term of agreement; conversion privileges.
3. Assignment of tax credit.
4. Description of deliverable items: system; documentation; all goods and services.
5. Definition of acceptance: performance criteria; time period.
6. Warranties provided: system, hardware, software.
7. Personnel assigned.
8. Special vendor services and charges: project management; consulting; training manuals; training courses, computer test time; travel and living expenses.
9. User responsibilities.
10. Penalties.
11. Protection against third-party suits for patent or copyright infringement.
12. Maintenance service and charges; options and costs; parts costs and warranty; hours available; spare parts allowance or costs; time and travel costs.
13. Right of ownership of software.
14. Upgrades available: what time period; any cost.
15. Handling of contract disputes: laws applicable; suit procedure; arbitration.

MINICOMPUTER TECHNOLOGY AND THE FUTURE

The minicomputer is not just another more advanced piece of data processing equipment; it is a new way of doing things. Although the full range and sizes of data processing peripheral equipment can be attached to the minicomputer, it is not just a lower-priced computer system. The minicomputer is the first of many new devices that have the capability to change our methods of doing business. It is an initial, visible part of a continuous spectrum of logic processing devices that includes the microprocessor and microcomputer, all of which will be used in business and the home in ways too numerous to mention. It is representative of the machines, the tools, and the instruments that extend man's brain and senses. It is also the forerunner of equipment that will be available in the home, in the office, in schools, and in the factory, and which can assist us in many invisible ways.

The technology that is now affecting our lives through the minicomputer is still new and growing. It is important to recognize its use both today and in the future. Technological advances in themselves do not improve life, working conditions, or business profits. Knowing the importance of the advances in technology, and understanding and guiding its use, are necessary to reach higher levels of achievement. Failure to understand the importance will not stop the adoption of new methods, for the economics of their use will favor the new ways. Failure to understand, appreciate, and take advantage of this significant development will mean that opportunities will be lost.

Without an appreciation of the significance of this advanced technology, the people who will be most affected by a new particular innovative method will not have sufficient awareness of its consequences to guide its use and protect and conserve their personal interests. The future of the new technology, epitomized today by the microprocessor, microcomputer, and minicomputer, is starting now, and the people who will be affected by it should know and understand both its power and its limitations.

Technology Forecast

The new integrated-circuit (IC) technology will continue to advance because of its power and constantly lower prices. However, the major thrust of its benefits will be extended horizontally to new products rather than vertically to continuing the trend toward lower-priced minicomputers. The price of the minicomputer hardware is so low presently that costs for peripherals, and particularly for personnel, are possibly 90 percent of the total system cost. Reductions in the processor cost will come about, but will not have a large effect on the total system cost.

The high-performance, low-cost IC technology will allow new applications and techniques to be developed. Increasing costs of business operations will also allow many new applications to be cost-justified. New equipment and new techniques will be prominent in the home, industry, and business because of the decreasing cost of electronic circuitry.

The cost of IC components, which has decreased from an average price of $60 in 1962 to $1.30 ten years later, illustrates the dramatic changes in electronic circuitry. Equivalent ICs would cost less than $0.15 today. The cost of a given electronic function has been declining even more rapidly than the cost of the integrated circuit, since the complexity of the circuits has been increasing as their cost decreased. The cost per bit has declined 35 percent per year since 1970, when the major growth of integrated circuits got under way. Most of the advances in the computer-related technology are based on this dramatic change.

Electronic technology has become increasingly pervasive in all our activities, and electronic techniques will continue to displace other modes of control. Because the microelectronic industry has been able to make ever more sophisticated elements at ever-decreasing costs, this trend will be accentuated. Mechanical elements of the calculator and the watch have been displaced by integrated circuits that are less expensive and offer more flexibility. Now the electronic and electromechanical functions of vending machines, pinball machines, and traffic signals are being displaced. In the near future the automobile engine will be controlled by computer with a consequent improvement in efficiency and reduction of pollution.

All these applications are simply extensions of the traditional application of electronics to the task of handling information in measurement, communication, and data manipulation. It has often been said that just as the Industrial Revolution enabled man to apply and control greater physical power than his own muscle could provide, so electronics has extended his intellectual power. Microelectronics extend that power still further.

By 1986 the number of electronic functions incorporated into a wide range of products each year can be expected to be a hundred times greater than it was ten years earlier. The experience curve predicts that the cost per function will have declined by then to a twentieth of the 1976 cost, a reduction of 25 percent per year. At such prices, electronic devices will be exploited even more widely, augmenting mail service and bank services, expanding the library and making its contents more accessible, providing entertainment, disseminating knowledge for educational purposes, and performing many more of the routine tasks in the home and office. It is in this exponential proliferation of products and services, dependent on microelectronics, that the real microelectronic revolution will be manifested.

Computer Power

Computer power, while constantly decreasing in cost, has been increasing , but the cost per instruction has been decreasing exponentially. Figure 12–1 indicates that the price of a computer CPU decreases by an order of magnitude every ten years. At the same time, as shown by Figure 12–2, the CPU performance has increased at about the same rate. In fact, since 1955 there has been an exponential growth rate in many factors that increase computer system performance, including:

Number of instructions processed per second.
Number of instructions processed per dollar.
Power of the central processor in terms of the number of logic circuits per processor.
File storage technology in terms of the number of bits stored in reasonable commercial applications.

The promise of mass-produced, large-scale integrated circuits suggests that this trend will continue. The large-computer CPU of the 1980s will cost approximately one-tenth of the equivalent-power computer of the 1970s because of the continuing drop expected in the manufacturing cost. The small computer, which sells for approximately $4,000 in a minimum system configuration now, is not expected to drop at quite the same rapid rate. The 1985 minicomputer—provided there is a device that can be identified as a minicomputer at that time—might be only one-fifth of its present cost, or under $1,000 for a complete system.

Computer Memories

Originally, memory was one of the most costly items in the computer; as a result, the declining memory prices have contributed greatly to the reduction in minicomputer costs. Studies show

Figure 12–1. Relative computer processor price.

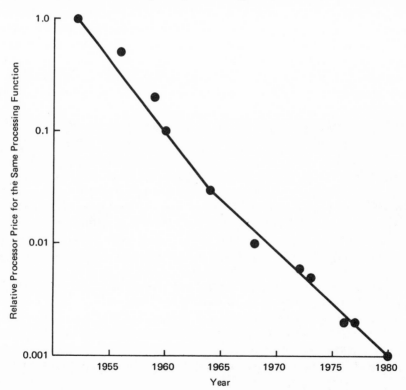

Figure 12–2. Relative computer processor performance.

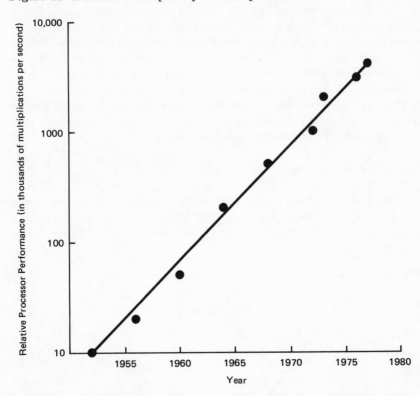

that costs of minicomputer core memories with comparable cycle times have declined more than 20 percent annually since 1966.

Memories consist of a large number of identical functions, and require high speeds and high reliability. Because of these requirements, semiconductor integrated circuits are ideally suited for the fabrication of computer memories. Because of their continuing cost reductions and higher packing densities, semiconductors are used increasingly for memories. This use, although not without its drawbacks, has established a trend that will continue well into the future.

Semiconductor memory costs have decreased an order of magnitude in the last ten years, as can be seen from Figure 12–3. If the present rate continues, memory will be essentially free of cost in 1990—which, although absurd, dramatizes the recent cost trends. However, the speed advantages of semiconductors are less significant in the dedicated computer or in the I/O-bound computer, so the

Figure 12–3. Cost of computer main memory. Cost per bit of computer memory has declined and should continue to decline for successive generations of random-access memory circuits capable of handling from 1K to 65K bits of memory. Increasing density and complexity of successive circuits are primarily responsible for cost reduction, but less complex circuits also continue to decline in cost.

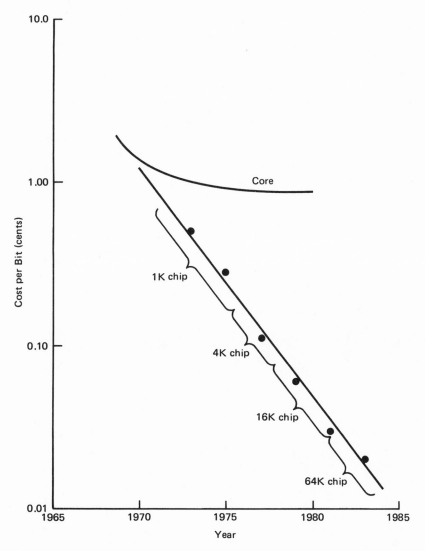

SOURCE: Robert N. Noyce, "Microelectronics," *Scientific American*, September 1977; and other industry sources.

highly reliable, nonvolatile core memory systems will continue to be available during the next five years.

A factor that may prevent universal acceptance of the semiconductor memories is their characteristic called "volatility." Semiconductors require constant power to maintain the intelligence that they are storing. Loss of power to a semiconductor memory in which a program is stored results in the loss of the program. A core memory does not require power to maintain the intelligence and would not lose the program if power were lost. Bubble-memory technology can also be made nonvolatile, providing a distinct advantage over semiconductors.

Read-only memory will be used in the same manner as it is used today, and probably in the same percentage of the applications. Semiconductor read-only memory will be used where extremely high-speed routines are necessary, and wired read-only core memory will be used to increase the reliability of the computer to make it more independent of the rough environment in which it will be working.

Microprogramming

Microprogrammed minicomputers and microprocessors will be increasingly used in repetitive applications because of their low fabrication costs and their high reliability. The uses of microprogramming are described below.

Control logic in all sizes of computers. Control logic takes advantage of the high speed and reliability of the semiconductor IC chip to perform repetitive, high-speed computer operations, particularly those dealing with transfer of data to and from peripheral devices and controllers.

Software replacement. With the increasing costs of software development and decreasing costs of semiconductor logic, a gradual shift toward performing more in hardware logic will come about. Only relatively stable functions will use this technique, but there are many of these kinds of functions. Standard functions such as code conversion, decimal-to-binary conversions, or serial-to-parallel bit stream conversions are examples of such functions. In addition, semiconductor logic will be used increasingly to convert, at run time, programs developed for other computers, thus reducing program development costs.

Special terminals. Terminals, frequently called *intelligent terminals*, will be tailored to the individual user's needs. The functions to be performed will be programmed by using semiconductor IC logic. These functions will include the steps for entering data, validating procedures, as well as the checking of data, temporary storage of data, and as many communication functions (dail-up, line surveillance, transmission control, error control, error correction, and similar operations) as are desired. This single use of integrated-circuit logic is the most important of all its uses, and will have an enormous impact on the method by which business will function in the future.

Auxiliary Storage

Random-access, rotating memory will be the primary mass storage technique used with small computers throughout the next decade. The inherent access delays and the relatively low reliability due to the electromechanical nature of the disk drives are the major problems. But their low cost, small size, and easy interfacing with any type of computer will make alternative storage means impractical.

An important way to compare various forms of auxiliary storage is to consider the cost and access time. In the currently available storage technologies, the access times vary from a millionth of a second or less for semiconductor memory to 10 seconds or more for magnetic tape memories. As can be seen from Figure 12–4, across a million-to-one range in price per bit, the pattern is uniform—for each two-orders-of-magnitude increase in access time, there is one order of magnitude of saving in price.

Cost of a disk storage unit will not decrease much more than it did in the 1970s. During this time, an 8-million-bit unit could be purchased for less than $2,000. Improvements were made in the packing density of this equipment, resulting in decreased cost per unit of storage, but because of the mechanical nature of the drive mechanism the units are not available for much less than $1,000. However, because of this low price, cassette storage units will decrease in use. The serial nature of accessing information on cassettes is inefficient and time-consuming. Since the price of a cassette drive will be in the same range as a disk unit, users will prefer the disk because of its random-access capability.

As a result of mechanical constraints, there is little likelihood for greatly reduced access times, which are now in the 20- to 100-millisecond range for small-computer disks. Multiple heads will be used to reduce access time, but it is doubtful if these access times will be reduced by 50 percent in the next decade.

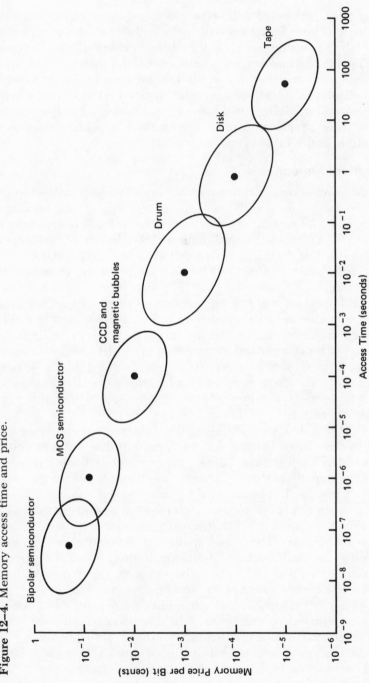

Figure 12–4. Memory access time and price.

There will be continued steady improvement in the cost per storage bit and in price/performance of the disk units. Because of advances in packing densities of the tracks on which the data is recorded, as well as in the number of bits per track, the storage capacity of the disk drives will be extended and the cost per bit will be decreased. A maximum fourfold increase in packing densities is projected in the next decade.

A number of new technologies that are being or have been considered for large-scale auxiliary storage are now in development. These include magnetic bubbles, charge-coupled devices (CCD), laser, electro-optical, and holographic techniques. There are always problems with new technologies, and even after many problems are solved and the technology appears to be cost effective, new problems in the application of the techniques will arise.

A number of promising memory technologies have not achieved commercial success in spite of their promise and the intensive research spent on them. Examples are the magnetic film memories, the electronic beam, and optical beam memories. Often the investment required to establish the use of a new memory technology at low cost and with high reliability has been considered too great in proportion to the risks and potential rewards.

The next decade is likely to bring substantial improvements in performance in both the moving-surface and electronic memories, along with reductions in cost. Increasing density of recording on magnetic surfaces together with improved electron-beam reading devices will permit at least a tenfold increase in the number of bits stored on a magnetic medium, and with little accompanying increase in the price of the system. Anticipated introductions of new techniques and fabrications of the microelectronic circuits should also make it possible to increase the bit density of these devices by a factor of 100, again with only minor increases in price per component. Thus, the expectation is that over the next ten years there will be a reduction of more than an order of magnitude in the price per bit of all forms of memory. The device cost will not decrease sharply, but the much greater data density will result in a much lower cost per bit.

Input/Output Devices

Most computer input/output equipment is largely mechanical, and for this reason only modest reductions in their cost effectiveness are expected in the next decade. The few electronic I/O devices will experience close to an order-of-magnitude improvement over the same period.

Electronic input/output devices. Devices such as CRT data-input terminals, nonimpact printers, and optical character readers, which are largely electronic, will steadily decrease in price over the next decade. In addition to the overall price decline, and to a large extent because of the price decline, smaller specialized units (especially CRT terminals and single-copy printers) will become available. This will result in much lower priced units.

Punch card equipment. The most significant development in punch card technology was the introduction of the 96-column card with the IBM System/3 in 1969. This card provides for 20 percent more information on a smaller card. If compatibility obstacles that exist between the 80- and 96-column card techniques are overcome, the smaller card can produce benefits well in excess of the 20 percent.

CRTs and other on-line data entry terminals have cut into a major use of punch cards, but because of the large existing base of punch card systems, their use is still increasing, though at a much lower rate than other systems.

In general over the past years, there have been only modest advances in the performance of card readers and only slightly better improvements in price. This has resulted in approximately doubling the price-performance ratio (as measured by the characters read per second per dollar of rental) every five to seven years. This trend is expected to continue.

Printers. The highly mechancial impact printers are relatively mature. There have been only modest improvements in their price-performance ratio in the past decade, and no more than a doubling of the price-performance ratio (measured by characters printed per second per dollar) is expected in the present decade.

The big advance in the printing segment of the computer peripheral market has been the introduction of many new types of printers that can fulfill the small computer user's needs without system overbuying. Until recently, the user could buy either a "data processing" type of line printer or a very slow character printer. Once the requirements of the job exceeded printing speeds of 30 characters per second, the large, expensive line printer had to be used. There is now, and will continue to be in the future, a full range of impact and nonimpact printers that can match the needs of the job, eliminating the need for costly overbuying. The benefit to specific users could be large, but the overall change in the cost effectiveness of impact printers is not expected to improve significantly in the future.

Some specialized applications never have need for more than one copy of a document. In these rare cases, a nonimpact printer, which is largely nonmechanical, can be used. Printers using photographic techniques were introduced around 1970 to handle great masses of printing at high speeds. Concentrated in the large-computer market, they have not helped the small-computer user to any noticeable extent. Over the 1970 decade, manufacturers will concentrate on reducing the costs of these printers rather than on improving or maintaining high performance. This will result in highly effective devices that will be priced in the $300 range. In effect, users whose needs can be satisfied by these printers will have a tenfold reduction in their printing costs over the next decade.

Software

The major obstacle to cost-effective system performance today is software. This problem will not only continue but will also be accentuated throughout most of the 1980s. New program development techniques and language translation techniques may improve performance significantly, but the rate of improvement in software will not approach the rate of improvement in hardware. As a result, software performance will fall behind hardware and will be relatively more of a problem than it is today.

Rather than make advances in software, the small-computer segment of the industry will compensate for the software ineffectiveness and do more in hardware. The use of microprogramming will become more prevalent in small-computer systems, as was discussed previously.

Languages. There are two distinct levels at which computer language considerations are relevant and important: that pertaining to development and that pertaining to use. Since the uses of a dedicated or turnkey system will continue to grow in numbers and value, many users will not be directly concerned with the development of the system. Even if the development is done by the same company that uses the system, the people who do the programming will likely be very far removed from the users. And since the user will directly interface with the computer in performing the job, this unsophisticated user will have to be able to "converse" with the computer to initiate procedures, change programs, recognize various error conditions, and correct data or system errors.

Because higher-level languages such as COBOL produce programs at considerably less expense than assembly languages, the continued acceptance of these languages is assured. As a result, they will be used to such a large extent that assembly language programming will be limited to special situations. The maturing computer industry has learned how to develop effective and efficient compilers, and this experience will be directly translated to the minicomputer systems.

New types of preprocessors will make the input source language even easier to handle than it is today. Presently accepted languages such as RPG, COBOL, and enhanced BASIC will continue to play a major role in business data processing. Developed systems will increasingly have a conversational mode of interaction with the user. Special user-oriented commands will be employed in these languages, which will be especially designed by computer manufacturers and sophisticated users. Users will find that a knowledge of computers is rarely required to interact with the system, just as a knowledge of the workings of an automobile is not required to be a successful driver.

Application programs. The application programming bottleneck has been the limiting factor in the case of small computers. Application packages are not the complete answer that many claim them to be. Applications are very personal and must be modified to suit each user. Sometimes this modification takes longer and entails more risk than would reprogramming of the entire application.

Considerable strides are being made in this packaging area, but these will not lead to standard programs. Rather, the techniques used through the 1980s will employ standard program modules that can be easily assembled into workable programs. These techniques will be extensions of presently used techniques such as modular programming, subroutine libraries, problem-oriented languages, and standard utility packages. To make these techniques effective, however, strong control over hardware and system development must be maintained. This can be done by an independent systems house or by a specialized development group of a knowledgeable user company.

Electronic Offices

The market for computers to manage clerical functions of the electronic office of the future is expected to be equal to the entire computer industry today. In 1985 the word-processing or electronic office market is expected to yield approximately $10 billion in annual revenue. Major computer and office equipment companies such as IBM, Xerox, Burroughs, Honeywell, and NCR are in the so-called word-processing market. This market goes well beyond the clerical operations usually associated with word processing. Cluster systems, including electronic mail, electronic file cabinets, indexing, and information storage and retrieval, are in the plans of these manufacturers for 1980, and the true work-station environment (of which word-processing functions are but a subset) is indeed around the corner. Many companies both in and out of the traditional computer industry are serious contenders for a marketplace share in this ever-growing area.

Communications

A number of important developments occurring within this decade will be as important as the electronic technology developments of the late 1960s. These developments pertain to transmittal of data between distant points. The specific technology involved applies to the use of commercial satellites and cable TV circuits for two-way transmission of signals and data.

Changes in cost of transmission. A number of new companies have entered the communication field to supply common carrier services. Because of this competition to the established communication companies, many predictions of drastically lower costs for data communication have been made. In general, these lower costs will not come about. The new transmission companies require enormous amounts of money to wire up the nation in the fashion they propose. These enormous sums will not be available and, as a result, only the heavy-volume circuits between major cities will be handled by these new carriers. The result will be a reduction in rates by the existing common carriers, if they are to remain competitive in these major routes. In order to maintain their necessary level of revenues, common carriers will have to compensate for the reduction of some tariffs by raising the costs of traffic on circuits that are not in competition. Therefore, the cost of heavy-volume transmission between major cities will be reduced, but the tariffs between the many lower-volume points will be increased. Thus, the net results, on the average, will not reflect rates very much different from those in effect at present. In fact only a 2 percent annual reduction is predicted.

Besides technical deficiencies of the existing telephone network for data transmissions, tariffs do not seem to be adequate for or responsive to the new telecommunication services. The costs are generally considered prohibitive for most telecommunication-supported computer systems. While computation costs decrease at about 50 precent every two years, communication cost reductions are estimated at only 2 percent per year. Consequently, costs of communication services may prove to be the limiting factor in the development of computer communication complexes. At present, communication costs make the development of many large systems prohibitive. In the future, although total system costs for equivalent systems will be significantly lower, communications will take up an increasingly heavy share of the expenses. As a result, other alternatives, which include on-site processing with minicomputers and distributed processing, will become increasingly attractive.

Commercial communication satellites. Satellites are the most recent means of communication whose capabilities of range, volume, and coverage are beyond those of any other form of communications. Two fundamental characteristics make satellites extremely attractive: (1) wide bandwidth, and consequently huge communications capacity; and (2) ability to serve points not specified in advance. Satellites have a much greater range of transmission than that of cables or microwave circuits. Satellites provide a flexibility that cannot be otherwise duplicated. They can be used in transmitting to fixed points or to moving receivers, and the transmission mode can be changed at will.

Cable TV circuits. Now more than just an entertainment medium, cable TV circuits provide the capability to communicate with every business and home in the nation. Originally designed for the transmission of entertainment and related pleasure-oriented programs, cable TV circuits are now required by a Federal Communication Commission regulation to have the capability of two-way transmission. Experimental systems to transmit individual, interactive data and video signals have been under way since 1970. Cable TV systems have enormous possibilities for handling a number of functions and services, including remote meter readings, security alarms, and banking and shipping functions.

On the other hand, coupling a community antenna head to satellite transmission means that any number of points within the country can be connected by a heavy-data-volume path, no matter how remote or close the points are. No cables will be necessary and no prior arrangements for connection will have to be made. Within the next ten years, transmission will be made from any point to any other point, and it will be just as easy to transmit between two cities that are thousands of miles apart as it will be to communicate between cities ten miles apart.

Costs of Future Systems

Changes of cost in various elements of the computer spectrum affect the user to varying degrees. We frequently hear how technology will improve equipment and reduce costs, but in the past we have not seen any decrease in operating expense. Part of this is due to the typical user preference of taking improved performance rather than reduced costs. However, a major factor in this continuous trend toward increasing costs, despite improving technology, is the increased cost for the human activities that interact with these systems. The same point of view applies to small-computer systems. Equipment cost is decreasing to such an extent that processing expenses will be negligible compared with the entire system cost.

The development of new systems still requires analysis, design, programming, testing, debugging implementation, documentation, and auditing. All these operations require human talents, and the cost of these talents is increasing. Furthermore, because the systems being developed are becoming more complex, the cost of system development by traditional means will increase exponentially. The same factors are involved in the use of the systems. Data-input functions are consuming an ever-increasing amount of the processing dollar. Added to this expense in large systems are the permanent staffs required for maintenance of complex operating systems and other support functions.

In order to attain at least part of the benefits of the new technology, the low-cost elements of the system—the processor and memory—must replace the high-cost elements—the people. The objective is not merely to have the computer do more, but to implement a shift of functions so that much of the work now performed by people will be done by the computer. The more advanced systems of today point this way toward the future.

Completely general, machine-independent languages based on COBOL will be increasingly used in business-related systems. Data management languages, used for data file access and processing, will eventually reach the same level of development and use. These languages and techniques will not be so efficient as the handcrafted, specifically tailored, assembly language routine or file access methods, but this does not matter. The performance improvements in the new hardware will more than compensate for any inefficiencies in the program.

In the future, the computer will be used to assemble the programs from a file of program modules and subroutines, thus reducing to a significant extent the amount of time and effort required to develop the system. System costs will depend almost entirely upon what resources are required in addition to the computer. Many small systems for handling common applications will be implemented at very low cost. These familiar systems, used largely for the information retrieval and data-entry functions, can be implemented with very little human assistance because they will be repeated very often. As a result, the development cost as well as the processing cost will be low. Therefore, many systems of this type will be economically justifiable and easily installed.

Larger, free-standing minicomputer systems will be implemented at relatively high costs, equivalent to the costs of the present-day systems. Again the user will accept technology advances in performance improvements rather than cost reduction. Personnel costs will be an increasing portion of the total system costs. Communication-oriented systems will be justified despite the costs of communications, which will be the highest-cost item in such a system. While the operating expense of a typical communication system today is distributed as 80 percent processing and 20 percent communication, the percentages will be reversed by the end of this decade.

The New Technology in Business

The opportunities brought about by technological advances and the minicomputer are very significant for the effective operation of a business. It provides large businesses with freedom from organizational constraints, but still allows the control capabilities. The new technology, when properly managed, also provides small companies and individual processing units of large companies with very cost-effective means for handling their business accounting and planning. Improvement can be achieved in many management areas such as planning and control, operating expenses, services, motivation of workers, development of managers, security, and customer relations. The minicomputer by itself does not provide all these benefits, but it does provide the means to achieve, or at least approach, a new level of benefits.

Data Needs of the Company

The concepts of organizational information needs, developed during the 1960s and early 1970s when the management information system (MIS) concepts were the rage, have been modified to more practical levels. We are now quite certain that a manager does not need available, and surely does not want, all company data before he makes a decision. But we also know that accurate and timely information is needed for proper control of business operations. The availability of low-cost data processing makes the hierarchical approach of information organization possible. While data is processed at lower organizational levels for operational needs such as billing or inventory control, summary information can be held for later transmission to regional or national centers for planning and control purposes. The minicomputer can accommodate all these necessary functions at a reasonable cost. Also, because of its programmable nature, it can be made to interface with many different systems and equipment types, and if future business requirements dictate changes some time in the future, the system approach can be modified without rebuilding the system from ground level.

Therefore, with this minicomputer flexibility, management can select its information needs and the organization can respond, rather than having management constrained by the information organization. In practical terms, this approach is not possible when using the large computer. Captain Grace Murray Hopper, a pioneer in the data processing field, whose continuous data processing experience dates back to the early computer developments at Harvard in the 1940s, is outspoken on the misuse and improper design of large computers. Captain Hopper claims that the computer industry is building dinosaurs and that the big machines will collapse under their own weight sooner or later. She claims that they should be broken up in the way a corporation president splits up his company into divisions. No successful executive insists on making every decision himself, or on reading every piece of mail. Rather, he coordinates the activities of the employees to whom he has delegated authority. Captain Hopper feels that jobs should be assigned to minicomputers, possibly specialized ones, which are interconnected and can use each other's results.

The minicomputer, or an organization of minicomputers, provides a hierarchical approach to information processing and collection. When the desired information is passed along "topside" to the organization executive level, a minicomputer-based system would then be used to provide planning information. With the data quantity reduced to manageable levels, the planning group could very effectively play the "what-if" game. The planners, with properly designed algorithms, could manipulate the assumptions and data to determine the effect of certain investments or decisions on long-range company prospects.

Organization Functions and Management Development

The possibility of performing some amount of data processing at various levels provides corporate management with new opportunities in manager development while retaining strong control of operations. If a field-level manager is responsible for his data processing rather than being dependent upon service from the central organization, a significant step toward complete accountability and the profit-center concept is achieved. This will result not only in better management development techniques but also in better control of field operations. It will allow a greater degree and more effective delegation of authority and responsibility within the organization, and will motivate managers to improve performance.

The dispersal of low-cost computing power that serves the managers at each organization level results in an exact match between the corporate organization structure and the information structure. These matching structures sharpen the distinctions between business functions, reduce overlap or uncertainity of responsibility, and produce a smoother, more efficient overall organization.

Security. Data security and physical data center security became major problems in the late 1960s, and concern continues to this day. Complete security is impossible to attain and anything approaching it is extremely expensive. Data center security is usually achieved more easily and effectively when all data processing is performed at one site rather than at numerous dispersed locations. Protection against disaster is achieved by backing up the main computer center with a compatible center that will accommodate, at least for a period of time, the critical data processing operations of the firm. This requires some duplication of facilities as well as retention and duplication of files and data. Data security is even more difficult to attain. When all data is funneled through the data center, no practical precautions can be taken that will absolutely assure the confidentiality of the data.

The distributed processing concept, made possible by the minicomputer, assures adequate backup; each center in the network could conceivably act as backup for every other center to provide the necessary physical security. Having the data files dispersed reduces the consequences of file destruction at a center.

The combination of on-site information processing together with user-operated systems in a private, secured environment provides a great measure of the total data security desired. This may not be possible for the substantial volume of the basic business processing of the organization, but is particularly pertinent to the sensitive non-mainline functions such as management compensation and shareholders' records. The data input/output in these sensitive applications can be performed only by the personnel associated with these functions at their office rather than by large unidentified numbers of support personnel.

Another proposed important function for the minicomputer which will aid data security is its use as a programmable data scrambler and unscrambler in interfacing communication networks with the data processing computer. This will deter and render ineffective any attempt to obtain company data by tapping communication line facilities.

On-line system advantages. Use of the electronic technology of the intelligent terminal and the minicomputer allows on-line systems to be cost effective. In fact, with this equipment, the direct interaction provided by this mode of operation seems natural and frequently costs less than historical data-entry means. A number of important advantages that were covered earlier in this discussion are derived from this approach: improved accuracy of data, earlier capture of data, reduced training, less skilled workers required, fewer workers required, fewer errors. As a corollary to these benefits, some important changes in the worker's performance and therefore the company's expenses result.

These on-line systems, where the worker is entering data in a conversational mode, get the worker involved. The method is more interesting than entering data by using pencil and paper or keypunching. In addition, the worker knows that the entire function is being performed by him and that he is not only responsible for doing the job but also accountable for its accuracy. This two-way motivation of the worker increases his productivity, with an obvious effect on the company.

The Consumer and the Computer

Besides the effect that minicomputer philosophy will have on business methods, it is likely to have other applications that affect our lives outside of business. These personal extrabusiness functions will follow organizational application implementations. However, the time lag will not be great, and the use of this technology in homes, schools, stores, banks, and in all those areas that touch personal affairs will act as a catalyst for even greater acceptance in industry.

Applications in the home. The 1969 Christmas catalog of a well-known Texas department store advertised a minicomputer for sale. This computer was programmed to assist the homemaker in planning menus. Although there were probably no buyers of this minicomputer which sold for about $10,000, it did indicate, even at that early date, a growing interest in its adaptability to home use. In 1977 a similar computer with software to process small personal business (check accounting and appointment recording) and a number of games was available for $4,000. Computers with less software were sold for $600 by hobby shops during the same year.

The microcomputer and minicomputer have developed a large following of hobbyists. Thousands of members of at least ten national organizations, as well as many individuals in all walks of life, built the hobby market to a very substantial $50 million in 1977. It is predicted that the following five years will see more than a threefold expansion of the hobby market, as shown in Figure 12–5. In addition there is a very substantial increase, estimated at $300 million, predicted for the consumer TV and recreation market.

The wired city. Twenty years ago the objective of community antenna television was to bring quality programs to communities in fringe TV viewing areas. Today, experimental cable TV systems are turning the home television set into a communications terminal hooked to computers to provide a variety of services. The requirements for having bidirectional signaling, and the government financing of equipment and experimental projects, will assure its rapid development. Special terminals containing logic elements, data buffering areas, a keyboard for data input, and a modulator/transmitter for communications have been developed and are being used experimentally. These systems are being planned to accommodate many functions, including educational TV for shut-ins, consumer shopping and services, banking services, household-security monitoring, voting, calculating, and pop entertainment such as playing competitive games with the computer.

Several companies have proved the economic justification of pay TV, security alarms, emergency alarms, shopping by TV, and credit-verification services. The minicomputer is involved in sev-

Figure 12–5. Revenues of computers sold to homes.

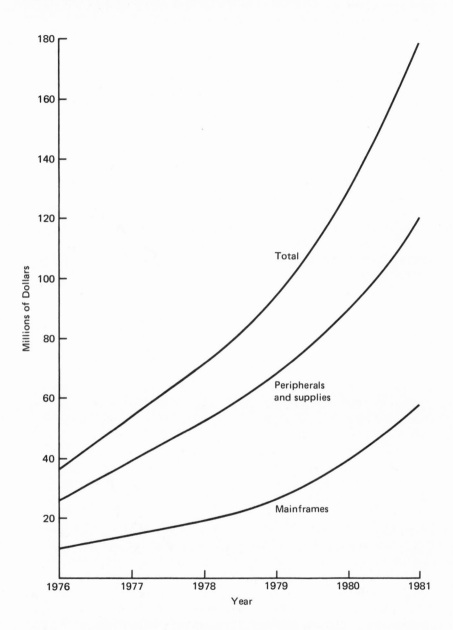

SOURCE: *Electronic News,* August 22, 1977.

eral ways. It is physically used to monitor and control all the communication functions in these systems. The more advanced input terminals, those able to store information and perform logic operations on the input/output, are built around microprocessors and microcomputers.

The philosophy involved in the use of these systems is identical to the point of view necessary for their full utilization in business and industry, and their application to everyday personal situations will further stimulate new uses in business.

Adjusting to the Future

The 1980 decade will produce major changes in information processing techniques, building upon the important changes in data processing methods that have already taken place. Minicomputers are in common use, but their number is just a fraction of the volume expected in the next few years. Their attractiveness has been enhanced by their low price, which justifies their use in applications where automation was never previously thought possible. This rapidly developing acceptance has been stimulated by people who require responsive computer systems. Even without the advent of minicomputer technology, the return to a true service function was imminent. The new electronic technology merely speeded it up, made it more noticeable, and provided the means for quick response to the user's cry for help. Minicomputers, and the technology that produced them, are here today. It is no longer a question of whether the approach is valid. Everyone will be touched by this technology. The question is how to react to this new force. The objective should now be to minimize the risks while obtaining a proper share of the benefits.

Before the enormous processor cost reduction came about, the processing of data could be done only on a very expensive machine. After users got over their initial awe of the machine and used it for cost-reduction purposes, they began to look for ways to improve its effectiveness. This meant monitoring and measuring the internal processing of the machine to assure that the costly computer was being utilized to its maximum. Machine throughput became the overriding objective. When a company upgraded to a more powerful—and inevitably a more costly—machine, the same objectives were followed with increased vigor. But, it does not necessarily follow that because it was proper to do this with a very expensive processor, it is proper to do so with all types of machines. The change in economic values changes the ground rules. Efficiency of the processor cannot be directly translated to efficiency of processing a business application when the major cost area is external to the processor. Although the cost of people exceeds the cost of the equipment by only a small margin now, this ratio is constantly increasing because processor prices are decreasing and salary and benefit costs are rising. This continuing trend invalidates the guidelines and evaluation criteria used in the past.

To plan properly for the distant future, certain assumptions should be made:

1. Computing processing power will be essentially free. Computing power will be treated in a manner similar to that for electric power. That is, people will know it will be available at a fairly reasonable cost when needed. No new applications will be rejected because of the cost of computing power. All other costs involved in system development and operation will so far outweigh the processor cost that processing will be a negligible expense.

2. The cost of people will increase because there will be a shortage of skills. This applies to both users and developers of information systems. A shortage of competent professional programmers will make it essential that nonprofessionals be able to communicate with the computer. Also, average people with no interest in the computers will be the users of these systems. Because of this shortage of skills, the information systems design will have to accommodate and handle successfully the introduction of improper information.

3. Functions usually performed by software will be performed in microprocessor hardware.

4. Communication systems will be available so that any location in the country can transmit to any other location. The availability of satellite transmission and two-way cable TV circuits will make this possible.

5. People will become familiar with and adapt readily to the concept of interactively communicating with a computer system.

If these guidelines are valid, then surely the approach that has resulted in the use of the minicomputer will be with us for years to come. The minicomputer and the technology it represents show every promise of being the means of bringing about the benefits that computers have been expected to deliver ever since their first acceptance in the business world in 1950.

APPENDIX

BID EVALUATION SHEET

Date:_____   Prepared by: _____

Rating values: 10, excellent; 8, very good; 6, good; 4, average or nominal
value; 2, poor; 0, unacceptable

A rating of zero for any asterisk factor is cause for rejection, regardless of
overall score.

Factor Evaluated	Weight	×	Rating	=	Score
I. Vendor Organization (40%)					
*Stability (years in business, project as a percent of business)	4	×		=	
*Financial rating	3	×		=	
*Experience with similar systems	7	×		=	
*Client satisfaction	4	×		=	
Maintenance and software support	5	×		=	
Timeliness of delivery	2	×		=	
Quality of proposal (revealed level of understanding)	4	×		=	
Level of staffing and management for project	3	×		=	
Project plan and organization	2	×		=	
Quality and cost control techniques	1	×		=	
Experience with proposal hardware/ software	5	×		=	_____

      Subtotal

Factor Evaluated	Weight	×	Rating	=	Score
II. Proposed System (60%)					
A. General (25%)					
*Suitability for user's intended solution (such as specified volume, timing, inputs, outputs, storage, retrieval, routing, controls, recovery, interrupts)	8	×		=	
*Capability compared to cost	3	×		=	
Simplicity	1	×		=	
*Compatibility	2	×		=	
Scheduling (realism, mileposts, accountability)	1	×		=	
Ease of installation, cutover plan	2	×		=	
Consideration of alternatives/ trade-offs	1	×		=	
Training	1	×		=	
Documentation	1	×		=	
Growth potential	2	×		=	
Test-acceptance plans	1	×		=	
Backup/recovery	2	×		=	_____
Subtotal					
B. Software (20%)					
*Suitability to problem (such as control, security, error handling, translation, file organization, formatting, sorting, updating)	7	×		=	
Modularity	2	×		=	
Use of previously developed hardware	4	×		=	
*Ease of revision and maintenance	4	×		=	
Versatility	2	×		=	
Report, printing, file, record-keeping capacity	1	×		=	_____
Subtotal					
C. Hardware (15%)					
*Suitability to project (such as terminals, computer, peripherals, capacity)	5	×		=	

Factor Evaluated	Weight	×	Rating	=	Score
*Performance compared to cost (storage capacity, speed, redundancy)	2	×		=	
*Reliability	2	×		=	
*Maintainability and manufacturer support	2	×		=	
*Number in use	1	×		=	
In-house experience	1	×		=	
Ease of changing configuration	2	×		=	_____
Subtotal					

Summation

Subtotal I   _____

Subtotal II—A   _____

Subtotal II—B   _____.

Subtotal II—C   _____

Total (maximum = 1,000)   _____

ADDITIONAL READINGS

Chapter 1

Abrams, Marshall D., and Philip G. Stein. *Computer Hardware and Software: An Interdisciplinary Introduction.* New York: Addison-Wesley, 1973.

Bylinsky, Gene. "Here Comes the Second Computer Revolution." *Fortune,* November 1975.

Matthies, Leslie H. *The Management System: Systems Are for People.* New York: Wiley & Sons, 1976.

Munyan, Jack. *So You're Going to Automate.* New York: Petrocelli, 1975.

Noyce, Robert N. "Microelectronics." *Scientific American,* September 1977.

Weinberg, Gerald M. *The Psychology of Computer Programming.* New York: Van Nostrand-Reinhold, 1971.

Chapter 2

"All About Minicomputers." Delran, New Jersey: Datapro Research Corporation, December 1976.

"All About Small Business Computers." Delran, New Jersey: Datapro Research Corporation, September 1977.

Pentages, Angeline. "IBM Series/1 Minicomputers." *Datamation,* December 1976.

Soucek, Branko. *Microprocessors and Microcomputers.* New York: Wiley Interscience, 1976.

Chapter 3

Amdahl, Lowell, "Computer Obsolescence." *Datamation,* January 1969.

Cassell, Stephen A. "Floppy Disk Drives and Systems." *Modern Data,* August 1975.

Computer Characteristics Review, Vol. 16, No. 2. Lexington, Mass.: GML Corporation.

Eckhouse, Richard H., Jr. *Minicomputer Systems: Organization and Programming.* Englewood Cliffs, N.J.: Prentice-Hall, 1975.

Knight, Kenneth E. "Changes in Computer Performance." *Datamation,* September 1966.

Miller, Frederick W. "The Non-Diminishing Printer." *Infosystems,* October 1977.

Stone, H. S. *Introduction to Computer Organization and Data Structures.* New York: McGraw-Hill, 1972.

Chapter 4

Eldin, Hamed K., and F. Max Croft. *Information Systems: A Management Science Approach.* New York: Petrocelli, 1974.

Glaser, George. "The Centralization vs. Decentralization Issue: Arguments, Issues, and Alternatives." Paper presented to the Fall Joint Computer Conference, 1970. Available from AFIPS Processing, Montvale, N.J.

Grochla, Erwin, and Norbert Szyperski (eds.). *Information Systems and Organizational Structures.* Berlin: De Gruyter, 1975.

Sharpe, William F. *The Economics of Computers.* New York: Columbia University Press, 1969.

Reynolds, Carl H. "Issues in Centralization." *Datamation,* March 1977.

Weinberg, Gerald M. *An Introduction to General Systems Thinking.* New York: Wiley & Sons, 1975.

Chapter 5

Guzeman, David J. *Microcomputer Applications Handbook.* Los Angeles: Iasis, Inc., 1976.

Jensen, F. J. "Centralization or Decentralization in Banking." *Datamation,* July 1976.

Langefors, Borje, and Kjell Samuelson. *Information and Data in Systems.* New York: Petrocelli, 1976.

Solomon, Martin B. "Economics of Scale and Computer Personnel." *Datamation,* March 1970.

Turnblade, Robert C. "The Case for Dedicated Computers." *Data Processing,* May 1971.

Chapter 6

Breslin, Judson, and C. Bradley Tashenberg. *Distributed Processing Systems: End of the Mainframe Era?* New York: AMACOM, 1978.

Champine, G. A. "Six Approaches to Distributed Data Bases." *Datamation,* May 1977.

Down, P. J., and F. E. Taylor. *Why Distributed Computing?* Rochelle Park, N.J.: Hayden Book Co., 1977.

Kallis, Stephen A., Jr. "Networks and Distributed Processing." *Mini-Micro Systems,* March 1977.

Severino, Elizabeth F. "Databases and Distributed Processing." *Computer Decisions,* March 1977.

Chapter 7

Bell, J. R., and C. G. Bell (eds.). *Minicomputer Software*. New York: North-Holland Publishing Co., 1976.

Brinch, Hansen P. *Operating System Principles*. Englewood Cliffs, N.J.: Prentice-Hall, 1973.

Curtis, G., and K. Falor. "Solve Your Software Headaches with a Generalized Program." *Computer Decisions*, February 1971.

Knuth, Donald. *The Art of Computer Programming*. New York: Addison-Wesley, 1975.

Maurer, Ward D. *Programming: An Introduction to Computer Languages and Techniques*. San Francisco: Holden-Day, 1968.

Meyers, Glenford. *Software Reliability: Principles and Practices*. New York: Wiley & Sons, 1976.

Morris, John J. "What to Expect When You Scale Down to a Minicomputer." *Control Engineering*, September 1970.

Tausworthe, Robert C. *Standardized Development of Computer Software*. Englewood Cliffs, N.J.: Prentice-Hall, 1977.

Chapter 8

Barish, Norman N. *Economic Analysis for Engineering and Managerial Decision Making*. New York: McGraw-Hill, 1962.

Brooks, Frederick P. *The Mythical Man-month*. New York: Addison-Wesley, 1975.

Forrester, Nathan B. *The Life Cycle of Economic Development*. Wright-Allen, 1972.

Grant, Eugene L. et al. *Principles of Engineering Economy*. New York: Ronald Press, 1975.

Grindley, Kit. *Systematics: A New Approach to Systems Analysis*. New York: McGraw-Hill, 1975.

Parker, Donn B. *Crime by Computer*. New York: Scribner's Sons, 1976.

Chapter 9

Anderson, R. H. "Programmable Automation." *Datamation*, December, 1972.

Fouri, William M. *Introduction to the Computer: The Tool of Business*. Englewood Cliffs, N. J.: Prentice-Hall, 1977.

Hinrichs, Karl. "The Impact of Minicomputers on Industry." *Computers and Automation*, December 1969.

Sackman, Harold. *Man–Computer Problem Solving*. Princeton, N. J.: Auerbach Publishers, 1970.

Wu, Margaret S. *Introduction to Computer Data Processing*. New York: Harcourt, Brace, Jovanovich, 1975.

Chapter 10

Braden, William, Jr. *How to Buy Minicomputers and Microcomputers.* New York: Wiley Interscience, 1976.

Corsiglia, Jack. "Matching Computer to the Job: First Step Towards Selection." *Data Processing*, December 1970.

Ein-Dor, Philip. "A Dynamic Approach to Selecting Computers." *Datamation*, June 1977.

Freed, Roy N. "Get the Computer System You Want." *Harvard Business Review*, November–December 1969.

Kenney, Donald P. *Application of Reliability Techniques.* New York: Argyle Publishing, 1964.

Martin, James. *Design of Real-Time Computer Systems.* Englewood Cliffs, N. J.: Prentice-Hall 1976.

Yourdon, Edward. "Reliability of Real-Time Systems." *Modern Data*, January 1972.

Chapter 11

Baker, L. H. "Consider the Alternatives Before You Upgrade." *Computer Decisions*, May 1972.

Brandon, Dick H. "Contracting for Software." *Infosystems*, September 1977.

Brandon, Dick H., and Sidney Segelstein. *Data Processing Contracts: Structure, Contents, and Negotiation.* New York: Van Nostrand-Reinhold, 1976.

Lettieri, Larry. "Negotiating the Contract Maze." *Computer Decisions*, April 1977.

Scalletta, Walsh. *Understanding Computer Contracts.* New York: Data Processing Management Association, 1976.

Chapter 12

Ackoff, Russell. *Redesigning the Future.* New York: Wiley & Sons, 1974.

Ernst, Morris. "Management, the Computer, and Society." *Computers and Automation*, September 1971.

Kay, Alan C. "Microelectronics and the Personal Computer." *Scientific American*, September 1977.

Kindred, Julian. "Role of the Minicomputer: Today and Tomorrow." *Computers and Automation*, December 1971.

Michie, Donald. *On Machine Intelligence.* New York: Halsted Press, 1974.

Sanders, Donald. *Computers and Management in a Changing Society.* New York: McGraw-Hill, 1974.

Turn, Rein. *Computers in the 1980s.* New York: Columbia University Press, 1974.

Index

DATE DUE			
OCT 5 1983			